The Routledge Guidebook to Moore's
Principia Ethica

G.E. Moore's *Principia Ethica* is a landmark publication in twentieth-century moral philosophy. Through focusing on the origin and evolution of his main doctrines, this guidebook makes it clear that Moore was an innovator whose provocative take on traditional philosophical problems ignited heated debates among philosophers. *Principia Ethica* is an important text for those attempting to understand and engage with some major philosophical debates in ethics today.

The Routledge Guidebook to Moore's Principia Ethica provides a comprehensive introduction to this historic work, examining key Moorean themes including:

- ethical non-naturalism
- the naturalistic fallacy
- the Open Question Argument
- moral ontology and epistemology
- ideal utilitarianism
- vindictive punishment and organicity
- moral intuition for epistemic justification in ethics
- theory of value

Ideal for anyone wanting to understand and gain perspective on Moore's seminal work, this book is essential reading for students of moral philosophy, metaethics, normative ethics, philosophical analysis, and related fields.

Susana Nuccetelli is Professor of Philosophy at St. Cloud State University, USA. Her most recent book is *An Introduction to Latin American Philosophy* (2020), and she is the author of *Engaging Bioethics: An Introduction with Case Studies* (with Gary Seay, Routledge, 2017) among other works.

THE ROUTLEDGE GUIDES TO THE GREAT BOOKS

The Routledge Guides to the Great Books provide ideal introductions to the texts which have shaped Western Civilization. The Guidebooks explore the arguments and ideas contained in the most influential works from some of the most brilliant thinkers who have ever lived, from Aristotle to Marx and Newton to Wollstonecraft. Each Guidebook opens with a short introduction to the author of the great book and the context within which they were working and concludes with an examination of the lasting significance of the book. *The Routledge Guides to the Great Books* will therefore provide students everywhere with complete introductions to the most significant books of all time.

Augustine's Confessions
Catherine Conybeare

Foucault's The History of Sexuality
Chloe Taylor

The New Testament
Patrick Gray

James's Principles of Psychology
David E Leary

Berkeley's Three Dialogues
Stefan Storrie

Smith's Wealth of Nations
Maria Pia Paganelli

Paine's Rights of Man
Frances A. Chiu

The Routledge Guidebook to Moore's *Principia Ethica*
Susana Nuccetelli

For more information about this series, please visit: https://www.routledge.com/The-Routledge-Guides-to-the-Great-Books/book-series/RGGB

The Routledge Guidebook to Moore's *Principia Ethica*

Susana Nuccetelli

Routledge
Taylor & Francis Group

LONDON AND NEW YORK

First published 2022
by Routledge
2 Park Square, Milton Park, Abingdon, Oxon OX14 4RN

and by Routledge
605 Third Avenue, New York, NY 10158

Routledge is an imprint of the Taylor & Francis Group, an informa business

British Library Cataloguing-in-Publication Data
A catalogue record for this book is available from the British Library

Library of Congress Cataloging-in-Publication Data
Names: Nuccetelli, Susana, author. | Seay, Gary.
Title: The Routledge guidebook to Moore's Principia ethica /
Susana Nuccetelli.
Description: Abingdon, Oxon ; New York : Routledge, 2022. |
Includes bibliographical references and index. |
Identifiers: LCCN 2021015744 (print) | LCCN 2021015745 (ebook) |
ISBN 9781138818484 (hardback) | ISBN 9781138818491 (paperback) |
ISBN 9780429275975 (ebook)
Subjects: LCSH: Moore, G. E. (George Edward), 1873–1958.
Principia ethica. | Ethics.
Classification: LCC B1647.M73 P7536 2022 (print) | LCC B1647.M73 (ebook) |
DDC 171/.2—dc23
LC record available at https://lccn.loc.gov/2021015744
LC ebook record available at https://lccn.loc.gov/2021015745

ISBN: 978-1-138-81848-4 (hbk)
ISBN: 978-1-138-81849-1 (pbk)
ISBN: 978-0-429-27597-5 (ebk)

DOI: 10.4324/9780429275975

Typeset in Times New Roman
by codeMantra

CONTENTS

PREFACE

This *Routledge Guidebook* is a critical introduction to the early
ethical doctrines of G. E. Moore as he formulated them in his
landmark monograph *Principia Ethica* of 1903. More than
a hundred years after its publication, a revisionist consensus
has begun to emerge about the relevance of those doctrines to
present-day ethics. While the contributions of Moore's writings
to early analytic epistemology, theory of perception, and philosophical method have never been in doubt, several generations
of successors in moral philosophy spent their professional lives
raising doubts about the contributions of *Principia Ethica* to
their field. Among the primary subjects of their skepticism has
been Moore's non-naturalism in moral semantics, metaphysics,
and epistemology. Although this set of doctrines came under
intense critical scrutiny and appeared dead a few decades after the
publication of *Principia*, some periodic re-evaluations and refor-
mulations suggest that there is much to learn by revisiting how
Moore sought to support them. In addition, we are now witness-
ing a renewed interest in the last two chapters of *Principia*, which
outline pioneering versions of a two-level consequentialist theory
and a pluralist, holistic account of value. Moore himself argued

that practical ethics is the chief goal of ethical investigation, and in those chapters offered insightful discussions of issues such as temperance and some other virtues, the asymmetry between the value of pleasure and disvalue of pain, and the deontic status of actions such as murder and retributive punishment. Among critics of his time, Bertrand Russell (1903a: 37) praised the quality of the chapters even when he objected to their excessively conservative reliance on the principles of common morality.

The present book examines all six chapters of *Principia Ethica*. In the course of doing so, it pays attention to some contemporary controversies that attest to Moore's ability to discover significant philosophical problems and put insights from a number of philosophical disciplines at the service of finding satisfactory resolutions. The closer look at *Principia* provided here shows that, by either identifying new questions or giving old ones a novel twist, Moore led the way for others to jump into the fray and advance the development of contemporary analytic ethics. First published when he was only 30 and judged harshly by him in retrospect, *Principia Ethica* is nonetheless what the vast majority of critics consider the best source for his philosophical ethics and normative theory. But as evident in the list of primary sources provided at the end of this book, also of interest for the study of his doctrines have been ethical works Moore published at various times consisting of essays, lecture notes, reviews, and two other monographs, *The Elements of Ethics* (1991/1898) and *Ethics* (2005/1912). The chapters that follow offer chiefly a reconstruction and an evaluation of Moore's philosophy of ethics (Chapter 3), classical non-naturalism (Chapter 4), the Open Question Argument and the naturalistic fallacy charge (Chapters 5 and 6), moral epistemology (Chapter 7), moral ontology (Chapter 8), conception of value and obligation (Chapters 9 and 10), and normative ethics (Chapter 11).

There are, however, a few exceptions to this general plan. The first two chapters, written in collaboration with Gary Seay, provide a biographical sketch and a discussion of the influence of Moore and his *Principia Ethica* inside as well as outside philosophical circles. Each of these chapters may be attractive to historically minded readers. Chapter 1 would be of interest to anyone curious about Moore's philosophical development and Chapter 2 to anyone curious about the impact and legacy of his philosophy, especially his ethical theory. In the absence of such interests, readers may skip these chapters altogether and jump to Chapter 3. In including some biographical and historical information we were motivated by the conviction that acquaintance with some facts about Moore's life and early interactions with certain philosophical and artistic circles at Cambridge and London can help to better understand the genealogy of some of his views in areas of philosophy pertaining to ethics and philosophical method. Moreover, such an acquaintance allows us to put in context a certain persisting question concerning the implications of Moore's practical ethics: are they inherently reformist or too conservative? This question, first posed in Chapter 2 in connection with our close look at the reception of *Principia* among philosophers generally and friends of Moore in the Bloomsbury group, receives a full answer in Chapter 11. This final chapter is followed by a brief assessment of the legacy of *Principia Ethica* and two reference lists providing facts of publication about cited materials.

Acknowledgments

Some of the views in this *Routledge Guidebook* have resulted from work done with Gary in two of our edited volumes, *Themes from G. E. Moore* (2007) and *Ethical Naturalism* (2012). In addition to Chapters 1 and 2, Gary Seay and I collaborated in writing Chapters 5 and 6 of the present book. He also read and edited the entire manuscript, for which I am very grateful. Among those who have provided useful comments on one or more chapters, I would like to thank especially Charles Pigden, whose insightful comments are acknowledged accordingly in the text. Harvey Siegel and Karen Kovach offered commentaries at two sessions of the American Philosophical Association in New York and Minneapolis that helped improve what were originally essays on Moore's Open Question Argument and the naturalistic fallacy charge. In personal communications, Brian McGuinness provided valuable historical information about Moore's interactions with some of his Cambridge peers. For general discussions of Moore's philosophy, I have a special debt to Charles Landesman and Phil Washburn. I have also benefitted greatly from discussions at one of Derek Parfit's seminars on metaethics at New York University, which I attended during a sabbatical year in the fall of 2012. Finally, I am most grateful to the editors at Routledge, especially to Adam Johnson whose patient and skillful guidance helped bring the project to fruition.

ABBREVIATIONS

See Bibliography for publication details.

A	"An Autobiography," 1942.
CIV	"The Conception of Intrinsic Value," 1922.
DCS	"A Defence of Common Sense," 1925.
E	*Ethics*, 1912.
EE	*The Elements of Ethics*, 1898.
IGQ	"Is Goodness a Quality?," 1959.
LP	*Lectures on Philosophy*, 1966.
NJ	"The Nature of Judgement," 1899.
NMP	"The Nature of Moral Philosophy," 1922.
OKB	*"The Origin of the Knowledge of Right and Wrong* by Franz Brentano," 1903.
OQA	Open Question Argument.
P1	"Preface," *Principia Ethica*, 1st edn.
P2	"Preface," *Principia Ethica*, 2nd edn.
PE	*Principia Ethica*, 1903.
PEW	"Proof of an External World," 1939.
RI	"The Refutation of Idealism," 1903.
RC	"A Reply to My Critics," 1942.

1

LIFE AND WORK

With Gary Seay

1.1 GROWING UP

A profoundly influential figure in twentieth-century British philosophy was the Cambridge philosopher G. E. Moore. Born in
1873 to a comfortably middle-class family, George Edward Moore
was the fifth of eight children, four boys and four girls. Since he
apparently disliked the name 'George Edward,' most of his contemporaries called him 'G. E. Moore' or simply 'Moore.'[1] His
father Daniel and his paternal grandfather were both physicians.
His mother, Henrietta Sturge Moore, came from a family of
some prominence among Britain's Quakers. In his autobiography
(A: 4–5), Moore tells us that she became estranged from the
Society of Friends because of the denomination's disapproval of
marriage between first cousins, which Henrietta and Daniel were.
As a result, she attended Baptist meetings, twice every Sunday,

DOI: 10.4324/9780429275975-1

with the whole Moore family in tow. Henrietta had some personal wealth that would later provide Moore with a convenient inheritance during a period he spent away from Cambridge between 1904 and 1911. This allowed him to continue his scholarly work while he had no teaching post.

But it was not only medical science and religion that were esteemed in the Moore household. The arts were also among things held in high regard. Moore himself cultivated singing and the piano. His eldest brother, Thomas Sturge Moore, grew up to become a celebrated poet, a friend of Yeats. He illustrated the first editions of Yeats's poems, and discussed with him the merits of G. E. Moore's early philosophical works in letters that are now in print (Bridge 1953).

Shortly before Moore's birth, his father retired from his medical practice. The family then moved to Upper Norwood in the southern suburbs of London so that the boys might receive an education at nearby Dulwich College, a recently improved boarding school that had a growing reputation among London's upper middle class, a group whose social status and political influence were on the rise. At age 8, Moore began as a day boy at Dulwich. According to his own recollections (A: 5), there he learned some mathematics as well as French and German. But above all, he developed an abiding interest in the classics curriculum that led him to spend most of these formative years translating English prose and verse into ancient Greek and Latin. During his last year at Dulwich, he took private music lessons from one of his teachers, E. D. Rendall. He learned organ as well as harmony and was able to sing *Lieder* by Schubert and Brahms, accompanying himself on the piano. He continued playing music and singing in social gatherings until late in life.[2]

While still at school, Moore suffered an embarrassment that might have affected his later views on religion and definitely left him uneasy when thinking about it in retrospect (A: 10–11). It came as a result of an episode he describes as "one of the most painful continued mental conflicts" he had ever faced. At around age 12, he was drawn into an ultra-evangelical Christian sect. One summer, while vacationing at a seaside resort with his family, he felt duty-bound to act on this newly acquired religious conviction by proselytizing for the group. He distributed its religious tracts, pressing leaflets into the hands of total strangers. This activity Moore felt embarrassing, especially in light of the presence at that very resort of two boys from Dulwich whom he admired. After about two years, Moore gave up his Protestant fundamentalism, and eventually religious belief altogether, embracing an agnosticism that remained his view for the rest of his life. In later years he was consistently skeptical about the existence of God. Tom Regan, in Chapter 2 of *Bloomsbury's Prophet* (Regan 1986), speculates that Moore was never comfortable with his agnosticism because it fueled for him a special concern about the grounds of morality. But it is far from clear that Moore's writings on the foundations of morality or religion support this speculation. Early in his career, Moore appeared quite comfortable with boldly declaring that his agnosticism about the existence of God rested on certain ontological and pragmatic considerations, including the lack of sound contrary reason or evidence. Accordingly, he wrote:

> It surely might be better to give up the search for a God whose existence is and remains undemonstrable, and to divert the feelings which the religious wish to spend on him, towards those of our own kind, who though perhaps less good than we can imagine God to be, are worthy of all the affections that we can feel; and whose help and sympathy are much more certainly real. We might perhaps with advantage worship the real creature a little more, and his hypothetical Creator a good deal less.
>
> (Moore 1901: 98)

In a 1955 letter to E. M. Forster, written just three years before his death, Moore still appeared resolutely agnostic. On his view, one or the other of these propositions must be true: either "there is no God," or "it is extremely doubtful whether there is any [God]."[3]

1.2 EARLY YEARS AT CAMBRIDGE

FROM CLASSICS TO PHILOSOPHY

Among Moore's teachers at Dulwich, he acknowledged especially the influence of A. H. Gilkes, the headmaster, and W. T. Lendrum, who later became a Fellow at Caius College, Cambridge. The study of Greek and Latin was at the time Moore's exclusive intellectual concern, since he "had no particular preference for anything else" (A: 5). Aware of Moore's talent for classics, Gilkes and Lendrum supported his application for a Major Entrance Scholarship to Trinity College, Cambridge. In the fall of 1892, Moore began his undergraduate study there, directing his efforts toward the completion of Part I of the Classical Tripos. He soon discovered that most of what was expected of him during this first year he had already studied at Dulwich.

But something was new: his intellectual and social circles had begun to expand, and with it he had begun to develop a growing new interest in philosophical problems – something he had not recalled happening before, not even while reading Plato's *Protagoras* as part of his instruction in classics. According to Moore's own, probably exaggerated, recollection in his autobiography, until his second year at Cambridge in 1893, he hardly knew "that there was such a subject as philosophy" (ibid.: 13). Crucial to his new interest in the discipline were some friendships Moore established with undergraduates and tutors in the Moral Sciences Tripos, the center of philosophical study at Cambridge at the time. That year Moore made two acquaintances who were to be most influential in the promotion of this new intellectual interest. One was undergraduate Bertrand Russell, one year Moore's senior but two years ahead of him at the university. Russell was about to leave Cambridge after completion of Part II of the Moral Sciences Tripos. The other was John McTaggart Ellis McTaggart, a young neo-Hegelian instructor who had been appointed to teach the history of modern philosophy for the Moral Sciences Tripos.

Conversations with them led Moore to some problems of philosophical method and substance that would become central to his thinking from then on. He later described them as problems facing neither ordinary nor scientific thinking but only philosophical thinking:

> [They are] first, the problem of trying to get really clear as to what on earth a given philosopher *meant* by something which he said, and secondly, the problem of discovering what really satisfactory reasons

there are for supposing that what he meant was true, or alternatively, was false.

(ibid.: 14)

McTaggart's punctilious regard for conceptual clarity and reasoned argument might have encouraged Moore's own detailed attention to matters of philosophical method. On consideration later, Moore said that what most impressed him about McTaggart's lectures was not his interpretation of Hegel, which he considered clearer than the original, though probably not faithful to it. It was instead that McTaggart seemed to Moore "immensely clever and immensely quick in argument" (ibid.: 18).

By 1894 (his third year at Cambridge), Moore was spending more time talking with philosophically-minded peers and tutors. Following what he recalls as Russell's advice (ibid.: 16), he decided to add the Moral Sciences Tripos to his undergraduate studies in Classics. Eventually he completed it, obtaining a First Class with a mark of distinction. At the same time he was preparing for the Greek philosophy section of the Classical Tripos Part II, which he completed in the same month with a Second Class.

In this period, Moore was focused primarily on developing his philosophical acumen under the guidance of his tutors. His autobiography acknowledges a debt to McTaggart's lectures on Hegel, James Ward's guidance on books to read and his lectures on all areas of philosophy except ethics, G. F. Stout's lectures on the history of modern philosophy, and Henry Jackson's lectures on Plato and Aristotle (ibid.: 16–19). The influence of Henry Sidgwick appears not to have originated in his lectures, which Moore's autobiography describes as dull and consisting of Sidgwick reading his papers to students. But in his writings, especially in *The Methods of Ethics*, Sidgwick developed some ethical doctrines that impacted Moore in a number of ways about which we'll have something to say later.[4]

THE CAMBRIDGE CONVERSAZIONE SOCIETY

Each of Moore's tutors, as well as fellow undergraduates such as Russell, were members of 'the Cambridge Conversazione Society,' a semi-secret fraternal circle that met periodically to debate short papers written by members. Commonly known to its members as 'the Society,' the group originally had only twelve members, and for that reason outsiders who knew of their existence dubbed them 'the Apostles,' a term still in use for members today. In its heyday (roughly between the 1890s and the beginning of World War I), the Society managed to enlist some very talented Cambridge men by means of a highly selective process of election. Discussions in the meetings of the Society played a crucial role in Moore's development of some of his characteristic philosophical traits.[5] At the time he began to show an interest in philosophy, the Society had enlisted, besides his tutors and other lecturers, many undergraduates who went on to occupy distinguished positions in Britain's public service, journalism, education, and culture.

Although since its founding the Society maintained rules of secrecy, a great deal of information about its practices during the years of Moore's active membership is now available from a number of sources. Among them are archival materials kept at Cambridge, the private correspondence of members, and memoirs published by some of the Apostles themselves (e.g., Russell's memoirs (Russell 1951a) and his autobiography (Russell 1951b)) or left for publication by their heirs (e.g., Sidgwick's memoir, posthumously published by his brother Arthur, himself an Apostle, and his wife Eleanor Mildred, based on Henry's notes and correspondence (Sidgwick 1906)). But Moore honored the rule of secrecy, as can be inferred from the fact that his autobiography never mentions the Society by name. At most, we might infer that he is referring to the Apostles when, after having acknowledged his philosophical debt to Russell, he reports "during part of these years I had a good deal of discussion with Russell, and I also learned a good deal from discussion with other *friends*. To mention one particular instance, the whole plan of the last chapter of *Principia* was first formed in a conversation with a *friend*" (A: 25, our emphasis).[6]

But from Russell's memoirs and autobiography we learn a lot more, including that the Society had a firm rule prescribing that, in its philosophical debates, "there were to be no taboos, no limitations, nothing considered shocking, no barriers to absolute freedom of speculation." As he recalls, "[w]e discussed all manner of things, no doubt with a certain immaturity, but with a detachment and interest scarcely possible in later life."[7] Generally consistent with Russell's recollections, Sidgwick also notes that "the pursuit of truth with absolute devotion" was central to that group of "intimate friends" from whom "absolute candour" in philosophical debates was expected. He adds,

[T]ruth as we saw it then and there was what we had to embrace and maintain, and there were no propositions so well established that an Apostle had not the right to deny or question, if he did so sincerely and not from mere love of paradox. The gravest subjects were continually debated, but gravity of treatment, as I have said, was not imposed, though sincerity was ...

(Sidgwick 1906: 34–35)

Based on textual evidence of this sort, Paul Levy (1979), W. C. Lubenow (1998) and other historians of the period converge in describing the Society, at the time Moore was elected to it, as a group of intellectually outstanding men, counting among them one or two undergraduates from each year at Cambridge, mostly from the colleges of Trinity and King's. They tended to have the socioeconomic background of a professional middle class whose influence in British intellectual and public life was growing rapidly at the turn of the nineteenth century. Compared with earlier Apostles, these were more distinguished, and at least at some point in their lives less sympathetic to religion, when not openly hostile to it, as illustrated by the agnosticism or open atheism of Apostolic philosophers such as McTaggart, Moore, Russell, Sidgwick, Stout, and Ward.[8] The Apostles' interest was chiefly that of engaging in reasoned debates to get closer to the truth about questions concerning a wide variety of philosophical questions, from the existence of God and the possibility of immortality to the unreality of time or space and many more.

The list of notable philosophers who had joined the Society in Moore's time, besides those already mentioned, must also include Alfred North Whitehead and Ludwig Wittgenstein. Among other eminent Apostles of the period were the poet Rupert Brooke, the novelist E. M. Forster, and mathematician G. H. Hardy. Flourishing in London in roughly the same period was the Bloomsbury circle, which, in addition to some Apostles such as economist John Maynard Keynes, public servant/editor/publisher Leonard Woolf, and biographer Lytton Strachey, included novelist Virginia Woolf and art critic Clive Bell, among others.[9]

About the Society during the period when he and Moore were undergraduates, Russell goes so far as to declare that it "had as members most of the people of any intellectual eminence who have been at Cambridge" (1951b: 92). He is critical, however, of the turn the group took in the hands of younger Apostles of the generation that followed, many of whom were also active members of the Bloomsbury circle. He finds them responsible for the Society's degradation due not only to their tendency to engage in "homosexual relationships" but, most important, because they had a conception of the good "as consisting in the passionate mutual admiration of a clique of the elite", whose origin they "unfairly" ascribed to Moore (ibid.: 99).

"BROTHER" MOORE

Moore's election as a "brother" or active member of the Society was a relatively easy matter once McTaggart decided to sponsor his candidacy. He was accepted in February 1894. Since membership was for life, after his resignation in January 1901, he became an "Angel" or Apostle who has "taken wings," which meant among other things that attendance at the Society's meetings on Saturday evenings was henceforth optional for him (by contrast, active members had to attend or pay a fine). Although during those meetings some records were kept and sardines on toast ("whales") and coffee served, what always took center stage was the reading of a paper written by a member on a previously assigned topic, followed by a philosophical debate. For the seven years of his active membership, Moore seems to have excelled at both activities: he wrote and presented about twenty short papers and proved to be an insightful debater. Russell (ibid.: 99) notes that he "first became aware of Moore's excellence" by observing his performance at the Society's meetings. These observations together with Moore's physical appearance created in Russell the fantasy that he personified the "ideal of a genius ... beautiful and slim, with a look almost of inspiration, and with an intellect as deeply passionate as Spinoza's" (ibid.: 85). Such standing would not last, however, since Wittgenstein would soon replace Moore in Russell's conception of the ideal of genius.

In any case, records by Moore's contemporaries suggest that his election to the Society carried mutual benefits. "This Society played a large part in Moore's life during his first period in Cambridge ... and Moore played a leading part in the Society" asserts a retrospective note by one of Moore's students (Braithwaite 1970: 18). On the other hand, historian of the Apostles and Moore biographer Paul Levy contends that many traits of analytic philosophy often taken to be characteristically Moorean were in fact part of the Apostles' dialectical lore, as codified in 1823 by the early Apostle J. F. D. Maurice, who later came to be celebrated as the founder of "Christian socialism." After reviewing the evidence from Maurice and others, Levy urges us to think that "[w]hen ... G. E. Moore demands of someone that he be precise, as to what question he is asking, it is this dialectical tradition of the Apostles that he is exemplifying" (Levy 1979: 69). Historian of the group, W. C. Lubenow takes a similar view (1998: 410–412).

In light of what he writes in his autobiography, Moore would probably say that it was McTaggart who best illustrated that tradition. Either way, Moore scored high in reasoned argument and relentless pursuit of clarity about philosophical questions. But when faced with this sort of question, he wrote, an emphasis on clarity is compatible with tolerating some degree of obscurity, which might always remain, owing to the complexity of some philosophical problems (A: 19). Perhaps, as Levy noted, this attitude resulted from Moore's adherence to Maurice's code for the Apostles. Yet it might also have been the other way around: Moore's excellence in pursuing conceptual clarity (owing in part to his background as a translator of Latin and Greek) might have helped in boosting the Society's adherence to the Maurice code.[10] In fact, many other hypotheses might contribute to explaining his excellence at this and other traits that later became ideals distinctive of analytic philosophy, such as the unconditional pursuit of truth and a willingness to follow an argument wherever it leads. All these are compatible with Levy's claim that those were the traits expected from any participant in the Saturday meetings. Most likely, Moore and the Society helped each other in sharpening many such traits now distinctive of analytic philosophy. But a later Moore, the one sometimes described as 'the philosopher's philosopher,' also showed a special mastery of argumentation strategies not at all prevalent in the work of many of his contemporaries. Here we have in mind his tendency, shown especially in his arguments against Cartesian skepticism, to respond to abstract philosophical speculation by invoking either the verdicts of common sense (Moore 1925) or his comparative greater certainty about the truth of his own view rather than that of Cartesian skepticism (Moore 1939; 1959). These argumentative strategies must have surfaced too not only at the Saturday meetings of the Society, which he continued to attend until late in life, but also at the meetings of professional groups such as the Cambridge Moral Sciences Club, of which he was a member, and the Aristotelian Society, which he joined in 1898.

COMPETING FOR A CAMBRIDGE FELLOWSHIP

Upon completion of the Classics and Moral Sciences Triposes in 1896, Moore decided to enter a competition at Trinity for a fellowship position that carried with it comfortable rooms, meals, and a 200 annual stipend. McTaggart and Russell had won such fellowships in 1891 and 1896 respectively. In an era before PhD programs became the norm for philosophers, Moore knew that winning this position was the way to launch an academic career in philosophy. Applicants for the prize fellowship had to write a dissertation on a philosophical topic of their own choice, which for Moore was the concept of freedom in Kant's major works in light of Kant's distinction between a "noumenal" reality of things as they are in themselves and a "phenomenal" reality of things as they are accessible to us through sense-perception. On Moore's view, this distinction entails that the noumenal self has an autonomous will while the phenomenal or empirical self lacks a will of this kind. That creates an inconsistency in Kant's moral theory because freedom of the will is a requirement of his normative ethics. And even if no such inconsistency were to arise, there would be at least a tension between Kant's moral ontology and his normative ethics. Submitted in 1897 with the title "The Metaphysical Basis of Ethics," this dissertation was unsuccessful in winning Moore the Fellowship. Neither Sidgwick, the philosophy faculty reader, nor Edward Caird, the Kantian-expert external reader, found his interpretation of Kant sufficiently convincing. In a two-page commentary Sidgwick did tell the electors that although "very promising," the dissertation shows "promise rather than performance." Sidgwick's knowledge of Kantian scholarship, by his own admission limited, was nonetheless sufficient for him to regard Moore's criticisms of Kant as a strawman. They "miss the real view," he wrote, by failing to consider both the relevant textual evidence from Kant, and "the changes of view … in works written with different aims during a period of 16 years" (Moore 2011: 97–98). Thinking about this dissertation in retrospect, Moore himself speculated that Sidgwick must have thought it complete "nonsense" (A: 21).

On the other hand, Caird produced a longer report of about twenty pages arguing that Moore's neo-Hegelian reading of Kant was unfaithful. Caird wrote:

> The difficulty partly arises from the fact that Kant is read so much through the eyes of Bradley and Lotze, which leads I think, to an imperfect realization of the best points in Kant's work, and an exaggeration of his inconsistencies.
>
> (2011: 99)

In retrospect, Moore agreed: his early interpretation of Kant was as unfaithful to Kant's philosophy as McTaggart's interpretation of the Absolute Idea was to Hegel's (A: 21). In fact, he declared "absolutely worthless" an essay based on the 1897 dissertation, "Freedom," which was published shortly afterward in *Mind*. But according to some accounts, Sidgwick had asked Ward, the internal reader of a revised dissertation that Moore submitted in 1898, to try to produce a charitable report of a revised version submitted a year later. Aware of those accounts, Moore wrote in his autobiography that Sidgwick might have judged his first dissertation "nonsense of the right kind."

His revised dissertation had the same title and some of the same materials as the previous one, together with some substantial new doctrines. It ended with an "Appendix on the Chronology of Kant's Ethical Writings" containing textual evidence from Kant's works, probably aimed at supporting his interpretation while avoiding the strawman charge implicit in the readers' critique of his previous dissertation. In spite of some similarities, a new preface of the revised dissertation warns readers that "some omissions and alterations, involving *an important change of view* have been made; and nearly as much again of new matter has been added" (2011: 117, our emphasis). In fact, this 1898 dissertation introduces a few "important changes," especially in an added Chapter 2 that takes issue with Kant's notion of reason, parts of which went missing but are believed to be the substance of an essay, "The Nature of Judgment" (NJ), that Moore published in *Mind* in 1899.[11]

The major change in Moore's 1898 dissertation, evident in NJ, was the abandonment of absolute idealism, the general metaphysical outlook then prevalent in British universities and championed by Francis Herbert Bradley, Bernard Bosanquet, and J. M. E. McTaggart among others. This form of idealism boiled down to a neo-Hegelian monism of ideas incompatible with any realist ontology since it denied the extra-mental existence not only of time, space, and matter and other quasi-scientific objects, but also of trees, tables, chairs and other everyday perceptual objects. Initially, Moore himself endorsed absolute idealism about scientific as well as ordinary perceptual objects even though in his autobiography he mistakenly claims that he always rejected as nonsense arguments for the unreality of time (cf. his 1897 "In What Sense, if Any, Do Past and Future Time Exist?," an article sympathetic to McTaggart's reasons for the irreality of time). But his idealism had a Kantian origin, especially the distinction between noumenal and phenomenal reality.[12]

However, in the 1898 dissertation, Moore took unprecedented first steps toward the rejection of idealism altogether and argued for a kind of realism compatible with the logical atomism later developed by Russell. Yet if the neo-Hegelian idealism of Bradley and McTaggart was offensive to common sense, the new realism of Moore was hardly less so. After all, it countenanced the exist-ence of neither scientific entities nor objects of ordinary percep-tion but only of mind- and language-independent concepts and propositions. It was thus as contrary to commonsense realism as to absolute idealism. Eventually Moore himself came to reject this heavy-duty Platonist ontology. In any case, his revised dissertation did win him the prize. At the age of 25, he became a Fellow of Trinity College, Cambridge, a position he held until 1904. During this period, he would write a book in ethics that would get the attention of the whole philosophical profession in the English-speaking world. Ahead of him lay the Golden Age of Cambridge philosophy.

PRINCIPIA ETHICA AND OTHER EARLY WRITINGS

Moore's early writings include his dissertations and other pieces produced up to about 1904. His most important work in ethics, *Principia Ethica* (*PE*) of 1903, belongs to this period. It unfolds along the lines of another early work, *The Elements of Ethics* (*EE*). Moore began working on *EE* in 1898, basing it on one of two sets of public lectures on ethics that he delivered that year.[13] In March 1902, he sought publication with Cambridge University Press but since he abandoned work on all the revisions requested by his edi-tor, he was unable to publish this book during his lifetime. Instead, by late May, he had decided to start a new book, *PE*, which turned out to be his masterpiece in ethics. That this book draws exten-sively from *EE* is clear, even when Moore himself wrote that *EE* merely provided the outline for all of *Principia*'s chapters except the last one, which he conceived in discussions with a friend.[14] For the next few decades this book had a wide and profound impact, shaping metaethical debate for a great part of the century – as demonstrated by the fact that it never ceased to have the status of a classic in debates between all varieties of naturalistic moral realism and their non-naturalistic competitors.[15]

In addition to these books, during his six-year fellowship at Trinity, Moore produced other influential works in the form of entries in reference volumes, reviews, and essays in journals, including "Truth" (1902), "Experience and Empiricism" (1902–1903), "Mr. McTaggart's Ethics" (1903b), "Kant's Idealism" (1903–1904), and the much celebrated "Refutation of Idealism" (1903a). Published in *Mind*, this article takes the revolt against idealism initiated with NJ a step further by targeting Berkeley's *esse-est-percipi* dictum, and with it, the phenomenalist type of idealism that was soon to be championed by A. J. Ayer and other logical positivists. Moore was determined to undermine all forms of this metaphysical doctrine, but how compelling were his arguments in this famous paper is still a matter of controversy.

1.3   THE PHILOSOPHER'S PHILOSOPHER

ETHICAL WRITINGS AFTER 1911

Between the years 1904 and 1911, Moore was away from Cambridge as well as from teaching. In 1904, his fellowship expired, but an inheritance allowed him to carry on his work in philosophy without the need of a teaching post. For some years, he shared a flat in Edinburgh with Apostle Alfred Ainsworth, his closest friend from Cambridge who, like Moore, had completed a Tripos in Classics and one in the Moral Sciences. Ainsworth, who later married one of Moore's sisters, had an appointment to teach classics at the University of Edinburgh. During this period Moore wrote a few papers and reviews mostly for a readership of professional philosophers who had expertise in questions of metaphysics and epistemology. Among them were well-received lecture notes on the problem of perception and on the philosophy of Hume that later appeared in his 1953 collection, *Some Main Problems of Philosophy*. Moore's writings during this period reveal the sharpening of his analytic power and a tendency to drift away from the writing style of the *Principia*, a book whose plainness appealed not only to philosophers but also to many amateur philosophers of his time.

This tendency also emerges in a book on moral philosophy that Moore wrote during this period, *Ethics* (*E*). Sent for publication in 1911, *E* appeared in print the following year but failed to attract the enthusiastic readership *Principia* had. On the whole, experts and non-experts alike found less to like about this book, in spite of the opinions of Moore and a few others, who thought it "much clearer and far less full of confusions and invalid arguments" than *Principia* (A: 27). Certainly, early reviewers were not impressed by either *E*'s clarity or its arguments. Tom Regan (1986: 288) goes so far as to state that "the book attracted no notice in the world of ideas." But a bold claim of this sort seems unsubstantiated since some chapters of this book such as that on free will have attracted long-lasting attention (Google Scholar shows about 22,000 hits). True, the debut of *E* with expert readers was overall weaker than that of *PE*. Perhaps contributing to this result might have been the fact that, like Russell's *Problems of Philosophy*, *E* was a short book aimed at non-experts and published in the Home University Library series. Nonetheless, the non-experts found Moore's new book confusing, perhaps because he was already deploying the powerful analytic method that later won him the description 'the philosopher's philosopher.'[16]

In *Ethics*, Moore introduced an important change to his views in *Principia*. For Moore now conceded that moral obligation is as basic as moral goodness, a point he revisited in an unfinished preface for *Principia*'s 1922 edition. He also abandoned the view that moral principles such as 'Right action is the action conducive to at least as much goodness as any alternative' are analytic, holding instead that they qualify as synthetic *a priori* truths. In addition, as pointed out by William Shaw (1966: x–xi), he offered perspicuous discussions of utilitarianism, subjectivism, relativism, and free will. But then, what if anything, can explain the comparative bad performance of *E*? The answer here seems twofold. On the one hand, *E* does not substantially advance what became classical Moorean themes in metaethics concerning the naturalism-versus-non-naturalism debate. On the other, since *PE* was extraordinarily successful in shifting moral philosophy's focus toward those themes in 1903, a 1912 book by Moore in which some other themes loom large was bound to receive less attention.

BECOMING THE PHILOSOPHER'S PHILOSOPHER

Although Moore did not become a Fellow of Trinity again until 1915, in 1911, he returned to Cambridge to take up a new appointment as a lecturer. This lectureship opened for him the option to teach either logic or psychology, and he chose the latter, a subject that was then understood as philosophical psychology or what we now call 'philosophy of mind.' For the next twenty-eight years he taught philosophy at Cambridge, lecturing there on philosophical psychology and metaphysics but never on ethics.[17] In 1921, Moore succeeded G. F. Stout as editor of the influential journal *Mind*, a position he held continuously until 1947. In 1925, he succeeded James Ward as professor of mental psychology and logic, though he focused on metaphysics (A: 30).

There are mixed accounts of Moore's work in philosophy in the decades that followed the publication of *Ethics*. Among unsympathetic readers, B. F. McGuinness (1988: 117) writes that Moore spent most of his time trying to understand Russell's *Principles of Mathematics*. Another such reader, G. J. Warnock (1968: 433), notes that Moore was trying to figure out the metaphysical and epistemic status that is presented to the mind in a perceptual experience, which he called 'sense data.' According to Warnock, in almost forty years of inquiry, Moore made little progress in determining whether sense data exist, and if so, what their mode of existence might be. By contrast, sympathetic readers take Moore to have made his greatest contribution to analytic epistemology and metaphysics during this period by making innovative uses of some insights of the commonsense tradition in philosophy, with which he became familiar mostly through his readings of Thomas Reid while living in Edinburgh. One such reader, Soames (2003; 2014) argues that, to these areas of philosophy, Moore introduced a "bottom-up" argumentation strategy against idealism and skepticism that has a pre-theoretical plausibility totally absent in the arguments of his challengers. But for Soames, Moore was unable to deploy similar successful strategies in moral philosophy and as a result, his achievements in this area fell short compared to those in epistemology and metaphysics.[18]

Be that as it may, Moore's mature work in philosophy shows two sets of features worth mentioning before concluding this biographical introduction. The first set concerns Moore's choice of topics in his publications after 1912. On this, there is no question that he was reading Russell closely, for he wrote a number of papers and lectures plainly connected to some of Russell's doctrines in metaphysics, theory of perception, philosophy of language, and epistemology. Yet in the course of studying Russell's doctrines, Moore made his own contribution to the topics at hand, as shown in his subtle observations about Russell's analysis of definite descriptions (Moore 1944).[19] Second, in contrast to his early writings, the Moore of this period showed little interest in reaching non-expert readers. Gradually his writings became more technical, his conclusions more tentative, and his tendency to dwell on details about the meaning of linguistic expression more pronounced (a kind of philosophical work later referred to as "linguistic botanizing"). He made regular explicit efforts to provide step-by-step arguments, to point to the weak aspects of his own doctrines, and to introduce, when possible, foundational questions concerning how to meet skeptical and idealist challenges or determine what was the proper business of philosophy. Examples of these developments include "A Defence of Common Sense" (his contribution to J. H. Muirhead's (1925) volume, *Contemporary British Philosophy*), "Certainty" (a paper he first read at a 1939 meeting of Cambridge's Moral Science Club), "The Justification of Analysis" (his 1933–1934 contribution to the first issue of the journal, *Analysis*, which he helped to establish), and his reply to William Frankena in the 1942 Schilpp collection.

Although Moore produced no monographs in this period, he wrote some influential papers and lectures, some of which appeared in the three collections of his own essays and lecture notes that he edited: *Philosophical Studies* (1922), *Some Main Problems of Philosophy* (1953), and *Philosophical Papers* (1959). The last collection was published posthumously by Casimir Lewy, a former student and collaborator in the direction of *Mind* while Moore was in the United States during World War II. In addition, Moore published two short pieces, "An Autobiography" and "Reply to My Critics," in Paul A. Schilpp's (1942) collection, *The Philosophy of G. E. Moore*.[20] And, in 1966, Lewy brought out two sets of selected writings by Moore. One consists of a compilation from nine of Moore's notebooks with entries from the years 1919–1953, six of which he had, before his death, labeled

The Commonplace Book. The other, *Lectures on Philosophy*, offers a selection of notes arranged in three parts, corresponding to three courses Moore gave in 1928–1929, 1925–1926, and 1933–1934. *The Commonplace Book* features records of discussions with students and other philosophers (e.g., Lewy, Georg Henrik von Wright, and Norman Malcolm) as well as thoughts prompted by the reading of Russell, William Ernest Johnson, Gottlob Frege, Wittgenstein, and others. Many of these entries are quite short and difficult to decipher. Gilbert Ryle (1971: 268) counted 190 such "odd" entries. Nearly half of all entries are about logical theory, including numerous detailed analyses of the meaning of 'if … then …' and other logical connectives. Only a few focus on a topic of ethics (fewer than ten), sometimes dealing with it in less than a page. The topics in *Lectures on Philosophy* range from the nature of classes, identity, incomplete symbols, and necessity, to propositions, truth, and sense data. There is no entry on ethics at all, but recall that ethics was not among the subjects he taught at Cambridge. Both books reveal Moore's growing interest, after the publication of *Ethics*, in topics of epistemology, theory of perception, metaphysics, philosophical logic, and meta-philosophy. Not counting his remarks on ethics in the 1942 "Reply to My Critics," the only three things he published on this subject after 1912 were the 1922 articles "The Conception of Intrinsic Value" and "The Nature of Moral Philosophy," and the 1932 article "Is Goodness a Quality?" (about which he had second thoughts in his reply to Frankena of 1942).

It is not uncommon to find commentators noticing that Moore's writings were by no means "copious" by comparison to his peers such as Russell (Warnock 1968: 435). True, but Moore's writings were quite influential, establishing him as an eminence in British philosophy, and this stature in the discipline landed him a series of distinctions. Among them, Moore was elected a Fellow of the British Academy in 1918 and became president of the Aristotelian Society that same year. He received two degrees *honoris causa*, a Litt.D. (doctorate in letters) from Cambridge in 1913 and an LL.D. (doctor of laws) from the University of St. Andrews in 1918. In 1951, he was appointed to the Order of Merit, the highest honor for a person of letters in the UK.[21]

In 1939, Moore retired from Cambridge, leaving a post in which he was succeeded by Wittgenstein. But he continued to lecture widely. He presented papers at Oxford and, in 1940, accepted an invitation to go to America, where he and his wife stayed until 1944. During this visit, he lectured in various places including Columbia University, Princeton, Berkeley, Swarthmore, Smith College, and Mills College in California. After his return to Britain, he continued to discuss philosophy with friends, though a stroke later limited his tolerance for longer conversations. He died in Cambridge in 1958, shortly before his 85th birthday, and his ashes are interred in St. Giles churchyard. He was survived by his wife, Dorothy Ely, a former student whom he married in 1916, and by Nicholas and Timothy, their two sons.

PHILOSOPHICAL PERSONA

Moore appears to have had an impact on analytic philosophy not only because of his doctrines in the various areas of his philosophical interest but also because of his personality. There is consensus among those who knew him that he had to a high degree some traits of an intellectual character that should be valued among philosophers. Most notably, inquisitiveness, integrity, and a determination to pursue the truth, however unflattering it might be for his own views. His student and friend Norman Malcolm summarizes Moore's best qualities this way:

> complete modesty and simplicity, saving him from the dangers of jargon and pomposity; through absorption in philosophy, which he found endlessly exciting; strong mental powers; and a pure integrity that accounted for his solidity and his passion for clarity.
>
> (1963: 167)

Like Braithwaite (1961), Levy (1979), and Ryle (1971), Malcolm too adds to this list of Moore's traits the virtues of candor and inquisitiveness in addressing philosophical questions, whether new or old, his remarkable enthusiasm for following an argument wherever it led, and his punctilious attention to detail in reasoning and conceptual analysis. There is also agreement that Moore showed great naïveté about ordinary, everyday matters.[22]

Some of these traits can be read right off Moore's works. Consider modesty. In his autobiography, for example, he describes himself as being "very lazy" by nature. Of NJ, his essay that marked the beginning of a revolt against absolute idealism in British philosophy, he later writes "there was probably some good" in it (A: 21–22). Moreover, it is not uncommon for him to refer to one of his own writings as "a dreadful muddle," "utterly mistaken," or even "a complete nonsense." About his celebrated article, "The Refutation of Idealism" (RI), he reflects in the preface of *Philosophical Studies* (*PS*) that "[it] now appears to me to be very confused, as well as to embody a good many down-right mistakes; so I am doubtful whether I ought to have included it" (*PS*: viii). Absent any evidence that such remarks were the expression of false modesty, we should take them to convey a humility rarely found among scholars of Moore's caliber.

NOTES

1   Baldwin (1996: 275). In a brief note in *The Commonplace Book*, Moore himself reveals that some people, including his wife Dorothy, called him 'Bill' and his siblings called him 'George' (see his entry "Proper Names," p. 248).

2   There is some evidence that after his return to Cambridge in the early 1910s, Ludwig Wittgenstein frequently played music with Moore, sometimes with both at the piano, other times with Wittgenstein at the piano and Moore singing. Moore's musical talent seemed to have been on display also at gatherings of the Bloomsbury group, which Wittgenstein sometimes attended. For more on that interaction, see McGuinness (1988).

3   Letter to E. M. Forster, August 10, 1955, cited in Lubenow (1998: 406).

4   The influence of Sidgwick on Moore is evident, for example, in *Prinicipia Ethica*'s vindication of Sidgwick as the sole writer in the whole history of ethics who did not commit the naturalistic fallacy.

5   The Cambridge Conversazione Society was founded in 1820 by George Tomlinson, who later became Bishop of Gibraltar. Originally, it consisted of a circle of exclusively men who met periodically to debate evangelical topics. In the 1970s, the Society began to accept some women, but little is known about the number of women who became members since then owing to the secret character of the Society.

6   That friend seems to have been fellow Apostle Hugh Owen Meredith (Levy 1979: 238), whose circles in London, like Moore's, also included the Bloomsbury group. Meredith later went on to teach economics at Queen's University, Belfast.

7   Russell (1951b: 92–93). For example, Russell recalls that, during this period, the Apostles had adopted in their communications some expressions of German metaphysics:

> The Society was supposed to be The World of Reality; everything else was Appearance. People who were not members of The Society were called 'phenomena.' Since the metaphysicians maintained that Space and Time are unreal, it was assumed that those who were in The Society were exempted from bondage to Space and Time.

8   For a complete list of Apostles of this period who either doubted or rejected altogether belief in the existence of God, see Lubenow (1998: 365 ff). A brief account of the history of the Society can be found in "A Cambridge Secret Revealed: The Apostles," King's College, Cambridge, available at: www.kings. cam.ac.uk/archive-centre/archive-month/january-2011.html

9   We examine the reception of Moore's doctrines in the Bloomsbury group in Chapter 2. For our purposes here, note that active in this circle were some of Britain's most eminent intellectuals and artists of the early 1900s.

10 Rosenbaum (1987: 218) also claims that Moore's quest for conceptual clarity "had its origins in his intensive training … as a classicist." However, Moore's cult of clarity eventually evolved into a mannerism that had an opposite effect. It became a distraction for his readers who were trying to follow the main line of the argument. A good example of this problem is Moore's reply to William Frankena in the 1942 Schilpp collection.

11 As suggested, for instance, in Chapter 3 of Regan (1986) and the "Editors' Introduction," in Baldwin and Preti (2011).

12 In the early writings, a remnant of idealism of either sort might account for Moore's reluctance to embrace an ontology consistent with common sense, one that can countenance the truth of propositions such as 'Here is a hand' or 'This is a pencil.' As is well known, he later changed his mind and vindicated the epistemic justification of commonsense beliefs, especially in some famous articles objecting to Cartesian skepticism. See Moore (1925; 1939), and the essays on these topics included in his (1959) volume *Philosophical Papers*.

13 *The Elements of Ethics* originated in some lectures Moore delivered in the Passmore Edwards Settlement at 9 Tavistock Place, London, that were organized by the School of Ethics and Social Philosophy as part of a new experiment in alternative education for students unable to afford private universities. Moore gave two sets of ten lectures there. One was focused on Kant's ethics. The other, devoted to general ethics, served as the source of this book. In every lecture, Moore read his notes for about an hour and then opened the discussion. For other facts about the genesis of *PE* and *EE*, see Regan's "Editor's Introduction" in Moore ([1991] 1898) and Levy (1979: 233).

14 That *EE* is the basis of *PE* would explain why Moore says in his autobiography that he spent most of his six-year fellowship at Trinity writing a book on ethics (*A*: 23–24). However, according to Tom Regan (1991), the editor of a posthumous publication of *EE*, these two books developed independently, though were related, given their common subject. Unquestionably, however,

the contents of *PE* and *EE* overlap, as can be seen in the comparison of their tables of contents that Thomas Baldwin includes in the 1993 revised edition of *Principia*.

15   According to Google Scholar, since 1903 to 2019, *Principia Ethica* has been cited in about 15,000 publications.

16   By the late 1950s, commentators such as J. A. Passmore (1957: 203) and Alan White (1958: 1) were using variants of the label 'the philosopher's philosopher' to echo at least in part Moore's own contention that, in philosophy, his interest was in neither the world nor science but in what philosophers say about either of these. By the late 1980s, however, in the writing of other commentators the label had become associated with Moore's mature style of philosophical inquiry, which gives a significant role to analysis of concepts and logical relations as well as rigor in argumentation (Regan 1986; Baldwin 1990). It is with the latter connotation that we use it here.

17   See Moore (A: 20–28), and Baldwin and Preti (2011: xxiii). Although Moore never taught ethics at Cambridge, he delivered courses in this subject at the Passmore Edwards Settlement in London, and the Morley College in Waterloo Road. He later acknowledged the influence of these courses in his published books in ethics (A: 23, 27).

18   More sympathetic readers of Moore think that Soames has not done enough to support his differential assessment of Moore's contribution to ethics, on the one hand, and metaphysics and epistemology, on the other. See, for instance, McGrath and Kelly (2015) and Hurka (2006).

19   In his autobiography, Moore acknowledges Russell as the major influence on his work, while at the same time conceding that he may also have been an influence on Russell. Most writers agree that these two giants of early analytic philosophy influenced each other. See, for example, Baldwin (1996: 277), Griffin (1991: 300), Sainsbury (1979: 12), and Chapter 2 of this book.

20   For a detailed bibliography of all of Moore's publications up to 1966, see "Bibliography of the Writings of G. E. Moore," initially compiled by Emerson Buchanan and Moore for the first edition of the Schilpp collection in 1942 and enlarged after Moore's death in a second edition of the volume. References to some posthumously published works by Moore that appeared after 1966 can be found in our list of writings of Moore in the Bibliography.

21   By the mid-1900s, Moore was one of only four Apostles who had received the Order of Merit, the others being Henry Jackson, G. O. Trevelyan, and G. M. Trevelyan. This fact did not go unnoticed by some of the proud Apostles, who gleefully took it to confirm their 'intellectual superiority'. A number of Apostles were also elected to the British Academy after its creation in 1902. For evidence of the Apostles' reactions to these distinctions, see Lubenow (1998: 41, 237).

22   Some of Moore's students and colleagues have passed on anecdotes which seem to confirm that Moore had character traits of these kinds in abundance. Two such stories, later revealed by Malcolm (1963: 165–167), have Moore's wife Dorothy as their source. One speaks of Moore's intellectual honesty: while at the railway station on the way to read one of his most celebrated

papers, "Proof of an External World," at the British Academy, Moore expressed to Dorothy his concerns with the quality of its ending, which seemed unsatisfactory to him. When she attempted to comfort him by saying that they would like it, he responded emphatically "If they *do*, they'll be *wrong*." Another anecdote recounted by Dorothy speaks of his candor about ordinary matters: after chatting briefly and politely with King George VI on the occasion of being awarded the Order of Merit, upon his return to the cab where Dorothy was waiting outside Buckingham Palace, Moore excitedly reported: "Do you know that the King had never heard of Wittgenstein!"

SUGGESTED READING

Baldwin, Thomas and Consuelo Preti, eds., *G. E. Moore: Early Philosophical Writings*, Cambridge: Cambridge University Press, 2011. Offers the text of Moore's (1897 and 1898 dissertations, both entitled "The Metaphysical Basis of Ethics," together with the comments by their respective readers (viz., Sidgwick and Caird; Ward and Bosanquet). See its useful "Editors' Introduction" (pp. xii–lxxxv) for a discussion of Moore's idealist beginnings and his change of mind in the 1898 dissertation.

Braithwaite, R. B., "George Edward Moore 1873–1958," *Proceedings of the British Academy* 47 (1961): 293–309. A eulogy for G. E. Moore by one of his former students. Contains interesting remarks about his impact on students, Bloomsbury, and other readers of his works.

Levy, Paul, *G. E. Moore and the Cambridge Apostles*, London: Weidenfeld & Nicolson, 1979. An ambitious, biographical account of Moore's early years at Cambridge, his troubled relations with Russell and Wittgenstein, and his interactions with other Apostles. But must be read with caution, since the author's speculative style often interferes with his ability to represent the facts. According to Russell scholar Nicholas Griffin (1991), such a defect is noticeable in Levy's account of why Moore's relationship with Russell became at some point strained.

Lubenow, W. C., *The Cambridge Apostles, 1820–1914*, Cambridge: Cambridge University Press, 1998. Looks closely at the history of the Cambridge Conversazione Society. Reveals how it recruited its members, what happened in the Saturday meetings, and what some prominent members believed on crucial issues, such as belief in immortality and the existence of God. At the end, Lubenow offers a helpful directory of members during the Society's heyday.

Malcolm, Norman, "George Edward Moore," in *Knowledge and Certainty*, Englewood Cliffs, NJ: Prentice-Hall, 1963, pp. 163–183. Contains biographical material focused on Moore's traits of character. Good source for anecdotal evidence concerning those traits. See also Stebbing (1942).

Moore, G. E., "An Autobiography," in Paul Arthur Schilpp (1942), pp. 3–39. Moore's own account of his personal and professional development. Although not always reliable, it contains interesting information about major influences in his work and the Golden Age of analytic philosophy at Cambridge.

Moore, G. E., *The Elements of Ethics*, Philadelphia, PA: Temple University Press, 1991 [1898]. Based on Moore's notes for a set of public lectures, it introduces his main doctrines in moral metaphysics and epistemology. On Moore's own account, it was the draft of all the chapters of *Principia Ethica* except for Chapter 6, "The Ideal."

Russell, Bertrand, *The Autobiography of Bertrand Russell, 1872–1914*, London: Allen and Unwin, 1951. Contains lively anecdotes of Russell's interactions with Moore and other Apostles during their early years at Cambridge.

Ryle, Gilbert, "G. E. Moore," in *Collected Papers: Critical Essays*, vol. 1, London: Hutchinson & Co, 1971, pp. 268–271. Ryle emphasizes the role of Moore's early attention to semantic clarity and philosophical analysis in the development of analytic philosophy. With regard to Moore's legacy as a teacher, Ryle notes that he taught his students "to try to assess and how to assess the forces of the expressions on which philosophical issues hinge," thus producing a drastic reorientation of the philosophical method that influenced Wittgenstein and others (p. 270). The article also includes warm anecdotal evidence of Moore's impact on his students.

Schneewind, J. B., *Sidgwick's Ethics and Victorian Moral Philosophy*, Oxford: Clarendon Press, 1977. Good discussion of the intellectual context (especially idealism and evolutionism) in which Sidgwick's and Moore's doctrines developed. Provides an overview of the history of British ethics from Reid's vindication of common morality and Bentham and Mill's classical utilitarianism to the time when Sidgwick wrote his *Methods of Ethics*.

Shaw, William, "Editor's Introduction," in G. E. Moore, *Ethics*, New York: Oxford University Press, 1966 [1912], pp. vii–xxxix. Disputes the view that after publication of *Principia* in 1903 Moore introduced no new ethical doctrines of any substance. Shaw is one of the few who seem to agree with Moore's judgment in his autobiography that *Ethics* is preferable to *Principia*.

Sidgwick, Henry. *Henry Sidgwick, a Memoir*, A. S. and E. M. S. eds., London: Macmillan, 1906. Published posthumously by Sidgwick's wife Eleanor Mildred and his brother Arthur, who, like Henry, was also an Apostle, this memoir includes an "autobiographical fragment" dictated to them by Sidgwick himself before his death, together with some of his notes and letters. Apparently, the inclusion of this material did not sit well at the time of publication with the Apostles, who considered the revelations added by the editors without Henry's approval a threat to the group's secrecy (Lubenow 1998: 36–37).

2

PRINCIPIA ETHICA IN ITS CONTEXT

With Gary Seay

Moore was only 29 when *Principia Ethica* came out in 1903. After winning a fellowship competition at Cambridge in 1898 and publishing his landmark article "The Nature of Judgement" (NJ) in 1899, he had quickly built a reputation for himself among philosophers as well as British artists and intellectuals. Moreover, his impact on each of these circles was not only doctrinal but also personal, as attested by many of Moore's acquaintances from inside and outside academic philosophy. In this chapter, we first consider the reception of his work outside academic philosophy, in particular, among the intellectuals and artists of the Bloomsbury circle. As our discussion reveals, some disputes about the source of Moore's popularity with them bear directly on what we should make of the normative theory in *Principia*, an issue we take up in Chapter 11. We then turn to some aspects of Moore's work that helped build his reputation

DOI: 10.4324/9780429275975-2

in philosophy and explain why he generally is (and should be) regarded as one of the founders of the analytic tradition in general, and of analytic ethics in particular.

2.1 THE NON-EXPERT READERS OF *PRINCIPIA ETHICA*

The publication of *Principia Ethica* in 1903 was an important event in philosophy. In addition to philosophers, it attracted the attention of many educated but "non-expert" readers of Moore's time. Numerous works of fiction and literary criticism, biographies, memoirs, and countless private notes and letters give abundant evidence that *Principia* generated an interest wider than what's usually expected for a monograph on the foundations of ethics.[1] Its non-expert readers came from the world of literature, music, the arts, journalism ... even economics, jurisprudence, and public policy. Although the group included some readers from Cambridge who were quite familiar with Moore's thought, others were not. But they all seemed especially attracted to the topics and style of ethical inquiry in *Principia*. They valued this book's vindication of conceptual clarity and reasoned argument as well as its claim to novelty. In fact, the preface to the first edition opens with the following remarks, which might have been appealing to the non-expert readers:

> I am inclined to think that in many cases a resolute attempt [at the analysis of any potential philosophical questions] would be sufficient to ensure success; so that, if only this attempt were made, many of the most glaring difficulties and disagreements in philosophy would disappear. At all events, philosophers seem, in general, not to make the attempt; and whether in consequence of this omission or not, they are constantly endeavouring to prove that Yes or No will answer questions, to which *neither* answer is correct, owing to the fact that what they have before their minds is not one question, but several, to some of which the true answer is 'No,' to others 'Yes.'
>
> (*PE*: 33)

Yet this passage shows of course a Socratic pedigree that ought to have been evident to many of the non-expert readers of *Principia*, who nonetheless went on to associate the book's pursuit of conceptual clarity, consistency, and reasoned argument with some characteristically Moorean set of standards. So dazzled were these readers with Moore's style of conducting philosophical inquiry that they ignored his occasional failure to live up to his own standards.

True, some of these readers belonged to the intellectual and artistic Bloomsbury circle, which had a strong connection with philosophy at Cambridge. Thus, they can hardly be considered non-experts.[2] The circle was most instrumental in spreading Moore's doctrines beyond philosophy. Many of its members, having overlapped with him at Cambridge during the time of his six-year fellowship at Trinity, had interacted with him at the Apostles philosophical society as undergraduates. They graduated shortly after publication of *Principia* and went on to form that circle, giving it the name of the London neighborhood where they lived. Although the exact date of its creation is unclear, according to one of its founders, Leonard Woolf, "there grew up in London during the years 1907 to 1914 a society or group of people which became publicly known as Bloomsbury" (Woolf 1960: 155). On his account, by 1904, "the foundations of what became known as Bloomsbury were laid" (ibid.: 180).[3]

By that time the group began to hold what were to become regular Thursday evening meetings. Besides Woolf and Moore, prominent participants who had a relation to Cambridge included biographer Lytton Strachey, novelist E. M. Forster, economist John Maynard Keynes, and journalist Desmond MacCarthy. Ludwig Wittgenstein, and Bertrand Russell sometimes attended the Thursday meetings which were held until the group dissolved in 1920. Afterwards, for about two decades some ex-Bloomsburyites attended the meetings of a new group, the Memoir Club, devoted to examining recollections of Bloomsbury by former members. It was for one of these meetings that Keynes wrote his (1949) memoir "My Early Beliefs," which like Woolf's (1960) *Sowing*, provides ample evidence that the Bloomsbury group embraced *Principia Ethica* as a moral bible – together with Moore himself, whom they came to consider a paradigm of the philosopher, ranking him higher than McTaggart, Dickinson, and Russell.

Accordingly, Keynes remembered that Bloomsbury "was all under the influence of Moore's method, according to which you could hope to make essentially vague notions clear by using precise language about them and asking exact questions" (1949: 88). Emulating Moore's analytic method, the Bloomsburyites would engage in lengthy discussions of the exact meaning of a given question because on their Moorean view this was a pre-condition for finding an adequate answer. They were particularly attracted to Moore's views on the "ideal" (i.e., what's intrinsically good to a high degree) discussed in Chapter 6 of *Principia*, "The Ideal." Particularly illuminating for the Bloomsbury group was Moore's claim that the value of some wholes need not equal the sum of the values of their parts. When a qualifying whole consists of, say, the contemplation of a beautiful object and the emotion of admiration, the principle sanctions that, although each of these might have little value by itself, a whole consisting in admiration in the contemplation of a beautiful object would have great value. Keynes recalled that the Bloomburyites focused on putting this principle to work in assessing the comparative value of alternative wholes in which sentiments such as enjoyment of personal relationships and beauty were at stake. But they ignored another important element of *Principia Ethica*: ideal utilitarianism, the normative theory offered in Chapter 5, "Ethics in Relation to Conduct," that we consider in Chapter 11 of this book. However, as we'll soon see, Keynes's "recollection" of this has been controversial.

For now, note that not all the amateur philosophers reading *Principia* came from the Bloomsbury circle, as evident, for instance, in the case of jurist Sir Frederick Pollock. A Cambridge Apostle and an expert in English Common Law, Pollock was about to retire as Corpus Professor of Jurisprudence at Oxford when *Principia* appeared. In a letter to Moore dated October 14 of that year, he welcomed the publication of the book, hailing it as "quite the most original and vital thing I have seen for a long time ..." Not only did Pollock agree with *Principia*'s arguments against naturalistic and metaphysical ethics, he went on to apply the principle of organic unities to jurisprudence generally, finding it well exemplified in the case of binding agreements. After all, he reasoned, although an agreement of just one person has no force, when combined with the agreement of another person, each of them count as a binding promise. "Here is a whole," wrote Pollock, "with a value not obtainable by any addition or multiplication of its parts, since each part separately is nothing" (cited in Lubenow 1998: 180–181). Moore's biographer Paul Levy cites this letter in the course of contending that, by contrast with Pollock, the Bloomsbury readers of *Principia* "were not capable of following Moore's dialectic in the way he patently intended" (1979: 237). However, as noted by Tom Regan, there is room to doubt the plausibility of Levy's claim since these non-experts "can hardly be regarded as fools."[4]

2.2   PRACTICAL ETHICS: REFORMIST FOR SOME, TOO CONSERVATIVE FOR OTHERS

Both Keynes's and Woolf's memoirs agree about the admiration the Bloomsbury group felt for Moore and *Principia*.[5] As "My Early Beliefs" puts it, the group found publication of this book "exciting, exhilarating, the beginning of a renaissance …" (Keynes 1949: 82). Its members were attracted primarily to Moore's methodology of inquiry and especially to his claims in Chapter 6 on the "Ideal," an expression Moore uses for things that are good as ends in a high degree. On his view, "[b]y far the most valuable things, which we know or can imagine, are certain states of consciousness, which may be roughly described as the pleasures of human intercourse and the enjoyment of beautiful objects" (*PE*: §113, 237). The Bloomsburyites found this claim congenial to their own evaluative preferences. But there is disagreement between these key figures of the circle about what the Bloomsburyites made (or rather, failed to make) of Moore's normative theory, especially his theory of right conduct outlined in Chapter 5 of *Principia*. According to Keynes:

> [W]hat we got from Moore was by no means entirely what he offered us. He had one foot on the threshold of the new heaven, but the other foot in Sidgwick and the Benthamite calculus and the general rules of correct behavior. There was one chapter in the *Principia* of which we took not the slightest notice. We accepted Moore's religion, so to speak, and discarded *his morals*. Indeed, in our opinion, one of the greatest advantages of his religion, was that it made morals unnecessary …
>
> (1949: 82, our emphasis)

Here 'morals' means Moore's theory of right conduct, which qualifies for what philosophers today regard as a two-level consequentialist theory. At the theoretical level, the theory embraces the principle that an action is morally obligatory just in case it would produce the highest balance of value compared to other actions available to an agent in the circumstances. At the decision-making level, it takes the rules of common morality to be generally adequate guides in determining the action that has the best overall consequences compared with all available alternatives (*PE*: §99, 213).

Contra Keynes's "recollection" Woolf thought that the Bloomsbury group ignored this normative theory *only* by 1914, but not by 1903 when its members were undergraduates. Instead, during the years before World War I, Moore's normative theory had become second nature among the group – or in his own words, it has "passed into our unconscious … we no longer argued about it as a guide to practical life" (Woolf 1960: 156). In 1903,

> The tremendous influence of Moore and his book upon us [the Bloomsburyites] came from the fact that they suddenly removed from our eyes an obscuring accumulation of scales, cobwebs, and curtains, revealing for the first time to us, so it seemed, the nature of truth and reality, of good and evil and character and conduct, substituting for the religious and philosophical nightmares, delusions, hallucinations, in which Jehovah, Christ, and St. Paul, Plato, Kant, and Hegel had entangled us, the fresh air and pure light of plain common-sense. It was this clarity, freshness, and common-sense which primarily appealed to us. Here was a profound philosopher who did not require us to accept any "religious" faith or intricate, if not unintelligible intellectual gymnastics of a Platonic, Aristotelian, Kantian, or Hegelian nature; all he asked us to do was to make quite certain that we knew what we meant when we made a statement and to analyze and examine our beliefs in the light of common-sense.
>
> (ibid.: 147–148)

Woolf also observed that the Bloomsburyites were attracted to *Principia* because of what they perceived as its emphasis on conceptual clarity as well as its reliance on reason and common sense for deciding the right thing do or believe morally. They thought Moore provided a normative theory far superior to the theories of classical utilitarianism and its competitors because it grounded moral decision-making in neither moral rules nor the moral virtues. As a result, they ascribed to it a liberating effect that contrasted not only with Aristotelian, Kantian, or utilitarian ethics but also with the principles of Victorian conventional morality.

Of course, not all agreed with this "liberationist" interpretation of *Principia*'s normative theory. Russell was one of the early dissenters who held instead that the book had certain "unduly Conservative and anti-reforming" implications.[6] If Russell is right, then Bloomsbury might have found *Principia* liberating only by misinterpreting it – something consistent with Keynes's claim that the group ignored the normative theory in Chapter 5 of the book.

But Woolf was not alone in proposing a liberationist interpretation since, among others, R. B. Braithwaite (1961) and especially Tom Regan (1986) too have regarded the normative theory of *Principia* as a vindication of individual freedom. On Regan's account, a celebration of reason and maximal freedom of the individual in moral decision-making is the "chief (but certainly not the only) lesson Moore's Bloomsbury followers learned" from the book (Regan 1986: xii). Elaborating on this point, he contends that:

> [Given Moore's] ethic of individual liberation ... we are to have the courage to act on our own, by our own lights, without being dominated by the oppressive demand to conform to widely accepted but unwarranted expectations about what is 'proper' and 'right.' The moral nerve of Moore's teaching is to free oneself from unreflective acceptance of tradition and custom in the conduct and direction of one's life.
>
> (ibid.: 24)

Regan took his interpretation of Moore's normative theory to rest on two pillars of textual evidence from *Principia*, each of which suggesting that individuals must generally decide for themselves what to do or believe morally, free from constraints from the rules of religion, common morality, or convention. First, Moore's claim that individuals cannot know all future consequences of their actions. Second, according to Moore, the situations in which people need to observe a rule of common morality are not likely to be more than a few, given his view that an existing rule of common morality must be observed only when it is required for social stability and very few such rules are so required.

At this point, the disagreement between liberationist and conservative interpretations of the normative theory of *Principia* has reached an *impasse* that can be resolved only by a look at the theory that is closer than what we can do in this chapter. Nevertheless, before moving on, let's distinguish two questions involved in the disagreement. One concerns the entailments of that theory as a decision procedure, which we consider in Chapter 11. The other is a factual question about what the non-expert followers of Moore generally made of Moore's ideal consequentialism. Did they interpret it in the liberationist way of Regan and Woolf, or in the conservative way of Russell and a few others? We must leave to the historians of Moorism a proper answer this question – but not without provisionally noting that Daniela Donnini Macciò (2015; 2016a; 2016b) has recently provided strong evidence that Moore's normative theory in fact fueled progressive agendas among its followers on matters of social justice and international relations. Although in *Principia*, Moore limited his discussion of justice to "vindictive punishment" (i.e., retributive justice), Donnini Macciò provides evidence that his "disciples" made attempts to apply his normative theory to some issues of the day involving social and economic inequities, and thus, distributive justice. Arguably, these disciples turned to a distributivist conception of justice under the influence of Moore's conviction that a nonegalitarian society cannot maximize the good for most people concerned.

In any case, Moore himself never directly addressed the question of what his readers from outside philosophy made of *Principia*. In fact, he never mentioned Bloomsbury in his autobiography, vaguely reporting that the outline of the last chapter of the book was suggested to him in conversation with "a friend" (supposedly, Hugh Owen Meredith, who was active in Bloomsbury and the Conversazione Society).

2.3   FROM ABSOLUTE IDEALISM TO NON-NATURALISTIC REALISM

AGAINST ABSOLUTE IDEALISM

According to a standard account of the origin of analytic philosophy, Moore's work is one of its principal sources. His NJ played a crucial role in the development of that tradition in philosophy because it advanced an ontological doctrine that is deeply at odds with the continental school of philosophy dominant in Britain during Moore and Russell's undergraduate years. As Russell puts it (1944: 54), NJ was "the first published account of the new philosophy." Here he is referring to the early realism of three pioneers of analytic philosophy at Cambridge: Russell himself, Moore, and Wittgenstein. To understand why Moore's NJ had that crucial role requires first recalling that during their undergraduate studies, Moore and Russell fell under the influence of J. M. E. McTaggart, one of their tutors who held a version of the neo-Hegelian idealism then in fashion in British philosophy. Particularly attractive to them was F. H. Bradley's *Principles of Logic* and its critique of John Locke's association of linguistic meaning with ideas in the mind, which was common in the work of other empiricists as well. Bradley rightly objected that a mentalistic conception of meaning is an obstacle to the development of logic and theories of truth because it entails that the meanings of ideas and judgments may vary from person to person and also change over time.

In NJ, Moore agreed with the basis of this objection to the psychologism of the empiricists but argued that the objection did not go far enough. In what is probably a strawman reconstruction of Bradley's own doctrine (Baldwin 1990: 13–15), Moore charged that it relies on a distinction between meaning and ideas still affected by the psychologism that Bradley sought to debunk. After all, Bradley said the meaning of an idea or sign consists in a part that is "cut off" from that idea and fixed by the mind. On Moore's new realism of concepts and propositions, Bradley should have said that concepts and propositions are radically different from ideas in the mind. Unlike these, they are objective and utterly independent of mind and language. Having these features, they cannot therefore be "fixed" by the mind. It follows that

Bradley's doctrine failed to go far enough in rejecting the mentalistic conception of meaning of the empiricists. At the same time, given the realism of concepts that Moore was thus entertaining, propositions are mind- and language-independent complexes of simple concepts that stand for simple objects of thought.

A conception of propositions along these lines has been widely influential in analytic philosophy, especially within the so-called Russellian theory of propositions, according to which the content of some such semantic entities is nothing over and above the objects they refer to. Many current writers on propositions in fact describe them in ways akin to Moore's account of them in some passages of NJ, for example, this one:

> A proposition is composed not of words, nor yet of thoughts, but of concepts. Concepts are possible objects of thought; but that is no definition of them. It merely states that they come into relations with a thinker; and in order that they may do anything, they must already be something. It is indifferent to their nature whether anyone thinks them or not. They are incapable of change; and the relation into which they enter with the knowing subject implies no action or reaction ... It is of such entities as these [simple concepts] that a proposition is composed. In it certain concepts stand in specific relations with one another. And our question now is, wherein a proposition differs from a concept, that it may be either true or false.[7]

Moore further claimed that in asserting a proposition or judgment, what is asserted is a connection between concepts (NJ: 180). While the act of judging occurs in the mind, the proposition is external to it. Neither simple concepts nor propositions can be subject to change or relative to space and time.[8] But while simple concepts are indefinable and lack truth conditions, complex concepts that qualify as propositions are, of necessity, true or false. Either of these truth values is, on Moore's view, a simple concept as well as a property of propositions. Being simple, 'truth' cannot be defined in terms of correspondence with reality or anything else. He went a step further to make the radical Platonist claim that reality itself consists exclusively of true propositions. Moore himself appeared surprised that his critique of Bradley led him to the stunning conclusion that anything that exists consists merely in a concept or a complex of concepts. "I am pleased to believe," wrote Moore, "that this is the most Platonic system of modern times."[9] However, since Moore could not find a compelling reason for such realism of concepts and propositions, he soon abandoned it. In later years he grew sympathetic to a kind of commonsense realism in metaphysics and epistemology inspired by Thomas Reid, whom he read during the years of 1904–1911 when he was away from Cambridge.[10]

Yet by contrast with the commonsense tradition, in *Principia Ethica*, Moore countenanced a richer ontology of *sui generis* non-natural properties and facts. As we discuss in Chapter 8, such properties and facts exist but somehow do not have being and of necessity metaphysically depend on some natural properties and facts. Although Moore did not provide a label for that relation of necessary metaphysical dependence, it is clear from *Principia* and other writings that he had in mind what we call today 'supervenience.' We consider Moore's understanding of this relation.

MOORE AND RUSSELL

Like Moore's, Bertrand Russell's early metaphysics was a form of realism of concepts or terms, the linguistic expression of concepts. But Russell's realist doctrine quickly evolved into logical atomism, a metaphysical position Moore never endorsed. Yet Russell credited Moore with having led the way to his own realism, and thus, with the leadership of the so-called revolt against idealism that took place in Britain at the turn of the twentieth century. Among other works, Russell credited Moore in this passage of the much-quoted preface to his *Principles of Mathematics*:

> On fundamental questions of philosophy, my position, in all its chief features, is derived from Mr G. E. Moore. I have accepted from him the non-existential nature of propositions (except such as happen to assert existence) and their independence of any knowing mind; also the pluralism which regards the world, both that of existents and that of entities, as composed of an infinite number of mutually independent entities, with relations which are ultimate, and not reducible to

adjectives of their terms or of the whole which these compose. Before learning these views from him, I found myself completely unable to construct any philosophy of arithmetic, whereas their acceptance brought about an immediate liberation from a large number of difficulties which I believe to be otherwise insuperable. The doctrines just mentioned are, in my opinion, quite indispensable to any even tolerably satisfactory philosophy of mathematics, as I hope the following pages will show.[11]

Peter Hylton (1990: 127–128) and David Pears (1957: 43) are among the scholars of early analytic philosophy who accept Russell's account of the things he learned from Moore. But others disagree, including Moore himself in his autobiography when considering the principal philosophical influences on his work. There he explicitly gave Russell a prominent role from the outset (A: 15). Most likely, Moore and Russell influenced each other as undergraduates and even later, once their early friendship had begun to fade, after Moore's return to Cambridge in 1911. Perhaps Russell exaggerated Moore's influence on his own metaphysics as a result of his awareness that many sources often went unrecognized in his writing, an error understandable in a philosopher as prolific as Russell (Griffin 1991: 56–58, 300 ff.). Be that as it may, the facts about their publications suggest that, while Moore was first to get the rebellion into print, Russell went deeper into its consequences, especially in philosophy of mathematics, logic, and language.

However this exegetical dispute gets settled, note that in spite of breaking with the metaphysics of the British idealists of the second half of the nineteenth century, the new realism of Moore and Russell did retain some elements of idealism, something that is evident, for example, in their objection to the psychologism of the empiricists. As a result, their "revolt" against neo-Hegelian idealism has been found to lack the sharp break with the past associated with a true revolution (Pears 1957: 41). Even so, in the course of carrying it out, these dissenters effected changes in the focus and manner of doing philosophy in Britain that soon became characteristic features of analytic philosophy. Of course, they were not alone in articulating this new philosophical tradition. A special place in its development must first go to the works of

German logician and mathematician Gottlob Frege.[12] In addition, the logical positivists and some of Moore and Russell's Apostolic friends at Cambridge played a key role in the advancement of that tradition – to name only a few, Ludwig Wittgenstein, Frank Ramsey, Alfred North Whitehead, and John Maynard Keynes.

NOT A SOURCE OF ANALYTIC PHILOSOPHY?

Our view of the sources of analytic philosophy thus conflicts with accounts that leave Moore out of that group, such as Michael Dummett's, according to which, "[i]mportant as Russell and Moore both were, neither was the, or even a, source of analytical philosophy" (1993: ix). Now surely this is a misreading of history, if ever there was one. Dummett is drawn to it because he thinks that the roots of analytic philosophy are to be found instead in the late-nineteenth-century phenomenology of the German-speaking world. Although Dummett admits that this school of philosophy appears precisely the antithesis of the analytic tradition, he none-theless contends that German phenomenology must be the source of analytic philosophy because this tradition was born with the so-called linguistic turn of contemporary philosophy taken by German phenomenology (ibid.: 5–6). Given that premise, assuming with Dummett that the linguistic turn was taken first by Frege, it follows that he is the source of analytic philosophy. Moreover, since Frege's philosophical views plainly fall within the phenome-nological school of philosophy, it would appear to follow too that analytic philosophy has its roots in German phenomenology and the standard account of its origin rests on a mistake.

Of course, the soundness of Dummett's argument hinges on the noted premises: namely, that (1) the linguistic turn of con-temporary philosophy was taken first by Frege, and (2) analytic philosophy emerged with that linguistic turn. By 'linguistic turn,' Dummett refers to a style of contemporary philosophy that arose when some philosophers began to regard natural language as an obstacle in their inquiry that could be overcome only by analysis of meaning and logical form. Frege was first in taking this turn since he was first in holding that "thoughts, and not the sentences that express them" are the subject-matter of philosophy, and in coming to regard natural language as an obstacle to philosophical inquiry in need of elimination by analysis.

But the standard account of the origin of analytic philosophy can concede Dummett's premise (1) while holding that Frege and others in the phenomenological school are not the *sole* source of analytic philosophy. After all, there is room for skepticism about the conception of analytic philosophy that fuels premise (2). Given that conception, this philosophical tradition consists in two theses: "first, that a philosophical account of thought can be attained through a philosophical account of language, and, secondly, that a comprehensive account can only be so attained" (ibid.: 4). Yet counterexamples to this conception are abundant. After all, not *all* strands of analytic philosophy set themselves, either as one of their goals or as their exclusive goal, to account for thought via an account of language. Consider the case of analytic ethics, which comprises many views that cannot be classified within the linguistic turn as described by Dummett. True, some schools such as prescriptivism (Hare 1952) and analytical descriptivism (Jackson 1998; 2012) offer metaethical accounts that might encourage thinking that these views are primarily in the business of analyzing moral language. But other schools, such as metaethical relativism and ethical naturalism, might not. And although the Moore of *Principia Ethica* pays some attention to questions of moral language, he denies that ethics, indeed philosophy, should devote itself to the sort of linguistic analysis that he ascribes "to the writers of dictionaries and other persons interested in literature" (*PE* §2: 54, §5: 57/58).[13] He seems far from considering natural language an obstacle to ethical inquiry into those questions, for he is quite content with the ordinary meaning of ethical terms and eager to determine the nature of the properties he takes them to denote. Here is a passage relevant to this point:

> A definition does indeed often mean the expressing of one word's meaning in other words. But this is not the sort of definition I am asking for. Such a definition can never be of ultimate importance to any study except lexicography. If I wanted that kind of definition I should have to consider in the first place how people generally used the word good; but my business is not with its proper usage, as established by

custom. I should, indeed, be foolish, if I tried to use it for something which it did not usually denote: if, for instance, I were to announce that, whenever I used the word 'good', I must be understood to be thinking of that object which is usually denoted by the word 'table'. I shall, therefore, use the word in the sense in which I think it is ordinarily used ... My business is solely with that object or idea, which I hold, rightly or wrongly, that the word is generally used to stand for. What I want to discover is the nature of that object or idea ...

(*PE* §6: 58)

It appears that neither Moore nor many other early analytic philosophers (think of Alfred Ayer or the Vienna Circle) have taken the linguistic turn that Dummett considers defining of this tradition of philosophy.[14] We may now conclude that Dummett lacks a conception of the tradition that is broad enough to include some major schools, and thus fails to mount a sound challenge to the standard view that Moore is one of its sources.

CONTRIBUTIONS TO ANALYTIC PHILOSOPHY

The Open Question Argument (OQA) is the most widely discussed contribution that Moore made to analytic ethics. But before introducing this argument, let's briefly review here some of his philosophical breakthroughs in metaphysics, epistemology, theory of perception, and ethics.

- Moore proposed a pioneering identification of a relation of necessary metaphysical dependence along lines now commonly referred to as 'supervenience.' Although Moore did not use this expression, he clearly had the concept of supervenience of the moral on the natural in mind when he wrote about the relation between these two orders.
- Moore discovered a subtle presupposition at work in statements such as 'P but I don't believe that P,' which create what has come be known as 'Moore's paradox.' Among philosophers who thought most highly of Moore's insight in discovering this quasi-logical paradox were Wittgenstein (Malcolm 1984: 56) and J. L. Austin (1963: 332). From

Austin's ordinary-language perspective, the paradox shows that Moore recognized the limits of any semantics focused exclusively on the meaning of declarative sentences, such as Frege's or Russell's semantics. After all, the conjunction 'The cat is on the mat but I don't believe it is' faces no logical contradiction but "misfires" in ways akin to any "null and void" performative such as a "I bequeath you my watch" uttered by a speaker who has no watch.

- Moore introduced some terms of art for objects and relations that previously were only vaguely or confusedly identified. Prominent among them are the terms 'entailment,' 'sense data,' 'naturalistic fallacy,' and the pair, '*analysandum/ analysans.*'

- Moore made a vigorous and creative use of some strategies of the commonsense tradition in philosophy. He deployed them most notably to argue against idealism and Cartesian skepticism – as illustrated by his appeal to comparative certainties in defense of commonsense metaphysics and epistemology and his "proof" of an external world.

- Moore forcefully argued for the instrumental value of conceptual analysis in philosophy. Since analysis can provide clarity and help solve philosophical puzzles, he considered it instrumental for knowledge, to which he ascribed some value on its own. The Preface of *Principia* in fact opens with this vindication of conceptual clarity:

It appears to me that in Ethics, as in all other philosophical studies, the difficulties and disagreements, of which its history is full, are mainly due to a very simple cause: namely to the attempt to answer questions, without first discovering precisely what question it is which you desire to answer.

(*PE*: 33)

In what follows, we offer an introductory look at two of these contributions that figure in *Principia Ethica*. One of them bears on philosophical method, the other bears on what is wrong with naturalism according to the OQA. However, readers who are familiar with these contributions may choose to skip the two sections that we consider next.

Philosophical method

Conceptual analysis or definition is essential to Moore's conception of the method of ethics and more generally philosophy. In his early writings he took it to consist in the decomposition of complex concepts into their simple "parts" or components, regarding it as instrumental in sharpening philosophical questions. In later writings Moore added two other types of analysis: analysis of forms of expression and analysis of propositions.[15] In any event, of interest to us now is the type of analysis found in *Principia Ethics*, which features a complex concept to be analyzed (the *analysandum*), standardly placed on the left-hand side, and what gives its analysis (the *analysans*), standardly placed on the right-hand side. The *analysans* consists in simple concepts into which the *analysandum* is decomposed. According to Moore, ordinary concepts such as 'brother,' 'horse,' and the like as well as quasi-scientific concepts such as 'quality,' 'change,' and 'cause' are complex and therefore good candidates for this type of analysis by decomposition.[16] For example, the analysis of relational concept 'x caused y' would have an *analysans* of the form, "x preceded y & whenever an event like x has been observed it has also been observed that an event like y followed the event in question" (*LP*: 156). Or consider a notorious example from Chapter 1 of *Principia*, where Moore held that by contrast with simple concepts, 'good' and 'yellow,' the concept 'horse' admits of decomposition by analysis in this way:

> My point is that 'good' is a simple notion, just as 'yellow' is a simple notion; that, just as you cannot, by any manner of means, explain to anyone who does not already know it, what yellow is, so you cannot explain what good is. Definitions of the kind that I was asking for, definitions which describe the real nature of the object or notion denoted by a word, and which do not merely tell us what the word is used to mean, are only possible when the object or notion in question is something complex. You can give a definition of a horse, because a horse has many different properties and qualities, all of which you

can enumerate. But when you have enumerated them all, when you have reduced a horse to his simplest terms, then you no longer define those terms. They are simply something which you think of or perceive, and to anyone who cannot think of or perceive them, you can never, by any definition, make their nature known.

(*PE*: §7, 59)

Moore's claims in this passage are exceedingly weak. For, neither is 'yellow' obviously simple nor is 'horse' obviously complex. After all, 'yellow' may admit of the following analysis: first, we determine by *a priori* means (i.e., just by thinking about our own concepts, to which we have privileged epistemic access) that 'yellow' is a color concept that picks out whatever property of objects is responsible for certain visual experiences under normal circumstances (good lighting, eyes opened, etc.). Second, we proceed to determine by empirical investigation what that property is. Moore simply assumed that 'yellow' is not susceptible of an analysis along these or any other lines, and this assumption weakens his attempt to support, by analogy with 'yellow,' the unanalyzability or indefinability of 'good.'[17]

At the same time, his attempt to draw a disanalogy between complex concept 'horse' and simple concepts 'yellow' and 'good' also fails because it conflates the concept 'horse' with its referent – namely, the species that this concept denotes. What Moore had in mind in the above passage (four legs, a tail, a head, a mane, etc.) might qualify as "parts" of a horse, but not as constituents of the concept 'horse.' In fact, on a popular externalist semantics for natural kind concepts, 'horse' picks out an essential biological property of paradigm horses, say, their DNA. The "parts" of 'horse' that Moore lists are inessential to the individuation of the concept.

In any case, note that Moore's examples above are neither instances of definitions that give the meanings of words nor instances of what Moore referred to as "verbal" definitions of the sort "'Cat' is a noun with three letters" (*RC*: 661 ff.). He often emphasized that his interest was not finding the meaning of some ordinary words, but the real nature of the object or notion denoted by them. Knowing the meanings of the words is for Moore a pre-condition for being able to the produce the real definitions that are a philosopher's true aim. In the following note from lectures delivered during 1933 and 1934, Moore made these views clear:

> What's the use of 'philosophic definition'? It is not verbal definition, of the sort that it may help you to read a foreign book, or to understand a foreigner when he speaks to you, & also to make yourself under-stood by him. But this is not the use of philosophic definition; because they're all of them definitions of words or forms of expression you already understand – you already know their meanings in the sense of being able to attach the common meanings to them when you use them or hear or read them, though you mayn't know their meanings in the sense of being able to make true props. of the form 'this means so-&-so'.[18]

Introducing the Open Question Argument

The OQA is Moore's master argument in *Principia Ethica* against naturalism in ethics and for his own non-naturalist moral seman-tics and metaphysics. Although the argument focuses on the con-cept and property captured by the term 'good' when used with its primary ethical sense, analogous OQAs can be run against natu-ralistic and metaphysical readings of other key ethical terms. The argument presupposes that competent users of 'good' can deter-mine by reflection alone whether or not the concept and property captured by this term could be identical to any given purely natu-ralistic or metaphysical *analysans*. Moore contended that it is an open question whether some analyses of either sort are correct, and concluded that no such analysis can be correct. Furthermore, there is no correct *analysans* of any sort for 'good.' This concept is indefinable and unanalyzable – or as he puts it, "good is good, and that is the end of the matter ..." (*PE*: §6). He drew similar conclusions at the ontological level for the property denoted by that simple term. Suppose someone attempts a naturalistic reduc-tion of 'good' by arguing it is equivalent to 'what's more evolved.'

Given the line of reasoning in this version of the OQA, if that equivalence obtained, the question 'x is more evolved, but is it good?' would be closed or tautological (just as would be the question of whether whoever is sister is a female sibling). Run for the concept expressed by 'what we desire to desire' the argument leads (or so Moore thought) to an analogous conclusion: the question of whether what we desire to desire is intrinsically good remains open. If the proposed equivalence obtained, competent speakers should eventually come to a 'Yes' answer to that question just by thinking. But in *Principia Ethica*, Moore felt confident that they would reject any such naturalistic equivalence of 'good' or any other ethical term. He introduced the expression 'naturalistic fallacy' to label the philosophical mistake fueling any attempt at either a naturalistic or a metaphysical analysis of key ethical concepts and properties. The expression also applies to any attempt at analysis of 'good,' a term that for Moore stands for the sole simple concept and property of ethics.

Thus, from a few examples of attempts at analyzing 'good' in fully naturalistic or metaphysical terms, Moore drew very ambitious generalizations. If compelling, his inference for those generalizations would support that no moral concept is synonymous with any non-moral concepts, and that no moral property is identical to, or reducible to, any non-moral properties.

But his inference has been met with heated controversies that we explore at length in Chapters 5 and 6. For now let us note that the OQA has been an influential inference in metaethics for more than a hundred years. Even a number of rivals of Moore's non-naturalism have accepted versions of the OQA. These rivals range from the non-cognitivists who deny any robust truth-aptness for moral judgments to the error theorists who consider them truth-apt but actually all false because there are no moral facts to act as truth-makers (the only exceptions being some negative judgments such as 'Euthanasia is not morally wrong'). At the same time, the OQA raises a huge challenge for a number of ethical realists who agree with Moore in thinking that there are mind- and language-independent moral properties as well as robustly true moral judgments, but hold these to be nothing over and above natural properties and truths.

In light of these and other contributions of *Principia* to philosophical ethics, we of course disagree with Sidgwick's comment about a draft of this book. It appears that after hearing (false) rumors about publication of *The Elements of Ethics* by Moore in 1900, Sidgwick wrote to a friend:

> Moore! I did not know he had published any *Elements of Ethics*. I have no doubt they will be acute. So far as I have seen his work, his *acumen*—which is remarkable in degree—is in excess of his *insight*.[19]

Be that as it may, by 1942, Moore himself seemed skeptical about the merits of his first published book in ethics and the OQA offered in it. He had come to believe that another argument provides the best reason against naturalism in ethics (RC: 605–606) and that his second monograph in ethics is stronger than *Principia*. "This book [*Ethics*]," wrote Moore, "I myself like better than *Principia Ethica*, because it seems to me to be much clearer and far less full of confusions and invalid arguments" (A: 27). Such an assessment should come as no surprise to us. In fact, as early as 1922, Moore already harbored doubts about the quality of *Principia*, which he expressed in an incomplete preface ultimately left out of this book's second edition. There he declared "the book, as it stands, is full of mistakes and confusions ..." (P2: 2). The defects appeared to him so significant that they could not be repaired in any way short of re-writing the whole manuscript. However, like almost everyone else, we disagree with Moore on this point. *Principia* is not only a much better source than *Ethics* for the study of his metaethical doctrines but also has had the wider influence in moral philosophy discussed earlier in this chapter. It was in part responsible for the fact that the combination of metaethical doctrines it forcefully defends – chiefly, a realist non-naturalist moral ontology, an intuitionist moral epistemology, and a cognitivist conception of moral thought and language – have enjoyed a sympathetic reception in the early decades of the twentieth century and continue to be an object of debate. In the chapters that follow, we take a closer look at these doctrines, beginning with Moore's philosophy of ethics.

NOTES

1   Historically-minded critics of Moore who have noted the wide reception of his *Principia Ethica* among non-expert readers include Griffin (1989), Hampshire (1987), Levy (1979), and Rosenbaum (1987).

2   If S. P. Rosenbaum (1987: 217) is correct, members of the Bloomsbury group hardly count as non-experts since they had read not merely *Principia Ethica* but *all* of Moore's writings up to 1920. Nonetheless, as evident in the list we provide next, few of them were academic philosophers.

3   This date is close to 1905, when the children of Leslie Stephen moved to 46 Gordon Square, Bloomsbury, after his death, and became active members of the group. Stephen's children were: Virginia (who eventually married Woolf and became a celebrity in the world of contemporary literature), Vanessa (a painter and interior designer herself who is often cited in connection with some romantic relationships that are sometimes noticed by historians of the group), and Thoby and Adrian (who were students at Cambridge). These two brothers helped to establish the Bloomsburyites' Cambridge and Apostolic connections. The case of Vanessa Stephen best illustrates the general rebellious attitude of the Bloomsbury group toward the Victorian moral code. Vanessa first married art critic Clive Bell, then left him for painter and critic Roger Fry, who soon lost her to painter Duncan Grant, whom she shared with novelist David Garnett. For more on that attitude, see Regan (1986. pp. 8 ff.).

4   Rees (1968) agrees with Levy and Keynes in thinking that the Bloomsburyites misunderstood Moore's ethical doctrines. But for an opposite view, see Griffin (1989), Regan (1986), and Rosenbaum (1987).

5   The Bloomsburyites professed "Moorism" as their philosophy. Paul Levy (1979) writes that they learned it not exclusively from reading *Principia* but also from their personal interactions with Moore. But scholar of the group, S. P. Rosenbaum (1987: 216) finds this account too simplistic, counter-arguing that there is evidence that not only did the Bloomsbury group read *Principia* but had among their core members some Cambridge graduates with an Apostolic background. This was especially true of Moore's closest friend in Bloomsbury, Apostle Desmond MacCarthy. And although E. M. Forster wasn't as close a friend, his novels have Moorean characters and themes, especially *Howards End* (Sidorsky 2007) – hardly something that could have resulted merely from Forster's personal interaction with Moore. In any case, Roger Fry is often mentioned as the only Bloomsburyite who completely escaped the philosophical influence of Moore and *Principia Ethica.*

6   Russell noted the conservatism of *Principia Ethica* immediately after the book appeared in print, in a letter to Moore of October 10, 1903 (cited in Griffin 1989: 85). An interpretation of the normative import of *PE* along similar lines can be found in Levy (1979), Baldwin (1988), Blackburn (1988), Klagge (1988), and Griffin (1989). For an analysis of Russell's early critique of the conservatism of *Principia*, see the introduction to Chapter 13 in Pigden (1999).

7   Moore (NJ: 179). Like Moore in this passage, present-day Russellians and Fregeans construe propositions as mind- and language-independent entities

that are the necessary bearers of a truth value, whether truth or falsity. The difference between these theorists arises in their respective accounts of the logical form of propositions containing ordinary proper names, indexicals, or any other expressions that Russellians would consider directly referential. At present, there is no agreement about which of these competing accounts best accommodates Moore's conception of propositions. While some think that Fregean semantics does so (e.g., Katz 2004: 83 ff.), others deny this, holding that Moore lacked a Fregean, two-tier semantics in which sense is different from reference. For example, Thomas Baldwin (1990: 44–45) contends that Moorean propositions are more akin to what Frege regards as the reference of a declarative sentence – namely, a truth value. But see "Contributions to Analytic Philosophy" in Section 2.3, where we return to Moore's conception of propositions.

8 A realism along these lines allowed Moore to draw a sharp divide between judging (the psychological act) and what is judged (the judgment or proposition), as well as between his own doctrine and the one he ascribed to Bradley.

9 Letter to Desmond MacCarthy, August 1898, cited in Baldwin (1990: 40). See also Griffin (1991: 300 ff.).

10 Inspired in the commonsense tradition are his famous "A Defence of Common Sense" and "Proof of an External World." These essays offer what is now considered a characteristically Moorean response to idealism and to Cartesian skepticism – one that appeals to our comparatively greater confidence in our own realist and anti-skeptical views and argues on this ground for (1) the truth of propositions about the existence of the ordinary objects of perception (*contra* the idealist), and (2) the epistemic justification of belief in those propositions (*contra* the Cartesian skeptic).

11 Russell (1903b: ¶7). Other works in which Russell credits Moore with the leadership of their revolt against idealism include his autobiographies of 1944 (p. 12) and 1951b (p. 37).

12 Note, however, that Frege's work was all but unknown in the English-speaking world when Moore and Russell parted company with neo-Hegelian idealism. There is no evidence that Moore was familiar with Frege's works. And although the evidence suggests that Russell became familiar with it around 1900, his interest then was Frege's logicist program – about which he learned when he attended a talk by the Italian mathematician Giuseppe Peano at the Second International Congress of Mathematicians in Paris. Later that year Russell read Frege's *Grundgesetze der Arithmetik*, published in 1893.

13 Moore further maintains that "verbal" questions "can never be of ultimate importance in any study except lexicography" (*PE* §5: 57).

14 Here we are not denying that in early analytic philosophy some practitioners sought an account of thought through an account of language. This goal is evident, for example, in Wittgenstein's *Philosophical Investigations* and the ordinary language philosophers whom he influenced. But neither logical positivism nor Quinean eliminativism – to list just two other strands of twentieth-century analytic philosophy – pursued that goal. However, it should

be noted that since the expression 'linguistic turn' has considerable vagueness, it is not at all clear which strands of analytic philosophy have taken that turn.

15   Inspirations for Moore's broader conception of philosophical analysis in *Lectures on Philosophy* (*LP*) were Broad's discussion in "Critical and Speculative Philosophy" (*LP*: 165) and Russell's theory of descriptions. For Moore, Russell's theory was a paradigm of analysis of forms of expressions. He agreed with Russell's analysis of definite descriptions of the logical form of negative existential with an empty term in the subject's position (e.g., 'The present king of France is not bald'). But he also noticed some subtle exceptions such as "The right arm is often slightly longer than the left" (ibid.: 162). Besides *LP*, other sources for Moore's mature conception of analysis include "The Justification of Analysis" (1933), "A Reply to My Critics" (RC, 1942), and "Russell's 'Theory of Descriptions'."

16   Moore illustrated this type of analysis by decomposition in some notes for a lecture (*LP*: 156–157) with the ordinary term 'brother' and contended that certain complex notions of the special sciences such as 'cause' admit of similar analyses.

17   This tentative analysis of 'yellow' is inspired by Michael Smith's analysis of 'red' (2000: 28). An alternative analysis holds that 'yellow' combines some stereotypical semantical components that are knowable *a priori* (e.g., that it is a color concept distinct from 'blue,' 'red,' and the like) with whatever property is responsible for *that portion* of the electromagnetic spectrum (pointing to the area occupied by a dominant wavelength of 570–590 nm, as determined by the experts).

18   Moore (*LP*: 166). Jerrold Katz (2004: 84) was probably alone in understanding Moore's analyses as definitions that provide the linguistic meanings of expressions. The traditional understanding has been that Moore took conceptual analysis to serve the purpose of producing *real* definitions of properties and facts (Nelson 1967; Baldwin 1990). Confirming the traditional understanding are passages of *Principia* such as the following, aimed at answering the rhetorical question of how 'good' might be defined:

> Now it may be thought that this is a verbal question. A definition does indeed often mean the expressing of one word's meaning in other words. But this is not the sort of definition I am asking for. Such a definition can never be of ultimate importance to any study except lexicography.
>
> (*PE*: §6, 58)

In later writings, Moore consistently denied that he had ever engaged in analysis of verbal expressions (RC: 661; *LP*: 166).

SUGGESTED READING

Beaney, Michael., "Moore," Supplement to "Analysis," 2014, accessed January 4, 2018, https://plato.stanford.edu/entries/analysis/s6.html#4. Insightful discussion of Moore's early conception of analysis as definition of complex concepts by decomposition. See also Beaney's "Analysis" and "Annotated Bibliography," in *Stanford Encyclopedia of Philosophy*, Edward Zalta ed., 2014/2003, respectively at https://plato.stanford.edu/entries/analysis/ and https://plato.stanford.edu/entries/analysis/bib6.html#6.4

Donnini Macciò, Daniela, "The Apostles' Justice: Cambridge Reflections on Economic Inequality from Moore's *Principia Ethica* to Keynes's *General Theory* (1903–1936)," *Cambridge Journal of Economics* 40 (2016): 701–726. Useful historical survey of the actual impact of *Principia* on the Bloomsbury group and Moore's Apostolic friends. Suggests that under its influence, some prominent figures in these circles such as J. M. Keynes, G. L. Dickinson, R. Hawtrey, and H. O. Meredith came to regard social justice as a means to maximize the good and accordingly advanced progressive agendas from the positions they occupied in British culture and institutions.

Dummett, Michael, *Origins of Analytical Philosophy*, London: Duckworth & Co., 1993. *Contra* the standard view that Moore and Russell are sources of analytic philosophy, this book advances the controversial thesis that neither of them should be considered a source. According to Dummett, analytic philosophy is rooted instead in the phenomenological school of philosophy, to which Frege subscribed. We take issue with this claim in Section 2.3.

Glock, Hans-Johann, *What Is Analytic Philosophy?* Cambridge: Cambridge University Press, 2008. Comprehensive discussion of the question in this book's title. Of particular relevance to Moore's contribution to the rise of analytic philosophy are Chapters 2 and 5, focused respectively on the Anglophone and the Germanophone origins of analytic philosophy and the account of its origins by Michael Dummett. *Contra* Dummett, Glock plausibly contends that Moore and Russell, together with Frege, played a role in the rise of analytic philosophy.

Griffin, Nicholas, *Russell's Idealist Apprenticeship*, Oxford: Clarendon Press, 1991. Historical account that pays some attention to Moore's and Russell's rejection of the neo-Hegelian idealism predominant in British philosophy at the end of the nineteenth century. For Griffin, these two giants of analytic philosophy influenced each other.

Hylton, Peter, "The Nature of the Proposition and the Revolt against Idealism," in Richard Rorty, J. B. Schneewind, and Quentin Skinner, *Philosophy in History: Essays on the Historiography of Philosophy*. Cambridge: Cambridge University Press, 1984. pp. 376–397. Historical account of Moore's and Russell's revolt against idealism, with an insightful analysis of Moore's theory of concepts and propositions in NJ.

Hylton, Peter, *Russell, Idealism, and the Emergence of Analytic Philosophy*, Oxford: Clarendon Press, 1990. In the course of tracing the evolution of Russell's early metaphysics, from a thoroughgoing Bradleyan idealism to an extreme form of realism, Hylton offers a good historical overview of Moore's metaphysics during the years 1898 to 1903.

Keynes, John Maynard, "My Early Beliefs," in *Two Memoirs*, New York: A. M. Kelley; London, Rupert Hart-Davis, 1949, pp. 78–103. *Locus classicus* for the view that the Bloomsbury circle misread *Principia Ethica*, since their members took from it only the message they thought consistent with their own unconventional moral outlook. Contends that their individualism as well as superficiality of judgment and sentiment led them to ignore the consequentialist normative theory of *Principia*. For an opposite view, see, for instance, Woolf (1960) and Donnini Macciò (2015; 2016a; 2016b).

Moore, G. E., "The Nature of Judgement," *Mind* 8(30) (1899): 176–193, available at: http://fair-use.org/mind/1899/04/the-nature-of-judgment. Excerpted from Moore's (1898) dissertation, it amounts to the first published work of the revolt against neo-Hegelian idealism that took place in British universities at the turn of the twentieth century. See also Preti's (2008) article on the influence of nineteenth-century psychology on Moore's theory of propositions.

Moore, G. E., *Lectures on Philosophy*, Casimir Lewy ed., London: Allen & Unwin. New York: Humanity Press, 1966. Selection of Moore's notes from three courses, arranged accordingly in three parts, of which Part III is the chief source for our discussion in this chapter of Moore's later conception of philosophical analysis.

Moore, G. E. (with Margaret Masterman), "The Justification of Analysis," *Analysis* 1 (1933–1934): 28–30. Masterman's notes of a lecture given by Moore on the subject of philosophical analysis. Discusses its value for sharpening philosophical questions and thereby contributing to the solution of puzzles. Argues that conceptual clarity is sometimes intrinsically valuable but always has instrumental value in weeding out questions that make no sense. But it does not *per se* solve any philosophical problem.

Regan, Tom, *Bloomsbury's Prophet*, Philadelphia, PA: Temple University Press, 1986. Argues that the reading of Moore's *Principia Ethica* by the Bloomsbury group is preferable to that of students of philosophy because it best captures Moore's celebration of individual freedom over any of the standard virtue- or rule-based normative theories.

Russell, Bertrand, "Review of G. E. Moore, *Principia Ethica*," *The Cambridge Review* 25, lit. suppl. (1903a): 37–38. Accessed January 20, 2018. Brief but informative outline of *Principia Ethica*. Shows an early Russell in broad agreement with Moore's ethical realism.

Russell, Bertrand, "The Meaning of Good," *The Independent Review* 2 (March 1904): 328–333. Argues that Moore's definition of rightness is vulnerable to objection from the Open Question Argument, which Russell reconstructs as showing that no definition of goodness can yield a semantic tautology (i.e., a statement of the sort 'A sister is a female sibling'). For more on this 'barren tautology' reconstruction, see Chapter 5 in this book and Pigden (2007).

Ryle, Gilbert, "G. E. Moore," in *Critical Essays, Collected Papers*, vol. 1, London: Hutchinson & Co., 1971, pp. 268–271. Locates Moore's contribution to analytic philosophy in his ability to put the early-twentieth-century tools of formal logic at the service of clarity and the demarcation of relations between philosophical doctrines.

White, Alan R., *G. E. Moore: A Critical Exposition*, Oxford: Basil Blackwell, 1958. Somewhat dated but still useful general introduction to the contributions of Moore in many areas of philosophy, including philosophical method, ethics, epistemology, and philosophy of language. White's assessment of Moorean ethics is heavily influenced by his own emotivist perspective.

Woolf, Leonard, *Sowing: An Autobiography of the Years 1880 to 1904*. New York: Harcourt Brace Jovanovich, 1966. Disputes Keynes's (1949) contention that the Bloomsburyites ignored the normative theory in *Principia Ethica*.

3

PHILOSOPHY OF ETHICS

With *Principia Ethica*, Moore did more than help establish a certain brand of moral semantics, metaphysics, and epistemology.[1] His theses about what ethics is and how it relates to other disciplines, our chief focus in this chapter, helped to shape the approach to moral philosophy that was predominant during the past century. Salient among them is the thesis that ethics has its own subject matter independent of the subject matter of the natural sciences and theology. As an autonomous area of philosophical inquiry, ethics comprises the three distinct but related branches that are now usually included in it: metaethics, general normative ethics, and applied normative ethics. In what follows, I discuss Moore's view of applied normative ethics first, after having a quick look at the organization of *Principia Ethica* and what Moore himself made of the book. Next I take up four theses of *Principia* that played a key role during the early twentieth century in making the subject matter of ethics into a large and self-conscious business in a way that it was not before. At least in part as a result of the wide

DOI: 10.4324/9780429275975-3

reception of these theses, metaethics began to function then as a separate branch of ethics, one that unlike normative ethics, does not deal with *first-order* questions about moral conduct, value, or virtue. Rather, it focuses on *second-order* questions of the sorts that Moore investigated in the first four chapters of *Principia*, which range from questions about the philosophy of ethics and the semantics of moral language and thought, to questions about the nature of moral properties, truths, and knowledge.

3.1 THE SUBJECT MATTER OF ETHICS

THE STRUCTURE OF PRINCIPIA ETHICA

Principia amounts to Moore's best attempt at developing what he sometimes referred to as a "scientific ethics." Of its six chapters, only the last two devote considerable attention to some issues of normative or practical ethics. By contrast, the initial four chapters focus mostly on topics of metaethics, a branch of ethics referred to as 'philosophical ethics' in his book. Chapter 1, entitled "The Subject-Matter of Ethics" (§§1–23), offers an extensive discussion of the *sui generis* nature of key ethical concepts and properties and its implications for the autonomy of ethics, especially from §1 through §4. It then proceeds to outline Moore's chief reasons against moral philosophers whose views he deemed had failed to understand that nature. The three chapters that follow – "Naturalistic Ethics" (§§24–35), "Hedonism" (§§36–65), and "Metaphysical Ethics" (§§66–85) – elaborate on Moore's reasons against naturalistic and metaphysical ethics by looking closely at a number of ethical theories that, in his view, have attempted to reduce basic ethical concepts or properties to non-ethical concepts or properties. Moore was eager to show that they all committed a "naturalistic fallacy" since they fell prey to what he treated as a conclusive objection raised by his Open Question Argument (OQA). Chapter 5, entitled "Ethics in Relation to Conduct" (§§86–109), turns to general normative ethics and defends a consequentialist account that since Rashdall (1907) has been known as 'ideal utilitarianism.' Chapter 6, "The Ideal" (§§110–135), lays out the ground of Moore's valued-based normative theory, namely, an invariabilist, pluralistic, holistic theory of value. In this chapter, often regarded as the book's greatest contribution to ethics (Russell 1904; Hurka 2011), Moore offered subtle analyses of some common candidates for intrinsic value or disvalue such as pleasure, pain, beauty, and knowledge – together with an insightful discussion of a consequentialist justification of retributive punishment that can accommodate commonsense intuitions.

Nevertheless, most chapters of *Principia Ethica* are devoted to metaethical inquiry on questions of the sort Moore considered a pre-condition for undertaking investigations of practical ethics. True, Moore said that such investigations are the very aim of ethics. But in the book's first four chapters, his focus is not any substantive question of practical ethics but rather determining "the fundamental principles of ethical reasoning; and the establishment of these principles, rather than any conclusions which may be attained by their use" (Preface, *PE*: 35). Also pointing to the priority of metaethical inquiry is the book's title, which plainly echoes the title of a book on the foundations of natural science that has drawn special attention from philosophers since its publication in 1687: Isaac Newton's *Principia Mathematica*. While, in this book, Newton set himself the goal of establishing the fundamental principles of nature, it seems that in his *Principia Ethica*, Moore quite immodestly set for himself an analogous goal for the principles of morality. In a similar vein, he declares in its Preface that the Kantian-inspired title "Prolegomena to any future Ethics that can possibly pretend to be scientific" would have been equally suitable.

At the same time, Moore's speculation about the best title for his book suggests that he had an inflated estimation of its achievement, something also evident in remarks scattered throughout the book that present his own philosophical ethics as a radical departure from all major schools of ethics, from Aristotle's to Sidgwick's. A similarly exaggerated picture of *Principia*'s role within the history of ethics, as we have seen, appears in the writings of Leonard Woolf and some other Bloomsbury admirers of Moore. But this picture conflicts with textual evidence indicating that, during the late nineteenth and early twentieth centuries, some of Moore's contemporaries in Britain, such as fellow non-naturalists Henry Sidgwick (1879; 1906), Hastings Rashdall (1903; 1907), and John McTaggart Ellis McTaggart (1901) held a combination of ethical doctrines in many respects consistent with Moore's. With Sidgwick, for example, Moore shared a non-naturalist moral ontology, an intuitionist moral epistemology, and a consequentialist normative theory. But Moore rejected Sidgwick's hedonistic utilitarianism while favoring, with Rashdall and McTaggart, an "agathist" or "ideal" variety of consequentialism. In his early work on ethics, Bertrand Russell (1903a; 1904; and, to some extent, Russell 1910) also held these core doctrines of *Principia*. A more balanced historical picture would credit this book not so much with having produced radical innovations but rather with having forcefully defended an ethical outlook characteristic of a group of theorists whom hereafter I refer to as 'classical non-naturalists.'[2]

MOORE ON THE NATURE OF ETHICS

The general metaethical questions that interested Moore most in *Principia Ethica* – together with his references to ethics as a "science" that is somehow analogous to physics and chemistry – appears to give credence to an objection by P. H. Nowell-Smith (1954: 36 ff.), according to which, in the early twentieth century, Moore and other classical non-naturalists had changed the subject matter of ethics. In Nowell-Smith's view, traditionally at least since Aristotle, ethics was considered to be in the business of answering practical questions concerning what we shall do (or more precisely what we *ought* to do). Yet under the influence of Moore and *Principia*, ethics became mostly concerned with non-normative questions such as 'What is the nature of goodness?,' 'May moral rightness be defined in terms of moral goodness?,' and 'What sort of properties and facts are denoted by moral terms and judgments?' Furthermore, given Moore's cognitivist understanding of judgments of the form 'x is morally good,' moral judgments of this form amount to theoretical judgments whose terms denote properties and may enter into any of the logical relations commonly holding between statements.

However, as it stands, there is an ambiguity in Nowell-Smith's objection. For it may say that nobody was interested in questions of metaethics until after the publication of Moore's book, in which case, the objection is simply false since there is a long and varied history in Western philosophy of concern with metaethical questions of the sort that figure prominently in *Principia Ethica*. Or it may say that after publication of *Principia*, for a great part of the past century, moral philosophers devoted considerable attention to metaethics, treating it as a branch of ethics related to but relatively independent from general and applied normative ethics. In this case, the contention is true but Mooreans can live with it, for surely a number of factors other than the negative influence of *Principia* may explain this result. Furthermore, that Moore was interested in the nature of ethical properties and truths and how we know about them *per se* amounts to *no* objection and cannot support the charge that his interest produced a "change" in the subject matter of ethics. Moore was of course not the first philosopher in the Western tradition to be interested in those types of question. For example, Aristotle in *Nicomachean Ethics* (1926: VI, viii, 1142a) devoted some attention to the nature of moral knowledge, which he took to be a kind of moral perception based on *phronesis*, practical wisdom or discernment. And, of course, in his *Treatise of Human Nature* (2010/1739: Bk. III, Part I, Section 1), Hume famously argued for the logical autonomy of ethics.[3] In addition, it is simply false that questions of practical ethics did not matter to Moore: Chapters 5 and 6 of *Principia*, whose significance for normative ethics is now being re-evaluated (Hurka 2006; Skelton 2011), count as evidence that Moore assigned great importance to those questions. Actually, Moore took them to be the very "aim" of ethical investigation.

In addition, in Chapter 1 of *Principia* (§4), Moore offered a qualified vindication of casuistry, construed in the traditional way as the art of applying moral principles to cases. But his was a principlist or generalist vindication that competes with the moral particularist vindication now common in certain branches of applied ethics where proponents of casuistry challenge the role of inference from general principles in moral decision-making about cases.[4] In Chapter 1 of *Principia*, Moore invoked Aristotle to object to the neo-Hegelians' rejection of casuistry. Being a realist, Moore agreed with some causists' assumption that there are moral properties that all right (or wrong) actions share. Noting this assumption, F. H. Bradley had argued that there are no such properties to be shared by all right (or wrong) actions. In addition, Bradley found the studies of casuistry "more detailed and particular" than the investigation of ethics (1922/1883: 269). Moore rejected these criticisms, replying that casuistry aims at "discovering what actions are good, whenever they occur" (*PE*: §4: 56). Casuistic investigations are therefore general and any difference in generality when compared with the investigations in standard branches of ethics is *of degree*, not *of kind*. To these reasons, Moore adds the following:

> [O]wing to their detailed nature, casuistical investigations are actually nearer to physics and to chemistry than are the investigations usually assigned to Ethics. For just as physics cannot rest content with the discovery that light is propagated by waves of ether, but must go on to discover the particular nature of the ether-waves corresponding to each of several colours; so Casuistry, not content with the general law that charity is a virtue must attempt to discover the relative merits of every different form of charity. *Casuistry forms, therefore, part of the ideal of ethical science: Ethics cannot be complete without it.*
>
> (ibid.: §4, 56; my emphasis)

For Moore, the problems facing casuistic investigations are due not to the discipline's particularity but to the complexity of the moral issues with which it deals and to the fact that there is no sufficient ethical knowledge on which to ground them. As a result, casuistry "cannot be safely attempted at the beginning of our studies, but only at the end" (ibid.).

We may now conclude that, on Moore's account of casuistry, this branch of ethics amounts to much more than the analogical method now popular in some areas of applied ethics. And by no stretch of imagination can it be construed in the particularist way noted above since casuistry requires knowledge of the general principles of ethics first, so that they could be put at the service of moral appraisal of cases.

3.2   CORE THESES OF MOORE'S PHILOSOPHY OF ETHICS

Moore held that investigation in either general or applied normative ethics requires prior knowledge of some major issues of philosophical ethics, the branch of ethics now known as 'metaethics.' Accordingly, he devoted the first four chapters of *Principia* to advance his doctrines on those issues and outline his philosophy of ethics. This I regard as consisting in four theses. One of them, the autonomy-of-ethics thesis, vindicates the semantical, metaphysical, and logical independence of ethics from theology and the natural and social sciences, including psychology. The three other theses concern the relevance of metaethics and its relations with other branches of ethics: they hold that metaethics has intrinsic epistemic worth as well as independence from and priority over other branches of ethics.[5] As noted above, these four theses were highly influential in the philosophy of ethics that prevailed during most of the twentieth century. They helped to demarcate the branches of ethics as we know them today, with the exception of theory of practical reason, which Moore neglected to consider but became a central concern of metaethics only later in that century. In addition, they can be shown to be consistent with the currently popular view that metaethics, though independent, has the potential to impinge on substantive questions of normative ethics.

THE AUTONOMY-OF-ETHICS THESIS

As offered in *Principia*, the autonomy of ethics is a thesis that follows from Moore's semantical and metaphysical non-naturalism. Given these forms of non-naturalism, both moral concepts and properties are non-natural or *sui generis* (unlike concepts and properties of any other kind). If so, then ethics has its own subject matter, completely independent of the subject matters of the sciences, metaphysics, and theology. The thesis of concern here can be construed as follows:

> Autonomy – Ethics has its own subject matter, independent of the subject matter of the sciences, metaphysics, and theology.

In Moore's time, just as today, major challenges to Autonomy stem from psychology and the theory of evolution. After all, if some key ethical concepts or properties were equivalent to, say, what has evolved more, then ethics would be a chapter of evolutionary science. This claim is unacceptable to the Moore of *Principia*, for whom all key ethical terms are reducible at least in part to 'good,' the only basic, irreducible term of ethics, including terms, such as 'right' and 'virtue.' Since 'good' is irreducibly ethical, no key ethical term can be reduced to one or more non-ethical terms, and the autonomy of ethics then follows. In *Principia*, Moore announces his anti-reductionist outlook in ethics from the out-set by featuring, opposite the title page, Bishop Butler's apho-rism, "Everything is what it is, and not another thing." Later he declares that most ethical writers, up to *Principia*, had failed to embrace this truth as it applies to ethics, something shown in their futile attempts at "defining" goodness in some non-ethical terms so that what in fact is the subject-matter of ethics would appear to belong to a science, metaphysics, or theology. In attempting to equate ethical terms with non-ethical terms, previous writers have committed the 'naturalistic fallacy' (*PE*: §10, 62). *Principia*'s master argument for this charge is the Open Question Argument (OQA), which, if compelling, also supports the irreducibility of 'good,' and with it, the irreducibility of any key ethical concepts or property into other kinds of concept and property. Thus, if compelling, the OQA would secure Autonomy – though as we'll see in Chapters 5 and 6, the force of the OQA and its associated naturalistic fallacy charge has been highly contested, especially when the OQA is construed ontologically as an argument for the irreducibility of ethical *properties*.

Moore later changed his mind about some of these arguments and doctrines of *Principia* – most notably, the doctrine that 'good' in its primary ethical use expresses the sole simple concept and denotes the sole property to which all other ethical concepts and properties can be reduced, at least in part. Later in his *Ethics* he claimed that 'right' and 'good' both are the sole basic terms of ethics. But this change of mind in no way affected his thesis about the autonomy of ethics since he continued to advance a non-naturalist moral seman-tics and metaphysics. Whether monist or pluralist about the basic ethical terms and properties, Moorean non-naturalism holds that some key ethical terms convey *sui generis* ethical concepts (i.e., con-cepts that are semantically unlike any other concept) which denote mind- and language-independent ethical properties that are also *sui generis* (i.e., properties that are ontologically unlike any other prop-erties in the universe). If so, those terms admit of neither seman-tic nor ontological reductive analyses in non-ethical terms. Moore consistently held this general anti-reductionist outlook in ethics, as shown in a posthumously published collection of class notes where he revisited the relation between ethics and the sciences. After making clear that the scope of his irreducibility claim included some ethical concepts beyond 'good,' there he cautioned about the perils of reductive naturalistic analyses in ethics, writing that

> *if* certain analyses of ['good,' 'ought,' 'right,' 'wrong,' 'valuable,' etc.] are right, then other ethical propositions ... wouldn't be philosophical at all, but belong to psychology, sociology, and the theory of evolution. If naturalistic analyses are wrong, then it seems to me some other propositions do belong to philosophy: e.g., Pleasure is not the only good.
>
> (*LP*: 196)

Now, there is some controversy about the relation between this defense of the autonomy of ethics and Hume's rule: namely, that no ought-conclusion (i.e., moral conclusion) can logically follow from is-premises (i.e., purely descriptive premises) alone.[6] There has been some skepticism about whether Moore could accommodate that rule because he made these claims about the relation between ethical and purely descriptive properties:

A. Ought-Implyingness: Some purely descriptive properties are ought-implying.
B. Metaphysical Supervenience: Ethical properties of necessity metaphysically depend on certain natural properties of the things or actions that have those ethical properties.

According to some critics (Baldwin 2010; Bruening 1971; Pigden 1989; 2019), anyone who, like Moore, holds A and B must deny Hume's ban on attempting to deduce ethical conclusions from purely descriptive premises alone. After all, since implication is closely related to deduction, Moore cannot claim the lack of deducibility from the natural domain to the ethical domain. So at stake here are in fact these three different, though consistent, autonomy-of-ethics theses:

1.a Logical Autonomy – The thesis that no ethical conclusions can be deduced validly from non-ethical premises alone.

1.b Semantical Autonomy – The thesis that no ethical concept is translatable into one or more non-ethical predicates without significant loss.

1.c Ontological Autonomy – The thesis that no ethical property is metaphysically identical or reducible to one or more non-ethical properties.

Of these three, 1.a, Logical Autonomy, amounts to the standard interpretation of Hume's rule. The critics of concern here question whether Moore held, or could have consistently held, 1.a in light of his endorsement of Ought-Implyingness and Metaphysical Supervenience. Less controversial is whether he could have held 1.b, Semantical Autonomy, and 1.c, Ontological Autonomy. Of these two, 1.b is vindicated not only by non-naturalism but also by non-reductive forms of naturalism in ethics such as non-cognitivism and non-reductive ethical naturalism, which may also seek support by invoking a version of the OQA.

But why think that the Moore of *Principia* could not have held a thesis along the lines of 1.a, Logical Autonomy? It is possible to show that he did hold such a thesis and did so consistently. Let's consider these two issues in turn, beginning with the textual evidence that Moore did hold the logical autonomy of ethics. Although in *Principia*, he was quite cagey about acknowledging the is-ought rule and did not mention Hume at all, in his review of Franz Brentano's *Origin of the Knowledge of Right and Wrong*, also published in 1903, he made remarks consistent with an acceptance of the logical problem identified in that rule. In this review, Moore explicitly accepted the *logical independence* of ethical judgments from purely descriptive (or factual) judgments, which amounts to accepting that no purely descriptive premise may logically entail an ethical conclusion. In addition, *contra* a purely naturalistic conception of intrinsic value, he argued

Obviously the conception of *"good,"* as Brentano defines it, *cannot be derived merely from the experience of loving, but only from that of "right loving" ... whereas the experience of loving has all the marks which are suggested by calling it a "concrete impression of psychical content," the "experience of right loving" – i. e., the perception of the rightness or a love– has not.* The quality of "rightness" is not a psychical content and the perception of it is not an impression in the ordinary sense of these words. A single mark is sufficient to distinguish it: by a "psychical content" we always mean at least an existent, and by "impression" the cognition of an existent, and "rightness" is not an existent.

(Moore 1903a: 118, my emphasis)

Consistent with this tacit endorsement of Logical Autonomy, Moore praised those philosophers who have come to a "recognition that all truths of the form 'This is good in itself' are *logically independent* of any truth about what exists" (1903a: 116, my emphasis).

What about the compatibility of the no-ought-from-is rule with Moore's convictions that (1) some of the natural properties of a thing may be ought-implying, and (2) ethical properties of necessity are metaphysically determined by some of the natural properties of the things that have them? These convictions need not commit him to a rejection of Logical Autonomy since, first, if properly construed, the relation of metaphysical determination of ethical properties by natural properties is a relation of metaphysical supervenience and need not be conflated with logical implication or entailment. Second, to subscribe to Hume's rule, Moore may follow C. D. Broad's lead (1961: 367) of using 'ought-inclining' instead 'ought-implying' when thinking about the relation between natural and ethical properties. Following Broad's lead, he can define 'ought-inclining' this way: "A property N is ought-inclining just in case if a thing has it that would provide some grounds for thinking that any agent who could bring the thing into being, ought to do so." Thus, if pleasure is intrinsically good, then it also is an ought-inclining property in the sense that the fact that an experience includes some pleasure would provide grounds for thinking that any agent who could bring pleasure about ought to do so. But there isn't anything logically contradictory in the assertion 'This experience will have some pleasure but I should not bring it about.' Its oddity seems pragmatic, just as seems that of assertions of the form 'It's raining but I don't believe it.'

Furthermore, Moore's painstaking discussion of the relation between metaphysical determination and logical entailment in his

1942 reply to Frankena suggests that his views need an update in light of what we know today about metaphysical supervenience. Once that knowledge is incorporated, it turns out that supervenience and logical entailment must not be conflated. Only if Moore were to accept that ethical properties are a special set made up of an infinite disjunction of natural, ought implying properties would he be committed to the identity of supervenience and entailment in the relation between ethical and natural properties. For then it would be guaranteed that the natural properties entail the ethical properties (McLaughlin 2005/2018). Moore himself contemplated the metaphysical possibility of such identity and rejected it.[7]

THE INDEPENDENCE THESIS AND THE PRIORITY THESIS

Independence and Priority are theses about the relation of meta-ethics with other branches of ethics that have *Principia Ethica* as their main source.[8] They run as follows:

> Independence – The thesis that not only does metaethics deal with higher-order questions about moral semantics, metaphysics and epistemology, but also it can carry out its investigations without unnecessarily pre-judging the lower-order, substantive questions of normative ethics.

> Priority – The thesis that investigation in neither normative theory nor casuistry can be properly conducted without clarity on some fundamental questions that constitute the subject matter of metaethics.

Given the impact of *Principia Ethica* in early analytic ethics, it is reasonable to believe that these theses had an influence among moral philosophers of the twentieth century in their general tendency to focus on questions of metaethics and neglect questions of practical ethics. As noted in Section 3.1 of this chapter, Moore showed his endorsement of these theses in his contention that inquiry within casuistry, though "the goal of ethical investigation," should be conducted only after gaining some knowledge about the nature of ethical notions and truths. Furthermore, he turned to questions of practical ethics in the last two chapters of the book, only after having devoted four chapters to foundational questions of metaethics. From the early pages of this book (*PE*: §2, 54), Moore devoted considerable effort to establish non-naturalism and the consequent autonomy of ethics, both issues of metaethics. He also paid punctilious attention to issues of moral semantics concerning the meaning of 'good' and other key ethical terms, writing that semantical investigation amounts to the most "necessary and important part of the science of Ethics" (ibid.: §5, 58). To substantiate that claim, he argued that moral philosophers cannot properly apply some complex predicates such as 'good conduct' unless they first have some clarity about the meaning of their parts – in this case, the meaning of 'good' (which is to be determined by ethics) and of 'conduct' (which is common knowledge). In order to establish that 'good' in its primary ethical use cannot be defined, he engaged in a lengthy discussion of the ambiguity of this predicate and the need to distinguish it from other concepts that are not ethical at all. In Moore's words, "this question, how good is to be defined, is the most fundamental question in all Ethics" (ibid.: §5, 57). All this suggests that the Moore of *Principia* regarded metaethical investigation as a task prior to and independent of any ethical inquiry into either general or applied normative ethics.

THE INTRINSIC WORTH THESIS

In Chapter 6 of *Principia Ethica*, Moore expressed the views that knowledge in itself has very little value, but knowledge of ethical truths is an organic whole that has great value. So we may ascribe to him:

> Intrinsic Worth: The thesis that knowledge of ethical truths is valuable as an ultimate end.

Although at first these views seem at odds, that oddity trades on certain ambiguities that require a closer look at what Moore in fact meant. First, he was referring to knowledge as ordinarily construed, something along the lines of 'reflective belief about what is true' (*PE*: §117, 243). Thus construed, for Moore, "the chief importance of most *knowledge*—of the truth of most of the things which we believe—does, in this world, consist in its extrinsic advantages: it is immediately valuable *as a means*" (ibid.: §118, 244). Relevant to this claim is a distinction concerning what is instrumentally valuable (i.e., valuable as a means, for its extrinsic advantages) and what is intrinsically valuable (i.e., valuable as an ultimate end or for its own sake). If metaethical investigation is valuable for the knowledge it yields, then, since knowledge on its own has little value, it seems to follow that metaethical investigation is merely instrumentally valuable. The problem with this argument is in its details since, for Moore, knowledge of metaethical truths is a complex state of affairs or organic whole and, as such, its value need not equal the sum of the values of its parts. Thus, he can consistently hold Intrinsic Worth in light of his holistic conception of value, which I explore in Chapter 11. That conception enables him to argue that, although knowledge retains whatever little value it has individually when it enters a whole, its presence *can* increase the intrinsic value of a whole considerably. Thus, the value of a whole containing knowledge of the truths of moral semantics, metaphysics, and epistemology can be far greater than the value of a whole containing just knowledge or knowledge of other truths (ibid.: §117, 243).

At the same time, Moore can say that metaethical investigation is also instrumentally valuable, as a tool for clarifying, for example, the philosophical questions that make sense to ask and the exact meaning of key ethical terms. He makes this point in the opening paragraphs of the Preface to the first edition of *Principia Ethica*, where he claims that many disagreements, not just in ethics but in philosophy generally, would be resolved with sufficient clarity about the meaning of the questions at stake. But he is not committed to ascribing to metaethics *only* instrumental value.

Finally, note that something along the lines of Intrinsic Worth might be what fuels objections such as Nowell-Smith's, according to which, Moore ascribed little value to questions of normative ethics. Clearly, in *Principia Ethica*, he devoted more attention to philosophical ethics and said that its aim is analogous to the aim of investigation in physics. Like theoretical physics, the chief concern of philosophical ethics is "knowledge and not practice" (ibid.: §14, 71). This branch of ethics is not in the business of pre-scribing how the ethical world ought to be but rather discovering how it is. Moore further declared:

> What I am concerned with is knowledge *only* – that we should think clearly and so far arrive at some truth, however unimportant: I do not say that such knowledge will make us more useful members of society. If anyone does not care for knowledge for its own sake, then I have nothing to say to him ...
>
> (ibid.: §37, 113; my emphasis)

NOTES

1   The legacy of *Principia Ethica* in contemporary metaethics was the subject of many discussions commemorating the centenary of its publication in 2003. Prominent among them are Terry Horgan and Mark Timmons (2006), based on a special issue of the *Southern Journal of Philosophy*, Nuccetelli and Seay (2007), and special issues of *Ethics* (vol. 113, no. 3, 2003) and *The Journal of Value Inquiry* (vol. 37, no. 3, 2003).

2   Together with the above-mentioned, the classical non-naturalists, also known as moral intuitionists, included C. D. Broad (1930), W. D. Ross (1930), and A. C. Ewing (1947; 1953). I'll have more to say about their school of moral philosophy in Chapter 4.

3   Non-cognitivists like Nowell-Smith need to show that there is something wrong with the moral realism and antiskepticism of the classical non-naturalists, including Moore's – something that, of course, they have attempted to do in a number of works. See, for instance, Ayer (1952/1936; 1971), Hare (1952), Nowell-Smith (1954), and Blackburn (1984; 1993; 1998) among others.

4   Following Jonathan Dancy (1993; 2004), casuists in various branches of applied ethics roughly maintain that since the background conditions of any moral case hardly transfer to another case, principles can be of no help in deciding what to do or believe morally in each given case. Instead, they pro-pose a thoroughgoing reliance on moral discernment to first determine the morally salient aspects of any specific case, and then decide the right course of action or belief in that case. Thus, what may justify one moral judgment in a context is not an inference from principles, but sensitivity to the particulars of the case at hand, together with sound reasoning. See, for instance, Jonsen and Toulmin (1988) and Jonsen (2005).

5   Cf. the theses that Terry Horgan and Mark Timmons ascribe to Moore in their "Introduction" to *Metaethics after Moore* (2006: 1–6).

6   In "Distinctions Not Derived from Reason" (2010/1739: Book III, Part I,
     Section 1 of *A Treatise of Human Nature*), Hume famously explained the
     is-ought problem in this way:

> In every system of morality, which I have hitherto met with, I have always
> remarked, that the author proceeds for some time in the ordinary way of
> reasoning, and establishes the being of a God, or makes observations
> concerning human affairs; when of a sudden I am surprized to find, that
> instead of the usual copulations of propositions, is, and is not, I meet with
> no proposition that is not connected with an ought, or an ought not. This
> change is imperceptible; but is, however, of the last consequence. For as
> this ought, or ought not, expresses some new relation or affirmation, it is
> necessary that it should be observed and explained; and at the same time
> that a reason should be given, for what seems altogether inconceivable,
> how this new relation can be a deduction from others, which are entirely
> different from it.

7   Moore (RC: 605–606). Broad (1961: 368–369) charged that Moore gave no
     good reason for rejecting a reductive definition of intrinsic value in terms of
     an infinite disjunction of natural properties along the lines of "'X has G' just
     in case 'X has some intrinsic natural property or other that is ought-inclining'."
     He speculated that Moore would reject this definition on the unconvincing
     grounds that one can think of the *definiendum* without thinking of the *definiens.*

8   Moore also gave evidence of his endorsement of these theses in "What Is
     Philosophy?" (WIP), an article written between 1910 and 1911 but published
     only in 1953. In WIP, he construes philosophical ethics as the part of ethics
     devoted to the study of fundamental metaphysical truths, since "it is certainly
     one of the most important facts about the universe that there are in it these
     distinctions of good and bad, right and wrong" (WIP: 26–27).

SUGGESTED READING

Baldwin, Thomas, "The Open Question Argument," in John Skorupski ed., *The
   Routledge Companion to Ethics*, London: Routledge, 2010, pp. 286–296. Argues
   that Hume's no-ought-from-is rule is compatible with Moore's claim that some
   natural properties are ought-implying.

Bruening, William H., "Moore and 'Is-Ought'," *Ethics* 81(2) (1971): 143–149.
   Interprets passages from Moore's (1942) 'Reply to my Critics' as inconsistent
   with Hume's no-ought-from-is rule and the fact/value distinction since they
   claim that some factual statements are also evaluative.

Darwall, Stephen, Allan Gibbard, and Peter Railton. "Toward *Fin de Siècle* Ethics:
   Some Trends," *Philosophical Review* 101 (1992): 115–189 (reprinted in Darwall,
   Gibbard, and Railton 1997). An influential survey of the development of metaethics from 1903 to 1992. Raises the puzzle of why *Principia Ethica* is considered a turning point in that development even when Moore's non-naturalism
   and his master reason for it, the Open Question Argument, were "defunct" by

the 1930s. To solve it, the authors contend that the book's "continuing vitality" stems from its having effectively argued that key ethical concepts are irreducibly ethical.

Horgan, Terry and Mark Timmons, "How Should Ethics Relate to (the Rest of) Philosophy? Moore's Legacy," in Terry Horgan and Mark Timmons eds., *Metaethics after Moore*, Oxford: Clarendon Press, 2006, pp. 1–16. Useful introduction to Moore's philosophy of ethics in *Principia Ethica*. It takes this book's legacy to be twofold: (1) metaethics itself, as a distinct branch of ethics, and (2) a combination of metaethical doctrines that continues to exert strong influence today (viz., non-naturalism, realism, and cognitivism). But among contemporary developments that Moore missed are the possibility of combining doctrines he thought incompatible, such as non-naturalism and irrealism, and of including metaethical investigations within the philosophical study of meta-normativity. The authors question what they regard as Moore's excessive focus on establishing meaning equivalences as well as drawing a sharp line between metaethics and applied ethics.

Jonsen, Albert and Stephen Toulmin, *The Abuse of Casuistry*, Berkeley, CA: University of California Press, 1988. A classic vindication of a casuistic approach to moral decision-making in applied ethics, especially bioethics. It attempts to ground casuistry in an anti-theory of the sort now advanced by particularists. Accordingly, it rejects moral reasoning about cases based on principles, which is the traditional business of casuistry according to Moore's discussion in *Principia Ethica*.

Moore, G. E., "Preface," in *Principia Ethica*, Cambridge: Cambridge University Press, rev. edn, Thomas Baldwin ed., 1993/1903b, pp. 33–37. In this Preface to the first edition of the book, Moore makes clear that his chief goal is distinguishing questions of philosophical ethics from questions of normative ethics. While the latter questions concern moral obligation (or what sort of actions are morally obligatory), the former questions concern intrinsic value (or what sort of things ought to exist for their own sakes).

Moore, G. E., "The Subject-Matter of Ethics," in *Principia Ethica*, Cambridge: Cambridge University Press, rev. edn, Thomas Baldwin ed., 1993/1903b, pp. 53–56. Occupying the first 23 sections of *Principia* (out of a total of 135 sections), this is by far the most read chapter of the book. Moore first deals with questions about the ambiguity of the predicate 'good' and the nature of ethics, considered a science-like inquiry into the reasons and principles that are sufficient for deciding the truth of many everyday judgments about moral conduct, values, and traits of character. He then takes issue with naturalistic and metaphysical ethics, against which he chiefly wields the Open Question Argument. Readers can find the early Moore's philosophy of ethics in §§1–4, views on the semantics of 'good' in §§5–9, his Open Question Argument against naturalistic and metaphysical ethics in §§10–14, his principle of organic unities in §§15–22, and a summary of these in §23.

Moore, G. E., "*The Origin of the Knowledge of Right and Wrong* by Franz Brentano," *International Journal of Ethics* 14(1) (1903b): 115–123. Review article that provides some evidence that Moore might have accepted Hume's rule that no ought follows from is. Most notably, he writes that some true propositions about what's intrinsically good are "logically independent" of propositions about the natural world (p. 116).

Moore, G. E., *Lectures on Philosophy*, Casimir Lewy ed., London: Allen & Unwin, 1966. Good source for Moore's more mature view of conceptual analysis. In Part V, devoted to questions of philosophical method, Moore defends the autonomy of ethics and shows awareness that, given reductive naturalistic definitions of key ethical concepts such as 'good,' 'ought,' 'right,' 'wrong,' and 'valuable,' it would follow that certain propositions containing any of them would be synthetic and belong to psychology, sociology, or the theory of evolution rather than to philosophy (p. 196).

Nowell-Smith, P. H., *Ethics*, Harmondsworth: Penguin, 1954. Good early non-cognitivist objection to the cognitivist realism of the classical non-naturalists, especially Moore's. Argues that while the great ethicists of the past took ethics to be primarily concerned with answering practical questions such as 'What shall we do?,' in the early twentieth century, the non-naturalists replaced that fundamental question of ethics with theoretical questions about ethical properties and truths of the sort that concern Moore in Chapters 1 through 4 of *Principia Ethica*. For Nowell-Smith, Moore's analogy of ethics with science is untenable on Humean grounds, since it lives out the role of emotion, rather than knowledge or reason, in motivating action and attitude.

Parfit, Derek, Chapter 29 in *On What Matters*, vol. 1, Oxford: Oxford University Press, 2011. Strong reply to a standard non-cognitivist objection to *Principia* that appeals to the role of motivation in ethics (Hare 1952; Nowell-Smith 1954). Parfit contends that this objection wrongly assumes that, if ethical judgments were capable of being true or stating facts, they could not guide action. But when an act or attitude has a normative property (e.g., is right or wrong, good or bad, etc.), that by itself guides action in the sense of being reason-providing.

Pigden, Charles R., "No-Ought-From-Is, the Naturalistic Fallacy and the Fact/Value Distinction: The History of a Mistake," in Neil Sinclair, *The Naturalistic Fallacy*, Cambridge: Cambridge University Press, 2019, pp. 73–95. Construes Hume's problem as vindicating the logical autonomy of ethics (i.e., as a ban on any attempt at logically deriving a moral conclusion from non-moral premises alone). Moore's naturalistic fallacy involves instead (1) semantical autonomy, the thesis that moral predicates admit of no reductive definition in terms of non-moral predicates; and (2) ontological autonomy, the thesis that moral properties admit of no reductive analysis in terms of non-moral properties. Hume must reject the semantical autonomy of ethics as well as Moore's naturalistic fallacy. After all, in his view, key moral concepts admit of definition in terms of our tendencies to approve and disapprove. For more details on these autonomy theses, see also Pigden (1989).

Prior, Arthur N., "The Autonomy of Ethics," *Australasian Journal of Philosophy* 38(3) (1960): 199–206. A retraction of Prior's (1949) endorsement of the autonomy-of-ethics thesis that follows from Hume's no-ought-from-is rule and

Moore's naturalistic fallacy. Invokes inferences such as 'Tea drinking is common in England, therefore, tea drinking is common in England or all New Zealanders ought to be shot,' and 'Undertakers are Church officers, therefore, undertakers ought to do what Church officers ought to do' to show that normative conclusions sometimes do deductively follow from descriptive premises alone. But arguably, such "counterexamples" fail to have any substantive normative conclusions. For a good outline of later challenges to the autonomy of ethics, see Jackson (2013).

Russell, Bertrand, "The Elements of Ethics," in *Philosophical Essays*, London: Longmans, Green, and Co., 1910, pp. 40–49. In the first part of this Moorean short monograph, "The Subject-Matter of Ethics," Russell offers a critique of ethics at the turn of the twentieth century, which he regards as unduly concerned with conduct and virtue. Like Moore, he distinguishes a branch of metaethics ("theoretical ethics") whose aim is discovering true propositions about morality, and a branch of normative ethics ("practical ethics") whose aim is determining good and bad conduct. Unsurprisingly, Russell's explanation of why some ethical truths have the status of being basic or underivative is easier to follow than Moore's.

4

MORAL LANGUAGE AND THOUGHT

Although the two final chapters of *Principia Ethica* pay attention to some issues of normative ethics, the other four chapters count as evidence of Moore's view that inquiry into the fundamental principles of philosophical ethics comes first. In the course of this inquiry, Moore offered certain principles of metaethics that clearly place him within the school of classical non-naturalism that flourished in Britain mostly during the first half of the twentieth century. In this chapter, I first introduce classical non-naturalism and then outline the chief doctrines that render the Moore of *Principia* a paradigm member of that school: namely, his minimalism and cognitivism in moral semantics, non-naturalistic realism in moral metaphysics, and intuitionism in moral epistemology. The availability of predecessors who held versions of these doctrines – most prominently Henry Sidgwick – suggests that Moore was not exactly the radical innovator he took himself to be in *Principia*.

DOI: 10.4324/9780429275975-4

Nevertheless, as I show in later chapters, Moore introduced some novel doctrines and arguments (often giving his own twist to those already in the literature) and managed to draw a great deal of attention to deep problems facing reductive programs of naturalistic and metaphysical ethics. In what follows, I also consider what Moore, among other classical non-naturalists, would say about some semantical distinctions of present-day metaethics, such as the distinction between thick and thin normative concepts.

4.1 MOORE'S MORAL SEMANTICS IN CONTEXT

CLASSICAL NON-NATURALISM

Some core doctrines of Moore's non-naturalist moral semantics and metaphysics, as well as his intuitionist moral epistemology were already on offer by some early representatives of classical non-naturalism when *Principia Ethica* appeared in 1903. Representatives of a school of moral philosophy active, roughly, from the turn of the twentieth century to the mid-century had advanced a number of versions of these doctrines. Initially Moore developed his own version of them in part as a reaction to the versions of some predecessors and contemporaries in the school, such as Henry Sidgwick and John M. E. McTaggart. C. D. Broad, a contemporary and successor in the group, also played a significant role in the shaping of Moore's chief metaethical doctrines.[1]

Accordingly, it is not surprising that Moore's claim to radical novelty in *Principia* gained little sympathy from some early reviewers of the book. Among them, in 1904, J. S. Mackenzie observed that "[m]ost of the points emphasized by Mr. Moore have already been brought out by other critics," quickly adding "but perhaps never so tersely and so clearly" (1904: 378). The same year, Bernard Bosanquet wrote "The book indicates throughout how strongly the author has been affected by Sidgwick's views ..." (1904: 255). Almost half a century later, in 1949, Arthur N. Prior undertook the task of showing that the so-called naturalistic fallacy charge that Moore directed against naturalistic and metaphysical ethics can be traced to some relevantly similar objection by some British moralists of the 1650s and 1800s.[2]

Yet even those who early noted that *Principia* was not alto-gether original explicitly credited Moore's presentation of the core doctrines of classical naturalism with many merits, and an entire new generation of philosophers at Cambridge came to regard the book as a breakthrough. According to one of these philos-ophers, G. H. Geach, *Principia* amounted to the *first* work in the whole history of ethics that gave the discipline a rigorous founda-tion. "This was Moore's own claim," writes his son Peter Geach (1979: 175), "the wonder is that men like Russell, McTaggart, and Maynard Keynes, accepted it." As puzzling as such a response by Moore's peers might seem, the book succeeded in putting the core doctrines of classical non-naturalism at the center of philosoph-ical debate, generating an interest in them that persisted until at least the 1950s. This phenomenon owes a great deal to *Principia*'s vigorous defense of a type of moral realism characterized by the theses that there are mind- and language-independent moral properties and truths, and entities of both kinds are *sui generis* (i.e., ontologically unique and therefore irreducible to any non-moral properties or facts). If so, the autonomy of ethics from the sciences and theology follows, for ethics has a subject matter all of its own, independent of these. Somewhat less emphatically, *Principia* also offers a defense of moral intuitionism, a kind of foundationalism in moral epistemology characterized by the the-sis that some moral truths are necessary and synthetic yet justified by rational intuition alone.[3]

But, by the 1950s, many were, on a number of grounds, critical of these metaethical doctrines. First, non-naturalism's ontology of *sui generis* moral properties and truths appeared too extravagant to fit within an austere, naturalistic conception of what there is, which was by then the prevailing metaphysical outlook in analytic philosophy. Philosophers of this metaphysical persuasion had seri-ous doubts about non-naturalism's ability to provide a plausible explanation of how such properties and truths might relate to the natural world, or why they should have normativity at all.[4] Critics were also skeptical about the intuitionist moral epistemology of non-naturalism, which some took to presuppose the existence of a quasi-perceptual faculty of moral knowledge for which there is no evidence. As the sense that classical non-naturalism faced these and other problems became more pervasive, interest in this school of moral philosophy faded considerably, to the point that by the second half of the twentieth century, it was mostly historical.

The decline of interest in non-naturalism went hand in hand with the rise of ethical doctrines that appear more congenial to philosophical naturalism. Among them were, first, emotivism and other forms of non-cognitivism, followed later by the error theory and several types of moral realism of a naturalistic persuasion. Since the turn of the past century, however, non-naturalism has been experiencing a modest though significant comeback.[5] In connection with this revival has been a renewed interest in *Principia Ethica* and the core doctrines of classical non-naturalism that it advances, to which I now turn.

CLASSICAL NON-NATURALISM ABOUT WHAT?

The principal contentions of the classical non-naturalism in moral metaphysics, semantics, and epistemology that Moore defended in *Principia Ethica* can be summarized as follows:

- Ontological Non-naturalism
  - *Moral realism*, the doctrine that there are mind- and language-independent moral properties and truths.
  - *Moral anti-reductionism*, the doctrine that some key moral properties and truths are *sui generis* and therefore neither equivalent to, nor reducible to, purely naturalistic or metaphysical properties and facts.
- Semantical Non-naturalism
  - *Semantical minimalism* – the doctrine that there is just one or at most a few ethical terms that express simple (i.e., basic or underivative) concepts or meanings and denote simple properties.
  - *Semantical anti-reductionism* (outside the ethical domain) – the doctrine that moral concepts and propositions are *sui generis* and therefore neither equivalent, nor reducible without a significant semantical loss to purely naturalistic or metaphysical concepts and propositions.

o   *Moral cognitivism* – The doctrine that (a) key moral terms denote moral properties and key moral judgments express belief-like propositional attitudes that are truth-apt in a robust sense, and (b) moral judgments do indeed have the declarative form that they appear to have and can therefore enter into relations governed by the standard rules of logic.
- Epistemological Non-naturalism or Moral Intuitionism
    o   The doctrine that some key moral propositions have the epistemic status of necessary, synthetic, yet self-evident truths justified by rational intuition alone.

These doctrines carve a distinct niche for classical non-naturalism in the landscape of metaethics. No rival position can accept the whole set, though different combinations of some of its members are compatible with a number of rivals. For example, non-cognitivism and non-reductive naturalistic realism can both accept Moore's conceptual anti-reductionism, while the error theory can accept his moral cognitivism. But none of these rivals can accept his ontological non-naturalism and all three doctrines that make up his semantical non-naturalism.

THE CONCEPT/PROPERTY DISTINCTION

In *Principia Ethica*, Moore's chief reason for ontological and semantical non-naturalism is the Open Question Argument (OQA), introduced here in Chapter 2 and considered in detail in Chapter 5. As noted there, the Moore of *Principia* conflated concepts and properties and this mistake weakens the force of his argument since he invalidly drew the unanalyzability of moral properties, a claim of moral ontology, from premises entirely about moral concepts. This problem is evident throughout Chapter 1 of *Principia Ethica* (especially §10, 61/62; §13, 66/69), where various formulations of the OQA move from claims about the semantical indefinability of the term 'good' to the conclusion that any reductive analysis of goodness in terms of some other property or properties commits the naturalistic fallacy. But in later ethical writings Moore no longer invoked the OQA as an argument for non-naturalism, though he continued to vindicate a non-naturalist moral semantics and metaphysics on other grounds. His sole hesitation about the truth of non-naturalism occurs in the course of his 1942 reply to C. L. Stevenson, whose emotivist program in ethics (1937; 1944) takes ethical concepts to reduce to psychological concepts and may count therefore as a variety of naturalism in ethics.[6] Arguably, the extreme referentialism of his early philosophy led Moore to conflate moral concepts with the moral properties he took them to denote. After all, in his first notable article, "The Nature of Judgment," Moore already advocated a Platonist form of realism about concepts and propositions that equates these semantical entities with properties and facts.

Philip Stratton-Lake (2014/2003) and Robert Shaver (2007) are among those who disagree with the common charge that Moore's OQA founders on his conflation of concepts and properties. After acknowledging that Moore did not draw a sharp line between concepts and properties, Shaver goes on to contend that such a conflation opens up the following, more charitable, reading of his OQA: it is an argument about the irreducibility of moral concepts throughout, and any reference to moral properties in it should be ignored. Shaver writes:

> If Moore's talk of non-natural properties is read as talk of non-natural concepts, the open question argument does not fail in (one of) the ways in which it is taken to fail, and, as far as I can see, Moore loses nothing of worth to him. For example, he does not lose his arguments against naturalism, given that he construes naturalists as offering analyses.
>
> (2007: 291)

On this reading, Moore's moral semantics turns out to be non-naturalistic but he is not committed to a non-naturalistic moral ontology. He must deny that 'good' may express a purely descriptive concept but may accept that it denotes a natural property. In my view, Shaver's proposal faces two problems. First, although it seems a charitable reading of Moore, it fails to be faithful to what he had in mind. And when charity conflicts with faithfulness in interpretation, faithfulness trumps. Second, it is untrue that under Shaver's reading "Moore loses nothing of worth to him." Consider the autonomy of ethics: on Shaver's reading, Moore gets only the semantic autonomy of ethics, but he has no argument for vindicating the ontological autonomy of ethics. After all, as Shaver recognizes, on his reading, "[it] would not follow that goodness is a property over and above those properties dealt with by the natural sciences." And on his reading, non-naturalism becomes indiscernible from non-reductive naturalism, a doctrine that most non-naturalists consider a rival of their own type of realism in ethics.[7]

By contrast with Shaver, who attempts to put Moore's conflation of concepts with properties at the service of a charitable reading of the Open Question Argument, Stratton-Lake argues that no such conflation occurs in *Principia Ethica*. He invokes textual evidence to the effect that Moore drew a sharp line between verbal and metaphysical definitions and argues that this distinction is "close enough" to a distinction between concepts and properties. However, this line of reasoning mistakenly assumes that by 'verbal definition,' Moore meant analysis of concepts. Yet in *Principia* and elsewhere, Moore called 'verbal' any definition needed for understanding the meaning of a term, of the sort provided by lexicographers. His central question in this book concerning the meaning of the term 'good' in its primary ethical use should not be construed as asking about whether a *verbal* definition of this term is possible given remarks such as the following:

> A definition does indeed often mean the expressing of one word's meaning in other words. But this is not the sort of definition I am asking for. Such a definition can never be of ultimate importance to any study except lexicography. If I wanted that kind of definition I should have to consider in the first place how people generally used the word 'good' ... My business is solely with that object or idea, which I hold, rightly or wrongly, that the word is generally used to stand for.[8]

This and other passages from Moore's writings on definition make it plain that, on his view, knowing the meaning of any term up for philosophical analysis amounts to a precondition for the possibility of the analysis. As a result, the textual evidence from those writings falls short of supporting Stratton-Lake's view that the Moore of *Principia* did not conflate concepts and properties.

In addition to this criticism of Moore's treatment of concepts and properties in *Principia*, there is the criticism that, in this book, Moore only invited further obscurity and equivocation by neglecting to observe any discernible convention for referring to terms, concepts, and properties or for making any consistent use/mention distinction. To avoid such problems in contexts where confusion might occur, I hereafter use these conventions: capitals for concepts (e.g., Good, Goodness), lower-case letters for properties (e.g., goodness, good), and the now customary scare quotes for the use/mention distinction (e.g., the term 'good' has four letters). Furthermore, I'll use 'concept' and 'property' over some alternatives found in *Principia* such as "ideas," "objects of thought," and "notions" for concepts, or "characteristics" and "qualities" for properties.

4.2   A GOODNESS-CENTERED SEMANTICAL MINIMALISM

Moore, like other classical non-naturalists, did not draw any sharp lines of the sorts that are now familiar in moral semantics between (1) ethical and moral concepts, (2) the Ought of morality, rationality, or prudence, and (3) thick and thin normative concepts. But the evidence I review here suggests that Moore would have rejected only distinctions (1) and (2). About distinction (3), he could have assimilated it into his own distinction of simple-versus-complex concepts, which draws a sharp line between definitionally prior or non-derivative concepts and reducible or derivative concepts. Yet given his moral semantics, he was committed to rejecting the thick/thin concept distinction *as drawn by* Philippa Foot (1958) and Bernard Williams (1985), which roughly says that some key *thick* normative concepts have definitional priority over any *thin* normative concepts. In this section I consider what Moore actually said or could have said about all three distinctions.

NORMATIVE CONCEPTS

First, note that although Moore and other classical non-naturalists did not draw a distinction between the terms 'ethical' and 'moral' (a practice adopted also here), there is room for a pragmatic defense of this omission, since it has some theoretical benefits. Plausibly, the omission allowed them to keep their focus on their chief concerns in ethics, which include some questions about the foundations of ethics and theory of value as well as substantive questions of normative ethics. Consider the case of *Principia*. Had Moore instead set for himself in this book the goal of drawing a moral-versus-ethical distinction, he would have been required to formulate suitable necessary and jointly sufficient conditions for isolating moral concepts within a broader set of ethical concepts. Arguably, the complex issues involved in attempts at formulating such conditions would have taken him far afield from the book's chief concerns of philosophical and practical ethics.[9]

Second, Moore's discussion of Goodness suggests that he would have rejected the present-day distinction between key normative concepts of the systems of morality, rationality, and prudence. In *Principia*, he regarded Ought as reducible in part to Goodness and considered both normative concepts indistinguishable from the parallel key concepts of rationality and prudence. On this view, either a moral, a rational, or a prudential Ought amounts to what an agent has a duty to do, something always assessable in terms of moral conduct. In *Principia*, it is clear from the outset that Moore did not draw a sharp line between kinds of normativity involving these three systems since he introduced moral judgment with examples such as 'Drunkenness is a vice' and 'Temperance is a virtue,' which under a common reading are prudential judgments. Moreover, he excluded from the interest of ethics judgments such as 'I am doing good now,' 'I had a good dinner,' and 'Books are good,' only on the basis that 'good' in them applies to facts that "are unique, individual, absolutely particular" and ethics is concerned exclusively with general judgments (*PE*: §4, 56). Although later in "The Nature of Moral Philosophy" he added epistemic, legal, prudential, and conventional Oughts to his examples of kinds of obligation, he took the moral Ought to be the most authoritative of a kind that ultimately determines any ascription of praise or blame for conduct.

Each of these sources of Moore's ethical theory assumes what Michael Smith (2013) has called the "signature doctrine of

moral rationalism," a doctrine Moore shared with other classical non-naturalists. Given this doctrine, rationality provides the
grounds of moral value and obligation, so that the facts about
what one has the moral duty to do are facts about what one has
reason to do. Beliefs about one's moral obligations are beliefs
about what one has *most* reason to do, from which it follows that
it is irrational to be immoral. Furthermore, the skeptical view
that denies a role to reason in morality, the so-called practical
moral skepticism, must be false. Moore thus committed himself
to holding that a question often asked by more recent ethical
writers sympathetic to that kind of skepticism, 'Why ought I to
be moral?' cannot rationally arise. Evidently, given the signature
doctrine of moral rationalism, that question makes no sense.
Although asking it was uncommon at Moore's time, in his early
The Elements of Ethics (1991/1898: 17–18), he did briefly address
the related question, 'Why should I do my duty?' He found this
question as puzzling and tautological as the question 'Why is my
duty my duty?'.

In *Principia Ethica*, the relation between the oughts of morality
and prudence surfaces only indirectly, in connection with Moore's
discussion of ethical egoism, the principle of which he did not
hesitate to construe as a *moral* principle. Since he held that the
goodness essential to that principle – the agent-relative concept
of prudence *good-for-me* or *my-own-good* – is wholly analyzable in
terms of moral goodness – construed as objective intrinsic value
from an agent-neutral perspective – he was therefore committed
to rejecting the view that there is a bright line between the key
normative concepts of prudence and morality.

Now, was it a serious flaw for the Moore of *Principia* to assume
that the key normative concepts of the systems of rationality and
prudence are moral concepts? Here there is room for presenting
once again the pragmatic argument offered above. If the ultimate
goal of ethics is, as he stated in that book, answering substantive
questions of normative ethics, then he can invoke our argument
for justifying his assumption of a univocal moral sense for all
such concepts. I am not alone in offering this line of reply to proponents of a distinction in *kind* between the normative concepts
of these three systems. Compatible replies have been offered, for

example, by Thomas Hurka in the course of examining Sidgwick's use of a single Ought. Hurka contends:

> If Sidgwick's conflict between egoism and utilitarianism is formulated using a single 'ought,' the issue is plainly the substantive one of which view has the stronger claim to determine what we ought to do. But if it pits a prudential against a moral 'ought,' the issue can seem to turn on conceptual issues about what prudence and morality in the abstract involve, which is misleading since substantive questions are never settled conceptually.
>
> (2014: 42)

In the case of Sidgwick's moral rationalism (1967/1874: 25–26), Ought (or as some would put it today, the concept of what an agent has most reason to do or believe in a circumstance) is the key normative concept grounded in reason. As such, this concept cannot differ in kind from the key Oughts of other substantive normative systems such as rationality or prudence even when, *unlike* Moore, Sidgwick did acknowledge the force of the Ought of prudence. This Ought concerns one's own interest or happiness in certain situations, and its dictates may compete with the dictates of a moral Ought. Some such conflicts, Sidgwick believed, amount to an irresolvable problem of practical reason: in fact, this creates a dilemma for any agent facing a situation in which there is no sufficient reason to choose between the principle of rational egoism and the impartialist principle of classical utilitarianism. We may construe these as recommending, respectively, 'I ought to do what's good for me' and 'I ought to do what's impartially good.' Although Sidgwick considered the dilemma irresolvable, the mere fact that he considered it *a dilemma* at all suggests that he took the Ought of prudence to ultimately be of the same kind as the Ought of impartialism, and thus, as a dilemma within morality. Furthermore, suppose Sidgwick were to accept a distinction in kind between prudential and moral Oughts. Then, as Hurka contends, his "dilemma" of practical reason would seem to involve primarily conceptual issues about the strength of these different Oughts instead of issues concerning conduct. Such an implausible consequence supports a pragmatic argument, according to which, at the end of the day, Moore's neglect of the conceptual distinctions discussed in this section gave him a theoretical advantage by allowing him to focus on substantive issues of philosophical and practical ethics.

THICK/THIN, SIMPLE/COMPLEX CONCEPTS

Moore could not have accommodated the distinction between thick and thin ethical concepts inspired in Bernard Williams (1985). Given that distinction, the divide between these categories of ethical concepts runs like this:

1. Thin ethical concept – Any ethical concept, the application conditions of which are contingent only on ethical norms or values.
2. Thick ethical concept – Any ethical concept, the application conditions of which are world-guided in the sense of *also* being contingent on the way things are.

Since concepts such as Goodness and Obligation appear not have any empirical constraints, they fall within the category of thin ethical concepts as defined here. By contrast, Bellicose and Selfish illustrate thick ethical concepts since their application conditions are constrained not only by some moral values or norms but also by some facts concerning actions, attitudes, and feelings. If Bellicose were to be applied to Mohandas Gandhi and Selfish to Mother Teresa, in light of these concepts' factual constraints, each of the resulting judgments would certainly misfire.

The early Moore is committed to saying that there is just one thin ethical concept. For he took any ethical concept other than Goodness to be reducible to a moral element (Goodness or its converse Evil) plus a factual, causal element concerning the production of Goodness. In Chapter 5 of *Principia Ethica*, he offered several two-part analyses of such complex concepts, thereby illustrating his own take on the general, classical non-naturalist approach to the essential division among ethical concepts: that between simple and complex concepts. Although this simple/complex distinction of ethical concepts is compatible with the present-day taxonomy of thick and thin normative concepts, the classical non-naturalists' semantical minimalism committed them to count very few ethical concepts as truly thin. For it entails that only a few ethical concepts qualify as having no factual constraints. As exemplified by Moore's early minimalism, except for Intrinsic Goodness and Evil, most other ethical concepts do have descriptive elements. If so, Moore must classify Rightness as a thick concept. In fact, his two-part analysis of this concept begins by noting that it equivocates between moral obligation and moral permissibility. When conveying obligation, it admits of a reductive analysis in terms of the act or omission that in a circumstance will produce most intrinsic goodness compared with any alternatives available to the agent. When conveying permissibility, it admits of a reductive analysis in terms of the act or omission that in a circumstance will produce as much intrinsic goodness as any other action available to the agent (*PE*: §17, 76; §89, 197/198). Furthermore, the Moore of *Principia* claims that the following consequentialist equivalences amount to analytic truths:

> 'I am morally bound to perform this action' = 'This action will produce the greatest amount of good in the Universe.'
> 'I am morally permitted to perform this action' = 'This action will produce as much intrinsic goodness as any other action available to the agent in the circumstance.'[10]

Either analysis entails two claims about moral concepts. First, Intrinsic Goodness, a thin concept, has definitional priority over Ought and Right, both of which would turn out to be thick ethical concepts. Second, the moral and descriptive components of these thick concepts are somehow detachable. It follows that *Principia*'s approach to moral concepts amounts to 'thin centralism,' a doctrine about the order of analysis of ethical concepts that ascribes definitional priority to thin concepts. For any key thick moral concepts, a thin-centralist analysis identifies two independent semantical components that constrain its application: a world-guided component in Williams's sense above, and a reason-giving component that is constrained only by norms and values. Competing with thin centralism are the doctrines of thick centralism, which reverses the order of analysis, and non-centralism, which amounts to a kind of coherentism holding that analysis runs both ways, from the thick to the thin concepts and vice versa (Smith 2013; Väyrynen 2016).

Although Moore did not fully spell out any systematic thin-centralist program of analysis, the thin centralism of his theory of moral concepts is evident in the above analysis of moral Obligation and Permissibility. Or consider his analysis of Virtue in *Principia*, the starting point of which is Aristotle's definition of virtue as a habitual disposition. After noting that this definition is fine "on the main" with regard to the descriptive component of the concept, Moore identified its moral component as concerning the performance of one's duty. But recall that in his view, Duty itself is a complex concept, analyzable in consequentialist terms as the act or omission that in a circumstance maximizes Goodness.[11] So his two-part analysis of Virtue must continue until the simple moral and non-moral components of this concepts are spelled out, which he did as follows:

> Virtue – "[A]n habitual disposition to perform certain actions, which generally produce the best possible results" (*PE*: §103, 221).

THE DISENTANGLEMENT ARGUMENT

Since Moore's theory of ethical concepts relies on the above reductive analyses, it appears vulnerable to the so-called disentanglement argument, which objects to the possibility of isolating the normative and the purely descriptive content of thick ethical concepts. Advanced by John McDowell (1981: 144) and echoed by Bernard Williams (1985: 140–142, 150–152), the disentanglement argument chiefly targets the two-part, reductive analysis of non-cognitivists (especially, Blackburn 1984: 148; Hare 1952: 121; 1963: 121–129; Stevenson 1944: 206–207). But if compelling, it can also undermine the minimalist moral semantics of Moore and the other classical non-naturalists, which relies on the possibility of reductive analyses of complex ethical concepts within the ethical domain. Briefly put, the disentanglement argument contends that, assuming that there is a divide between thick and thin ethical concepts, no thick ethical concept can be reduced to a thin ethical concept *plus* a descriptive concept or concepts. For, given any reductive analysis of that sort, the descriptive content of a concept up for analysis determines its denotation. But then, if it were possible to disentangle the descriptive content of a thick ethical concept, it would be possible to know the concept's denotation without any knowledge of its normative content. Since that is impossible, it follows that no such reductive analysis can succeed.

Moore and the other classical non-naturalists might reply to this argument by invoking Daniel Elstein and Thomas Hurka's (2009: 530–531) line of reasoning, according to which that argument mistakenly presupposes that *any* reductive analysis of thick ethical terms must reject the premise that it is not possible to disentangle the moral and the descriptive components of thick ethical concepts. However, the non-naturalists *can* accommodate that premise. Consider Moore's and Sidgwick's analyses of Virtue: although they differ, they are both consistent with each other as well as with the ordinary concept of Virtue. Crucially, neither provides a fully determinate specification of the descriptive content of virtue, a specification that may allow knowing the denotation of this thick concept independently of any knowledge of its ethical component. For Moore's analysis in terms of a dispositional relation provides no such determinate specification, and Sidgwick's analysis in terms of a causal relation provides only a *partly* determinate specification. Neither of these reductive analyses, Elstein and Hurka submit, needs to offer any *fully* determinate specification of the descriptive elements of Virtue. More generally, a non-naturalist's analysis of a specific virtue or vice needs only locate the general area of the relevant act, state, or dispositions, thereby constraining the scope of application of the concept. It would be enough to locate Bellicose or Selfish in a general area of how someone responds to warfare and the interest of others, respectively, to capture the application conditions of these concepts and explain why Bellicose does not apply to Gandhi or Selfish to Mother Teresa. Applying them in these ways amounts to a misunderstanding of the concepts. In addition, since Moore's and Sidgwick's analyses are both compatible with the ordinary concepts, these non-naturalists are not talking past each other and can have a genuine disagreement.[12] Compare Elstein and Hurka's analysis of Benevolence, which runs along these classical non-naturalist lines: 'x is benevolent' means 'x is good, and there is some relation R (not specified) that is a positive or favoring relation, such that it stands in R to something good, and standing in R to something good makes anything that does so good.' Arguably, this analysis is consistent with the crucial premise of the disentanglement objection and with the possibility of substantive disagreement about the causal and the intentional relation at stake, since

> The exact extension of 'x is benevolent' will then depend on which positive relation is good-making, and here the two views [the dispositional/intentional view and the causal view] can come apart. Consider a world where the desire to cause others pleasure somehow regularly causes them pain. An intentional view like Rashdall's will call this desire benevolent and virtuous; a causal view like Sidgwick's will not. While each view uses the same partly determinate concept of virtue, each specifies it in a different way and therefore generates a different extension for 'benevolent'.
>
> (ibid.: 531)

It appears now that Moore can avoid McDowell's objection. He might simply respond by acknowledging that is not possible to produce a *full* disentanglement of the moral and the descriptive contents of a thick ethical concept. At the same time, he can insist that thick ethical concepts are complex concepts and as such, they admit the two-part reductive analysis within the ethical domain illustrated above for the concepts of moral Virtue, Duty, and Permission.

NOTES

1   In *Principia Ethica*, Moore praised Sidgwick for having avoided the naturalistic fallacy but devoted several sections to argue against his hedonism (*PE*: §§49–57). Another early writing attesting to the impact of some classical non-naturalists on Moore is his 1903 review of McTaggart's *Ethics*. In his autobiography, Moore credited the influence of Bertrand Russell in changing his mind about *Principia*'s claim that the ethical term 'right' admits of a reductive analysis in terms of the act that produces most intrinsic goodness.

Classical non-naturalists whose impact was less clear include Hastings Rashdall, H. A. Prichard, A. C. Ewing, and W. D. Ross. For a close look at the doctrines of this group of moral philosophers, see Hurka (2011a; 2014).

2   Prior (1949: 104–107). In this survey of the history of the naturalistic fallacy, Prior suggests that it was in fact Sidgwick who in the late nineteenth century drew attention to the pattern of mistake in ethics that Moore later labelled 'naturalistic fallacy.'

3   Besides *Principia Ethica*, works providing versions of these core doctrines of classical non-naturalism include Sidgwick (1967/1874), Russell (1987/1910), Ross (1930), and Ewing (1947).

4   Motivating these critics of non-naturalism, who themselves represented some competing metaethical positions, was one conviction: philosophical naturalism – or, the view that all there is, is the world as revealed by science. This general metaphysical outlook appears incompatible with the inflated ontology and the mysterious epistemology of non-naturalism. After all, it seems implausible that natural science could count non-natural properties and facts on its list of what exists in the universe, or rely on rational intuition for knowledge of such properties and facts.

5   Among present-day representatives of non-naturalism are David Enoch (2011), William FitzPatrick (2011; 2014), Michael Huemer (2005; 2016), T. M. Scanlon (2003; 2014), Russ Shafer-Landau (2003), Philip Stratton-Lake (2002b), Ralph Wedgwood (2007), and the late Derek Parfit (2011).

6   Although Moore did write that Stevenson might be right (RC: 554), this occasional concession is insignificant: not only did he disavow it later (Ewing 1962), but most important, it conflicts with the doctrines in his ethical writings after *Principia Ethica*.

7   For an exception, see Cuneo and Shafer-Landau (2014).

8   Moore (*PE*: §6, 58). Moore made a similar point in other passages of *Principia* as well as in a lecture note where he writes that the qualifier 'verbal,' for him, applies to any definition of the sort that

> it may help you to read a foreign book, or to understand a foreigner when he speaks to you, & also to make yourself understood by him. But this is not the use of philosophic definition; because they're all of them definitions of words or forms of expression you already understand—you already know their meanings in the sense of being able to attach the common meanings to them when you use them or hear or read them, though you mayn't know their meanings in the sense of being able to make true props. of the form 'this means so-&-so.'
>
> (*LP*: 166)

9   As far as I can tell, no broadly accepted conditions are available, even to distinguish moral and non-moral Oughts. Michael Smith (2013) offers a good discussion of the problems facing one of the most influential conditions: R. M. Hare's universalizability requirement. According to this requirement, an Ought is moral just in case it belongs to a normative system that is

necessarily aimed at removing particular dangers and securing certain benefits. But Hare's requirement faces strong counterexamples stemming from retrospective Ought-to-Bes of the sort 'The HIV/AIDS epidemic ought not to have occurred in poor West Africa.' As Philippa Foot pointed out (2002: 6–7), such judgments seem moral yet aim at neither removing harms nor securing benefits.

10 Consistent with these analyses of moral obligation and permissibility, in *Principia*, Moore also writes:

> Our 'duty' ... can only be defined as that action, which will cause more good to exist in the Universe than any possible alternative. And what is 'right' or 'morally permissible' only differs from this as what will not cause less good than any possible alternative. When, therefore, Ethics presumes to assert that certain ways of acting are 'duties' it presumes to assert that to act in those ways will always produce the greatest possible sum of good.
>
> (*PE*: §89, 198)

11 Thus, Moore writes:

> Virtues ... are habitual dispositions to perform actions which are duties, or which would be duties if a volition were sufficient on the part of most men to ensure their performance. And duties are a particular class of those actions, of which the performance has, at least generally, better total results than the omission ...
>
> (*PE*: §103, 221)

12 For Elstein and Hurka (2009: 531), the dialectical situation facing Moore and Sidgwick on their disagreement about the analysis of Virtue is comparable to that of proponents of egalitarian and desert-based specifications of Distributive Justice.

SUGGESTED READING

Baldwin, Thomas, *G. E. Moore*, London: Routledge, 1990. A comprehensive introduction to Moore's philosophy that is relevant to the issues raised in this chapter. Provides textual evidence for thinking that Moore conflated concepts with properties (pp. 44 ff.), and ascribes to Moore a Russellian semantics, according to which moral judgments load directly the simple property of goodness (or its converse badness) in the expressed propositions.

Darwall, Stephen, "How Is Moorean Value Related to Reasons for Attitudes?" in Susana Nuccetelli and Gary Gary Seay eds., *Themes from G. E. Moore: New Essays in Epistemology and Ethics*, Oxford: Oxford University Press, 2007, pp. 183–202. Argues that although Moore and Sidgwick shared a non-naturalist moral metaphysics, a minimalist moral semantics, and a consequentialist normative theory, they disagreed about the nature of the sole ethical concept each claimed to be definitionally prior. Sidgwick assigned that role to Ought rather than Goodness, and therefore was closer than Moore to a plausible response-dependence account of moral responsibility, according to which ethical judgments are characteristically reason giving.

Elstein, Daniel Y. and Thomas Hurka, "From Thick to Thin: Two Moral Reduction Plans," *Canadian Journal of Philosophy* 39(4) (2009): 515–536. A reply to McDowell's disentanglement objection to the reductive, two-part analyses of paradigm thick ethical concepts proposed not only by R. M. Hare (1952) but also by the classical non-naturalists, especially Sidgwick and Moore. Argues that paradigm thick ethical concepts such as Distributively Just and Benevolent admit of certain analyses into their normative and non-normative semantic components. Those analyses are consistent with the premises but not with the conclusion of that argument.

Foot, Philippa, "Moral Arguments," *Mind* 67 (1958): 502–513. A precursor of the thick/thin ethical concept distinction. Intended as an objection to philosophers sympathetic to Hume's no-ought-from-is rule, it maintains that a purely descriptive premise (e.g., 'x causes offence by indicating a lack of respect') can entail an evaluative conclusion (e.g., 'x is rude'). Though originally directed against the prescriptivism of R. M. Hare (1952), the objection would, if compelling, undermine the moral semantics of Moore and the other classical non-naturalists by questioning some of their assumptions about the existence of a fact/value divide and an is-ought problem.

Hurka, Thomas, "Common Themes from Sidgwick to Ewing," in Thomas Hurka ed., *Underivative Duty: British Moral Philosophers from Sidgwick to Ewing*, New York: Oxford University Press, 2011, pp. 6–25. Excellent overview of the historical context of Moore's non-naturalism. Provides accurate summaries of the chief metaethical doctrines of classical non-naturalists as well as of some major objections facing some of them. Shows that the classical non-naturalists made up a school in ethics characterized by those doctrines.

Hurka, Thomas, *British Ethical Theorists from Sidgwick to Ewing*, New York: Oxford University Press, 2014. Chapters 1 and 2 ("Minimal Concepts" and "'Ought' and 'Good'") offer helpful outlines of the moral semantics of major classical non-naturalists. Shows that although they shared substantive doctrines about ethical concepts, they differed on the question of *which* ethical concepts are basic.

McDowell, John, "Non-Cognitivism and Rule-Following", in Steven H. Holtzman and Christopher M. Leich eds., *Wittgenstein: To Follow a Rule*, London: Routledge, 1981, pp. 141–162. The *locus classicus* for the so-called disentanglement argument, which roughly contends that the purely descriptive component of a thick concept cannot be separated from its normative component because if it could, then it would be possible to determine the concept's extension by looking solely at that component, something that seems not possible.

Moore, G. E., *The Elements of Ethics*, Tom Regan ed., Philadelphia, PA: Temple University Press, 1991/1898. Features a passage (pp. 17–18) that reveals Moore's view that the key normative concepts of morality, rationality, and prudence do not differ in kind.

Moore, G. E., *Principia Ethica*, Cambridge: Cambridge University Press, rev. ed., Thomas Baldwin ed., 1993/1903. Moore's best attempt at showing that Goodness is the sole simple, irreducible ethical concept. An excellent source also for his reductive, two-part analysis of key ethical concepts such as Right and Virtue. See especially Chapters 1 and 5.

Moore, G. E., *Ethics*. London: Williams & Norgate, 1912, New York: Henry Holt, 1912 (reprint New York: Oxford University Press, 1966). Revises *Principia*'s contention that Right admits of a reductive definition in terms of the act or omission that produces the most goodness in a circumstance. Right, together with Good, is now considered a basic or indefinable ethical concept.

Smith, Michael, "On the Nature and Significance of the Distinction between Thick and Thin Ethical Concepts", in *Thick Concepts*, Simon Kirchin ed., Oxford: Oxford University Press, 2013, pp. 97–120. Questions the significance of the thick/thin distinction for ethical concepts, arguing that all ethical concepts are somewhat thick. But some are maximally thin and therefore have definitional priority over thick concepts that are not maximally thin. On this view, the basic ethical concepts of the classical non-naturalists count as maximally-thin, thick concepts. Their definitional priority is thus preserved.

Stratton-Lake, Philip, "Intuitionism in Ethics," 2014, in *Stanford Encyclopedia of Philosophy*, Edward N. Zalta ed., 2003/2014, https://plato.stanford.edu/entries/intuitionism-ethics/ *Contra* the prevailing view, Stratton-Lake argues that the Moore of *Principia Ethica* did not conflate concepts and properties.

Sylvester, Robert Peter, *The Moral Philosophy of G. E. Moore*, Ray Perkins and R. W. Sleeper eds., Philadelphia, PA: Temple University Press, 1990. An introduction to Moore's moral semantics and ontology up to the 1920s that contains insightful comments and a critical bibliography by the editors. Like Hurka (2014), Sylvester sees a continuity in the doctrines of *Principia Ethica* and *Ethics*. On his interpretation of Moore's moral ontology, goodness comes out as a universal that lacks existence but is intelligible and has a reality outside space-time (p. 137). It also metaphysically depends on the natural properties of a thing, a relation of supervenience that Sylvester calls "ingression."

Väyrynen, Pekka, "Thick Ethical Concepts," in *Stanford Encyclopedia of Philosophy*, Edward Zalta ed., 2016, https://plato.stanford.edu/entries/thick-ethical-concepts/. Good discussion of the disentanglement argument and complex issues at stake in current debates over the thin/thick distinction of ethical concepts.

Williams, Bernard, *Ethics and the Limits of Philosophy*, Cambridge, MA: Harvard University Press, 1985. Introduces the terminology of 'thick' and 'thin' concepts in current metaethics in the course of having a closer look at Foot's (1958) objections to the prescriptivism of R. M. Hare. On Williams's account, thick ethical concepts (Coward, Brutality, etc.) have definitional priority over thin ones (Good, Right, etc.) and normative conclusions may follow from purely descriptive premises. Accordingly, not only is Moore's program of two-part reductive definitions of complex ethical terms mistaken but his Open Question Argument has no plausible interpretation.

5

THE OPEN QUESTION ARGUMENT

With Gary Seay

5.1 RECONSTRUCTING *PRINCIPIA*'S OPEN QUESTION ARGUMENT (OQA)

AN OQA AGAINST SIMPLE SUBJECTIVISM

As we saw earlier, for the Moore of *Principia Ethica*, the term 'good' expresses the sole indefinable ethical concept and denotes the sole unanalyzable ethical property. Neither 'good' nor any other ethical term admits of a reductive analysis in naturalistic terms such as 'what is more evolved,' 'what I approve of,' and 'what we desire to desire' – or in metaphysical terms such as 'what is commanded by a free will,' 'what is willed by God,' and 'what is an object of rational choice.' Moore later acknowledged the difficulty of finding a set of necessary and sufficient conditions for a

DOI: 10.4324/9780429275975-5

term to fall under either of the naturalistic category or the metaphysical category (*PE*: 2: 13) but continued to rely on *Principia*'s broadly epistemological criteria to distinguish these categories of term. According to these criteria,

- A term is purely *naturalistic* or *descriptive* just in case it denotes a property relevant to the study of the natural or the social sciences.
- A term is *metaphysical* just in case it denotes a property relevant to the study of speculative philosophy or theology.

Moore's chief reason in *Principia* for opposing attempts at reducing 'good' to terms of either of these two kinds is the Open Question Argument (OQA), from which Moore drew the corollary that such attempts commit the naturalistic fallacy. In the first four chapters of the book, Moore offered some examples of attempted reductive analyses of 'good' vulnerable to the OQA. Among them is an argument against a simple doctrine of emotivism that may be reconstructed in this way (*PE*: §26, 93):

1. If simple emotivism is true, then the term 'good' is identical to 'my feeling of approval.'
2. If the term 'good' is identical to 'my feeling of approval,' then the question 'I approve of x, but is x good?' would be closed (i.e., it would be non-debatable).
3. But the question 'I approve of x, but is x good?' is open (i.e., it is debatable).
   Therefore,
4. 'Good' is not identical to 'my feeling of approval' and simple emotivism is false.[1]

Representatives of simple emotivism in Moore's time included Edvard Westermarck, a Finnish philosopher and psychologist with whom he took issue in "The Nature of Moral Philosophy" (NMP: 332). On Moore's account, Westermarck advocated a reductionist thesis according to which to call an action 'right' or 'wrong' hinges on whether the action produces in us certain feelings of approbation or disapprobation respectively. Crucial to the force of his OQA against this type of emotivism are premises 2 and 3 above. Given these premises, Westermarck's definitions of 'right' and 'wrong' are incorrect. By attempting to provide them, he committed the naturalistic fallacy.

In Moore's view, arguments along relevantly similar lines can defeat any attempt at equating the concepts and properties captured by key ethical terms with the concepts and properties captured by either purely naturalistic or purely metaphysical terms. These arguments would show that any such putative equation always remains open or unsettled. As a non-naturalist realist who conflated concepts with properties, Moore believed the failure of a representative number of putative naturalistic or metaphysical analysis of 'good' demonstrated not only that the expressed concepts are indefinable but also that the denoted properties are unanalyzable. Thus, Moore thought that in addition to defeating naturalistic as well as metaphysical ethics, his OQA indirectly supports his own brand of semantical and metaphysical non-naturalism – an ambitious conclusion that, as we show later, his OQA fails to support, given some alternative hypotheses about why ethical discourse cannot be reduced to purely descriptive or metaphysical discourse.

MOORE'S CHANGING VIEWS ABOUT *PRINCIPIA*'S OQA

In *Principia Ethica*, the OQA amounts to Moore's chief argument against naturalistic and metaphysical ethics as well as for his own brand of semantical and metaphysical non-naturalism. Although the argument was somewhat familiar by the time of publication, Moore gave it not only the catchy name by which it is still known in ethics and beyond, but also an original twist and an energetic defense.[2] Yet his own enthusiasm about the OQA was short-lived. By 1912, in his book *Ethics*, he made no mention of the argument, by 1922 in an unfinished preface to *Principia*'s second edition, he was critical of some of its conclusions (P2: 2–21), and by 1942 in his "A Reply to My Critics" (RC: 605–606), he offered an entirely different argument as the "best reason" against naturalistic ethics.

Nevertheless, at least motivating the OQA and his other arguments against naturalistic ethics is Moore's pluralistic theory of value: such reductive analyses conflict with the truth of his pluralism about the things that have intrinsic value.[3] In his view, any reductive naturalistic analysis of goodness is committed to equating this ethical property with a single natural property, since he also rejected the possibility of equating ethical properties with the disjunction of naturalistic properties (ibid.: 605–606). But Moore provided no reason for ruling out an *analysans* of a key ethical property that is a disjunction of natural properties.[4] He would further oppose any reductive analysis of intrinsic goodness in terms of the disjunction of all *ought*-inclining intrinsic natural properties. Here his reason would likely be that having intrinsic goodness before the mind does not *eo ipso* amount to having a (possibly infinite) disjunction of such ought-inclining properties before the mind (Broad 1970: 368–369).

However, the invalidity of an appeal to what is transparent to the mind to support a claim concerning the nature of some properties has been plainly demonstrated in the case of Descartes' argument for mind-body dualism. Moore's appeal to the OQA might be as indefensible as Descartes. In what follows we look closely at the OQA construed primarily as an objection to reductive naturalistic realism. But now and then we'll remind the reader that Moore also offered this argument as an objection to metaphysical ethics (*PE*: §10, 61/62, §26, 90).

TWO FORMULATIONS OF THE OPEN QUESTION ARGUMENT

The barren-tautology formulation

Principia Ethica features at least two formulations of the OQA, each of which invokes ordinary intuitions about the irreducibility in content and reference of ethical vocabulary into purely descriptive vocabulary in support of the conclusion that 'good' is not identical to any descriptive predicate. The "barren-tautology" formulation occurs prominently in §11 and reappears in §14, §24, and §26.[5] It argues that if judgments such as 'Pleasure is good' stated the semantical identity of 'good' and 'pleasure,' then this judgment would be as informative as 'Pleasure is pleasure' or 'Good is good.' But these are obvious tautologies, a result that conflicts with the strong intuition that 'Pleasure is good' is not. This judgment seems not to amount merely to a statement of sameness of conceptual content but to express instead a substantive proposition of practical ethics. As Moore put it, "When they [the hedonists] say 'Pleasure is good,' we cannot believe that they merely mean 'Pleasure is pleasure' and nothing more than that" (*PE*: §11, 64).

Other attempts at drawing semantical equivalences between 'good' and any naturalistic terms appear to face similar challenges from a suitable barren-tautology OQA. If so, then Moore may plausibly conclude that no such semantical equivalences obtain. Among classical non-naturalists who at least briefly agreed with him on this objection was the Bertrand Russell of the *Elements of Ethics*. Russell argued that 'good' cannot be semantically equivalent to any naturalistic predicate because, if 'good' were equivalent to, say, 'the desired,' then the principle 'The desired is the only good' would amount to the tautology 'The desired is the desired.' But that principle expresses an informative proposition. In Russell's own words,

> When we are told that the good is the desired we feel at once that we are being told something of philosophical importance, something which has ethical consequences, something which is quite beyond the scope of a dictionary to tell us.
>
> (1987/1910: 23)

Note that, thus formulated, the OQA does not rule out ethical paraphrases of 'good,' such as those that Moore himself used: 'intrinsic value,' 'what ought to exist for its own sake,' and the like. But it does rule out paraphrases of 'good' in terms that are not semantically identical to it. His argument assumes that, whenever two terms mean exactly the same (think of 'sister' and 'female sibling'), one term may substitute for the other in any direct context without significantly altering the proposition expressed. Since the naturalistic definitions targeted by this OQA would render propositions of practical ethics into barren tautologies, that outcome alone is sufficient for them to fail.

Another way to look at Moore's objection concerns the fact that reductive theories of either a naturalistic or a metaphysical type construe their principles as having normative force. Proposing definitions of key ethical terms does not seem to be their aim when advancing those principles since such barren tautologies lack normative force. Moore hinted at this normativity problem while noting, in the case of naturalistic philosophers, that they seem "anxious to persuade us that what they call the good is what we really ought to do" (*PE* §11, 64). Of course, not all naturalistic philosophers may be so eager to offer principles with normative force: some may in fact wish to produce analyses of ethical concepts. For example, at some point, Russell advanced ethical principles conceived as naturalistic reductive analyses of ethical terms that are relevant to explaining moral motivation.[6] So there appears to be room for contending that the barren-tautology OQA begs the question against some naturalistic programs in ethics. Yet even if these programs evade objection from the barren-tautology OQA, they can fall prey to the formulation of the argument to be considered next.

The debatable-equivalence formulation

The debatable-equivalence formulation of the OQA, originally Moore's, occurs prominently in §13 (pp. 62–65) of *Principia Ethica*. It also crops up in other sections, most prominently in §10 and §§14–17, and we find it at work in the objection to simple emotivism discussed above. Since it amounts to the more standard formulation of the argument, hereafter we'll refer to it as simply 'OQA' and construe it as an argument against naturalistic reductive analyses of ethical terms. In the case of 'good,' the argument invokes semantical intuitions to rule out any such *analysans*. Once it shows that the same conclusion holds for a representative number of naturalistic reductive analyses of 'good' (and any other key ethical term), it concludes that key ethical predicates admit of no reductive naturalistic analyses. An analogous conclusion follows in the case of reductive metaphysical analyses.

To illustrate this argument, let's consider how it would run against a naturalistic analysis of 'good' in terms of 'what we desire to desire.' The OQA objects that, if presented with the question, 'Is what we desire to desire always good?,' speakers who are competent with the meanings of both terms would consider it closed. That is, no amount of *a priori* reflection would allow them to settle the question of the identity of the concepts involved. Since the question remains open, the proposed analysis cannot get off the ground. After thus raising skepticism about a representative number of other naturalistic reductive analysis of Goodness, Moore seems entitled to conclude that no such analysis can be correct. Now whether he can also conclude from such premises, as he did, that no ethical property is reducible to a purely descriptive property amounts to a disputed matter that we take up in our assessment of the argument. For now, let's summarize one instance of this formulation of the OQA as follow:

1. If a certain variety of naturalism in ethics is true, then Goodness is analyzable in terms of What We Desire to Desire.
2. If Goodness is analyzable in terms of What We Desire to Desire, then the question, 'Granted x is what we desire to desire, but is x good?' is closed.
3. But that question is open.
4. *Therefore*, Goodness is *not* analyzable in terms of What We Desire to Desire.

On Moore's view, relevantly analogous lines of argument can be run to challenge any attempt at analyzing Goodness in terms of other purely descriptive concepts. This result shows not only that such analyses fail but also that,

5. *Therefore*, Goodness is an unanalyzable, *sui generis* concept.

However, some considerations to which we now turn suggest that the OQA falls short of supporting conclusion 5.

PRINCIPIA'S OQA AGAINST NATURALISTIC REALISM

Metaphysical naturalistic realism

Moore used a simple label "naturalistic ethics" for what is in fact a broad family of meta-ethical doctrines. He touched hardly at all on the big divisions within that family separating varieties of naturalism in ethics according to whether they qualify as forms of cognitivism or non-cognitivism, realism or anti-realism, and semantical or metaphysical naturalism. In this section we look closely at the divisions within this family that bear directly on an assessment of the force of the OQA. As commonly objected, this argument appears quite weak against varieties of naturalism in ethics that can accommodate a negative conclusion, holding that ethical terms/concepts admit of no reductive naturalistic analyses. But we agree with critics that find it persuasive as an argument against reductive varieties of naturalistic realism, especially those that are semantical, definist, or analytical. To this group belongs analytical descriptivism, the reductive program of Frank Jackson (1998; 2012), to which we turn after having a closer look at what is meant commonly by the expression 'ethical naturalism.' Narrowly construed, this expression refers to a group of realist moral philosophers at Cornell University in New York who countenance the possibility of either reducing or identifying ethical properties and facts with natural properties and facts but reject any naturalistic reduction by semantical reduction of ethical concepts and propositions.[7] By contrast, most vulnerable to Moore's OQA are definist realists of a naturalistic persuasion in ethics who expect to reduce the ethical to the natural at the metaphysical and the semantical levels.[8] Given that Moore conflated concepts with properties, he took naturalistic realists of either type to be in the business of attempting a naturalistic reduction of ethical properties and facts by means of a naturalistic reduction of ethical concepts and truths. Had he distinguished concepts from properties and propositions from facts, he might have noticed that while the OQA may challenge semantical naturalistic realism, it falls short of refuting the metaphysical variety of naturalistic realism. In addition, its first conclusion is compatible with non-reductive competitors, such as moral non-cognitivism and the error theory, a compatibility to which we turn below. But before we do that, let's have a closer look at the central doctrines of these two realist competitors of non-naturalism:

- *Semantical Naturalistic Realism (SNR)* – A doctrine that combines realism about ethical properties and facts with the

thesis that both the content and the reference of ethical predicates and sentences admit of suitable naturalistic reductions.
• *Metaphysical Naturalistic Realism (MNR)* – A doctrine that
combines realism about ethical properties and facts with the
thesis that only the reference of ethical predicates and sentences admits of a suitable naturalistic reduction.

Since both these doctrines are instances of naturalistic moral realism, each countenances mind- and language-independent moral
properties and truths, as well as the possibility of a naturalistic
reduction of those properties and facts. SNR further advocates the
possibility of a naturalistic reduction of the concepts and propositions respectively expressed by ethical predicates and sentences.

In addition to their characteristic core claims, proponents of
MNR are committed to rejecting an account of the epistemic
justification of moral judgment by some current proponents of
SNR, which claims the *a priori* justification of reductive naturalistic analyses of key ethical vocabulary. The MNR proponents are
committed to an empiricist account along lines like this:

• *Epistemic Ethical Naturalism (EEN)* – Any correct account
of ethical properties and facts may have no other justification beyond that attainable through the standard methods of
empirical investigation and science.

The contrast between reductive naturalistic realism of semantical
and metaphysical persuasions (i.e., SNR and MNR) is best drawn
starting from SNR's claims

1. Ethical vocabulary is reducible without any ethical remainder
   to purely descriptive vocabulary.
2. Ethical properties and truths are reducible without any ethical remainder to purely descriptive properties and truths.

MNR accepts (2) but may reject (1). By rejecting (1), MNR theorists allow for irreducible differences in content between moral
and purely descriptive terms and sentences, and can therefore
vindicate the autonomy of ethics just like Moore (Brink 1989:

149 ff.). In fact, like Moore, they can be in the non-reductive realist camp.[9] To put it differently, the MNR theorists can resist Hume's is/ought problem as well as the debatable-equivalence formulation of Moore's OQA. Among other strengths might be that, by contrast with non-naturalism, their doctrine posits neither ontologically mysterious non-natural properties and facts (Railton 2010; Sturgeon 2003), nor a faculty of moral intuition about which there is no scientific evidence (Dreier 2012; but cf. Brink 1989: 109). We'll consider these objections to non-naturalism in due course.

Semantical naturalistic realism

Frank Jackson's analytical descriptivism, a present-day form of semantical naturalistic realism, rests on two core claims, each of which is vulnerable to the OQA. Given one of them, key ethical terms such as 'good' and 'right' are semantically equivalent to some sets of purely naturalistic terms. Given the other, certain purely descriptive premises entail ethical conclusions. According to Jackson (1998: 118 ff.), these claims follow from the global supervenience (S) of the moral on the natural. (S) says that any possible worlds whose descriptive nature is identical must be identical ethically.[10] That is, the descriptive nature of a world metaphysically 'fixes' its ethical nature. If so, from D (i.e., the way things are descriptively in a world), it would be possible to deduce E (i.e., the way things ought to be ethically in that world and in any world descriptively identical to it).

Consider a world in which no action may count as ethically obligatory unless the action satisfies at least one of a possibly infinite disjunction of properties such as being the saving of a life, or the preventing of harm, or the promoting of social cohesion, etc. If we knew this implication, then we could deduce the ways we ought to act in that world. Suppose an action X is right in that world if a certain specification of the world's descriptive nature D_1 obtains, e.g., X is the saving of a life. Typically, there would be other specifications of the descriptive nature of that world (and any world like it) that would support a cluster of implications from D to 'X is right'– something like 'If D_1, then X is right;' 'If D_2, then X is right;' and so on. Equivalently, the relevant implications can be formulated as a single conditional with a complex, possibly infinite, disjunction in its antecedent – something like 'If D_1, or D_2, or…, then X is right' (e.g., 'If it is the saving a life, or the promotion of social cohesion, or …, then X is right'). Now we seem in a position to assert the *a priori* equivalence between rightness and that complex set of descriptive properties by holding that, necessarily, in that possible world and in any world descriptively identical to it, the disjunction of all complete descriptive natures of each possible right action logically and metaphysically entails rightness, while rightness logically and metaphysically entails at least one of the disjuncts of a possibly infinite disjunction listing the descriptive natures of right actions.

(S) opens the possibility of analogous reductive analyses of other key ethical terms, by invoking other sets of complete specifications of the descriptive natures of all things that are good, all actions that are wrong, etc. Here is how Jackson argues for this general conclusion:

> [Given (S)] each world at which E is true will have some descriptive nature: ethical nature without descriptive nature is impossible (an evil act, for example, must involve death or pain or…). And, for each such world, there will be a sentence containing only descriptive terms that gives that nature in full. Now let w_1, w_2, etc. be the worlds where E is true, and let D_1, D_2, etc. be purely descriptive sentences true at w_1, w_2, etc. then the disjunction of D_1, D_2, etc., will also be a purely descriptive sentence, call it D. But then E entails and is entailed by D. For every world where E is true is a world where one or other of the D_i is true, so E entails D. Moreover, every world where one or other of the D_i are true is a world where E is true, as otherwise we would have a violation of (S): we would have descriptively exactly alike world differing in ethical nature. Therefore D entails E.
>
> (1998: 122–123)

Given this account, analytical descriptivism follows from a plausible thesis about the supervenience of the ethical on the purely descriptive or natural. Jackson has provided seemingly solid grounds for thinking that, necessarily, in any possible world where E is true, D would be true and vice versa – which amounts to saying that, necessarily, fundamental ethical properties and natural properties are *a priori* equivalent. As a result, he seems to have provided a definist account that can resist the OQA and bridge the is-ought gap because it allows for at least some ethical truths to logically, semantically, and metaphysically follow from factual truths.

But analytical descriptivism faces some challenges. First, since any disjunction equivalent to a key moral predicate would be infinite, it cannot be thought and therefore stated – something that undermines confidence in ever achieving the reduction of the ethical to the natural (Baldwin 2010). Furthermore, the account presupposes that the referents of ethical expressions are always descriptive properties, something that conflicts with the practice of ordinary moral appraisal whereby "we sometimes attribute ethical properties to ethical entities, for example in saying that wickedness is worse than naughtiness" (Williamson 2001: 627). In addition, global supervenience (S) at most says that no ethical properties or facts obtain unless some or other non-moral properties or facts also obtain. This is compatible with the absence of any *patterned* connections going from descriptive properties to ethical properties that could support a reading of the relation of supervenience as entailment in the case of moral properties.[11] Finally, suppose Jackson's argument is sound. To render it also cogent he would still need a plausible response to the strongest version of the OQA, which he takes to be R. M. Hare's version (Jackson 1998: 153). According to this version, definist naturalism in ethics, by seeking to make ethical judgments derivable from statements of fact, neglects to take into account that such judgments have an irreducibly prescriptive or commendatory force (Hare 1952: 82). Moore's OQA emphasizes that there is a problem facing any reductive naturalistic analysis of ethical terms and sentences, Hare's OQA explains why that is the case.[12] Since Moore's most plausible conclusion from the OQA is consistent with Hare's, we need to look closely at how analytical descriptivists as well as other critics of the argument have thought to meet the challenge that it raises for reductive naturalistic realism.

5.2 ASSESSING THE OPEN QUESTION ARGUMENT

WHAT'S WRONG WITH MOORE'S MORAL SEMANTICS?

Non-reductive ethical naturalists can reply to Moore that his OQA is invalid since it draws a conclusion about the nature of ethical properties from premises about the concepts expressed by some ethical and descriptive predicates. To elaborate on this line of reply, they may appeal to reasons offered by R. G. Durrant, Gilbert Harman, and Hilary Putnam among others. For Durrant, the problem facing Moore's attempt to undermine naturalistic and metaphysical ethics with the OQA stems from wrongly assuming that different concepts cannot denote the same property. Moore failed to consider that 'good' and some naturalistic predicate, such as 'what we desire to desire,' may differ in their expressed meaning or concept but have the same denotation – just as, to use Frege's famous example, 'the evening star' and 'the morning star' differ in meaning but each denotes the planet Venus. In light of this plausible line of reply, the OQA of *Principia* fails to support that intrinsic goodness cannot be identical to a natural property. Once its invalidity is revealed in this way, the argument also fails to support Moore's positive conclusion that the denotation of 'good' is "a unique property not denoted by any other expression" (Durrant 1970: 361). To this reply, William Frankena added that since the OQA is invalid, by offering it against his naturalistic rivals in ethics Moore simply begged the question.[13]

An influential, non-Fregean reply to the OQA which is nonetheless compatible with Durrant's came in the 1970s with the development of the direct-reference theory of natural kind terms. Inspired in that theory, Gilbert Harman and Hilary Putnam have argued independently that the OQA is invalid because it draws a conclusion about the reference of two terms – one ethical, the other descriptive – from premises about the concepts expressed by those terms. Any difference between those concepts would fall short of entailing a difference in the reference of the relevant terms. Both the ethical and the descriptive terms at stake in the OQA can refer to the same natural property, just as do pairs of natural kind terms such as 'water'/'H_2O,' 'temperature'/'mean molecular kinetic energy,' and 'gold'/'element with the 79 atomic number.' Given the direct-reference theory, the terms in these pairs may differ in meaning yet refer to the same natural kind (Kripke 1972; Putnam 1975). Surely speakers may attach different descriptive meanings to the terms in each of these pairs, and even be wrong about the descriptions they associate with them. But such errors need not translate into a failure to pick out the same property when used in speech or thought.

To Harman and Putnam, semantical considerations of this sort suggest that the OQA is invalid.[14] Harman (1977: 19) offers this line of reply by drawing an analogy between the natural kind term 'water' and the moral term 'right.' In a thought experiment, he invites us to assume that he does not know that water is H_2O and claims that in this scenario, an OQA can 'prove' that water is not H_2O. His OQA *à la* Moore runs this way: If 'water' and 'H_2O' are synonymous, the question of whether water is H_2O would be as trivial or closed as is whether water is water. But for anyone who is ignorant about the nature of water, the question 'Is water always H_2O?' seems open. Thus, in this scenario, reasoning from true premises along Moore's OQA wrongly leads to the conclusion that water is not H_2O. Evidently, the OQA is invalid. Ergo, it falls short of demonstrating that an ascription of moral rightness to an action is not the same as an ascription of a certain purely natural property. However, note that this appeal to direct-reference semantics construes Moore's OQA in the barren-tautology formulation. It need not land a fatal blow to the debatable-equivalence formulation when charitably understood as an objection to reductive analyses of key ethical terms. In addition, Harman's thought experiment assumes that terms of this type are analogous to natural kind terms – a controversial assumption also present in Putnam's (1981: 206) critique of the OQA.

But Putnam's critique adds to Harman's an ontological/epistemic angle concerning how we know certain necessary truths involving the reference of natural kind terms: we know that 'temperature' and 'mean molecular kinetic energy' refer to the same natural kind empirically, through a process of scientific discovery. Thus, their identity in reference counts as a synthetic necessary truth. Why couldn't the relation between moral terms and some descriptive terms be semantically akin to that between these or other natural kind terms? If it can be, then the truth about their identity in reference should qualify as something to be discovered empirically, ultimately by science. Now Putnam charges that the OQA falsely assumes that conceptual *definition* or *analysis* can only involve the *analytic* identity of concepts. In having such a conception of analysis, Moore was among those in a long philosophical tradition who "implicitly denied that there could be such a thing as synthetic identity of properties" (ibid.). These philosophers were wrong, for the synthetic identity of properties now has the status of a well-established principle in science. If its traditionalist detractors were right, then many well-accepted scientific discoveries involving the exact meanings of terms like 'temperature' and 'water' would have been impossible, since they require learning empirically that certain property terms that seem different in their meaning do in fact designate the same property.

This appeal to the semantics of natural kind terms against the OQA has turned out to be an attractive strategy for the Cornell realist naturalistic response to Moore, as illustrated by Richard Boyd (1988), David Brink (1989; 2001), and Nicholas Sturgeon (2003). Yet Moore has some logical space for a defense of the OQA provided he accommodates Durrant's less controversial objection and offers a compelling rejoinder to the more controversial direct-reference accounts of Harman and Putnam. To accommodate Durrant's objection, Moore may recast the OQA as an argument vindicating the irreducibility of ethical concepts to descriptive concepts through and through. To reject the direct-reference account, he can note that although that account may have some intuitive appeal in the case of natural kind terms, it seems an implausible semantics for ethical terms (Pigden 2012). True, not all agree with this assessment. For example, Geoffrey Sayre-McCord believes that there is a lot to say in defense of direct-reference semantics for ethical terms since it explains some features of moral disagreement and in addition "helps to make sense of why no robust analytical definitions are available" (1997: 269).

However, a Fregean semantics of the sort Kripke calls a "cluster theory of descriptions" can also account for the possibility of genuine moral disagreement in the scenario that concerns Sayre-McCord. And it is far from obvious that any two persons who do not share any of the descriptions associated with a certain ethical predicate could nonetheless succeed in communicating with each other by means of that term. In addition, there are many reasons against a direct reference account of moral terms. For one thing, how might direct-reference theory proceed to make a strong case for considering *empirical discovery* the sole factor necessary in settling what denotation key moral terms might have, if any? Surely, science does not appear to be in the business of discovering the essence or real structure of any moral kind. Furthermore, as suggested by the debate on moral twin earth, there are good reasons for doubting the existence of any such kinds (Horgan and Timmons 1991; 1992; Kim 1997). Given these difficulties, even philosophers who sympathize with a direct-reference semantics for moral terms theory tend to qualify their endorsement. In the case of Sayre-McCord (1997: 270), after giving some reasons for the theory, he finally settles with the view that moral terms "operate" like, but are not akin to, natural kind terms.

Note, in addition, that on the assumption that moral terms are semantically analogous to natural kind terms, it remains underdetermined whether moral realism or nihilism (the theory that there are no moral properties) is true. After all, 'good' and 'right' could be like 'phlogiston' and 'ether,' two pseudo-natural kind terms that, contrary to the intuitions of our medieval peers, turned out to refer to no property at all. At the same time, we should follow Durrant in holding that the standard OQA of *Principia Ethica* fails to show that moral terms cannot denote the same properties denoted by some purely descriptive terms. But in due course we'll show that, when Moore's OQA is properly reconstructed, it can accommodate Durrant's challenge as well as the objection considered next.

DOES THE OQA FACE THE PARADOX OF ANALYSIS?

Although the OQA falls short of amounting to a strong objection to metaphysical naturalistic realism, semantical naturalistic realism claims that ethical discourse reduces to naturalistic discourse and cannot therefore invoke the invalidity objection to the OQA discussed above. But a different line of reply to the OQA has proved attractive to these ethical naturalists: the so-called paradox of analysis, which amounts to a puzzle for the conception of analysis in the OQA.[15] As first stated by C. H. Langford, that conception raises the paradox of analysis because

> [i]f the verbal expression representing the *analysandum* has the same meaning as the verbal expression representing the *analysans*, the analysis states a bare identity and is trivial; but if the two verbal expressions do not have the same meaning, the analysis is incorrect.
>
> (1942: 323)

The barren-tautology formulation of the OQA makes clear that Moore held that the naturalistic analyses of 'good' cannot be correct, given that they lack the appearance of trivial statements of bare identity. They have instead the appearance of unobvious, informative, ethical principles. Yet some current proponents of semantical naturalistic realism maintain that from Langford's paradox "[w]e could equally well conclude that naturalistic analyses may be unobvious and informative, and yet be correct for all that" (Smith 1994: 37). Jackson would agree since he theorizes that reductive naturalistic analyses of ethical discourse can proceed in two stages, one just by reflection, the other requiring empirical investigation. The first stage yields identification of certain key ethical predicates with natural properties of the sort that folk morality associates with each of those predicates. In the case of 'right,' this *a priori* stage yields an identification like this: action A is right if and only if it has whatever property it is that plays the rightness role in mature folk morality, which is still under negotiation (Jackson 1998: 151). The second stage involves an *a posteriori* investigation of the natural properties that play that role in folk morality, which may likely yield a set of disjunctive properties. This result is to be expected given the complexity of the analyses that establish equivalences between ethical and purely descriptive terms. The OQA question concerning any analysis of that sort may seem open when it is in fact closed. Such a result can only undermine the assumptions about the nature of philosophical analysis that fuel Moore's chief argument against ethical naturalism in *Principia Ethica*.

There is, however, logical space for Moore to dissolve the paradox of analysis and vindicate the cogency of a properly construed OQA. *Contra* Langford and Moore's own view in *Principia*, a Moorean reply to this objection first notes that not all *a priori* analyses need be trivial or uninformative: think of mathematical and logical equations as well as syntactic or semantical identities (Katz 2004: 83–88). Like these identities, those at issue in the OQA also qualify for informative but knowable just by thinking: they are putative identities between concepts. In the crucial step of the OQA, the Moorean now claims that the correctness of reductive naturalistic and metaphysical analyses of key ethical concepts is debatable on *a priori* grounds. After all, it appears that speakers competent with the concepts involved in a representative sample of analyses of the relevant sort can doubt them just by thinking. Of course, they could be wrong since apriority entails neither infallibility nor incorrigibility. Their intuitions count with support from the fact that there seems to be no self-contradiction in affirming any such analyses' *analysandum* while denying its *analysans*.[16]

5.3 RECASTING THE OPEN QUESTION ARGUMENT

We believe that, charitably construed, an OQA can generate skepticism about certain reductive programs of naturalistic and metaphysical ethics. The argument we have in mind runs this way:

OQA*

1. If 'good' reduces to 'pleasure,' then the question of whether these predicates are content-equivalent is not open to doubt on *a priori* grounds.
2. But the question of whether these predicates are content-equivalent is open to doubt on *a priori* grounds.
   Therefore,
3. 'Good' does not reduce to 'pleasure.'
4. Steps (1) through (3) can be iterated for a representative number of reductive naturalistic or metaphysical analyses of 'good.'
   Therefore,

5. 'Good' admits of no reductive naturalistic or metaphysical analysis.

6. Steps (1) through (5) can be iterated for a representative number of reductive naturalistic or metaphysical analyses of other key ethical terms.

Therefore,

7. No key ethical term admits of a reductive naturalistic or metaphysical analysis.

Conclusions 3, 5, and 7 are justified by *a priori* inference from the semantical intuitions of competent speakers, which plainly qualify as *a priori*. Those intuitions are strong enough to support premise 2, the view that any reductive analysis of naturalistic and metaphysical ethics is debatable on *a priori* grounds. They thus put the burden of argument on ethical theories of this semantical sort. At the same time, the argument does not presuppose the obviousness or triviality of correct analyses. It plausibly presupposes the *a priori* warrant of speakers' intuitions concerning some recurrent failure of content-equivalence between ethical and naturalistic or metaphysical terms whose meanings they master. A suitable reply by semantical reductive programs in ethics needs to explain away the speakers' *a priori* doubts about the key analyses of those programs.

In 1939, W. K. Frankena suggested that the OQA begs the question against naturalists in ethics because where Moore sees two radically different properties, the naturalists see only one property. But it should be evident that, reconstructed as the OQA*, Moore's argument avoids this objection in light of having a far more limited, semantical goal. And if we are right, the OQA* amply achieves this goal. It does this not by mounting an ambitious refutation but by placing the burden of proof on the reductive semantical analyses of some ethical naturalists who must now make a case for them that is strong enough to overcome the *a priori* doubts generated by Moore's argument.

Moore was not alone in attempting to undermine naturalistic realism in ethics by reasoning along the lines of the OQA. He found sympathetic readers for this charge from two unexpected quarters of naturalism in ethics: non-cognitivism (e.g., Blackburn

1998: 80; Hare 1952: 82–86) and the error theory (e.g., Mackie 1967: 51, 60–61; Pigden 2007: 258–259). These rival theorists agreed that Moore's argument, at the semantical level, captures a radical difference separating ethical concepts and judgments from purely descriptive concepts and judgments. The non-cognitivists and error theorists fully embraced the argument's negative conclusion against the reductive variety of ethical naturalism while offering their own account of the problem detected by the OQA.[17] Thus, from the non-cognitivist quarter, R. M. Hare wrote that Moore had captured something deep when he concluded from the OQA that 'good' cannot be fully translated into any purely descriptive term or terms. He went on to recast this argument in ways that would make clearer what is wrong with reductive ethical naturalism. Accordingly, on Hare's view "Moore's refutation (or a recognizable version of it) is valid ... what is wrong with naturalist theories is that they leave out the prescriptive or commendatory element in value-judgements, by seeking to make them derivable from statements of fact" (1952: 82). From the error-theory quarter, J. L. Mackie agreed with Hare's assessment of the negative conclusion from the OQA, according to which the reductive ethical naturalists miss the commendation force that is attached to ethical uses of the term 'good.' In Mackie's view, there is more to say about what Moore captured with the OQA: the argument trades on the indeterminacy of 'good,' an ambiguous term that presupposes different requirements when applied, for instance, to what is conducive to pleasure and to what is ethically good. For Mackie, "if we ask, 'Though x is conducive to A's pleasure, is it good?' we indicate, just by asking this question, that we are bringing some other requirements into view" (1967: 60–61). Moore could agree in part with Mackie since in Chapter 1 of *Principia Ethica* he draws attention to the ambiguity of the term 'good.' But he would firmly oppose Mackie's further claim that, as used by the hedonists, 'good' has requirements or presuppositions that differ from those at work when it has another use.

To sum up, it did not occur to the early Moore that some such rivals of non-naturalism could agree with his negative conclusion from the OQA while rejecting his positive conclusion and advancing their own competing accounts of the failure of ethical naturalism to pass the semantical test that is crucial to that argument. Being of a *philosophical* naturalist persuasion themselves, the non-cognitivists and the error theorists propounded moral ontologies incompatible with all varieties of ethical realism, including Moore's non-naturalism. Although these fellow travelers suspected Moore himself of being ontologically closer to supernaturalism than naturalism, they joined forces with him against reductive naturalistic realism in ethics. This alliance no doubt contributed to the eclipse of ethical naturalism during a great part of the past century. Nevertheless, since the 1980s, the appeal of ethical naturalism has been on the rise, a phenomenon in part due to its ability to accommodate (1) moral properties and facts within what is a widely attractive naturalistic outlook and (2) everyday intuitions about how to understand moral terms and sentences. Moore's non-naturalism has no problem accommodating (2). Yet it faces problems in accommodating (1), and thus, in being consistent with the widely held naturalist outlook that all there *is* is the world as construed by mature science. We'll return to these questions of moral and general metaphysics in Chapter 7, after considering a corollary of the OQA: the naturalistic fallacy.

NOTES

1   By holding that the identity between the relevant predicates obtains, simple emotivism would in addition commit the naturalistic fallacy – a charge that we examine in Chapter 6.

2   A. N. Prior traces a proto OQA to Ralph Cudworth, Lord Shaftesbury, and Francis Hutcheson, Richard Price, Richard Whately, and Dugald Stewart. Some classical non-naturalists who preceded Moore also anticipated versions of that argument. Among them, Hastings Rashdall (1897: 214), Henry Sidgwick (1967/1874: 109), and T. H. Huxley (1894: 162).

3   As discussed in Chapter 11, Moore thought that several simple and complex things qualify for having various degrees of intrinsic value, from pleasure and knowledge to enjoyment of a personal relationship, admiration of a beautiful object, and many more.

4   As noted by C. D. Broad (1970), Moore never gave a reason for his own opposition to countenancing disjunctive properties. Among those who have argued for their unreality is David Armstrong (1978: 19–23).

5   Here we follow Pigden (2007; 2018) in calling this formulation of the OQA 'barren-tautology'. It can be found not only in Sidgwick's *Methods* but also in the works of some of the early British critics of naturalism mentioned in note 1.

6 Charles Pigden (2007) makes this remark in connection with the Russell of "Is Ethics a Branch of Empirical Psychology?" A similar remark applies to the descriptive analyses of some contemporary moral functionalist which are inspired in the work of David Lewis.

7 Among current representatives of non-reductive naturalistic realism are philosophers of the Cornell group, which includes Richard Boyd (1988), David Brink (1989), and Nicholas Sturgeon (1985; 2003). Although not at Cornell, Peter Railton (2006; 2010) shares the core theses of the group.

8 Reductive naturalistic realism is best represented by some moral functionalists of the so-called Canberra plan who argue for the possibility of naturalistic reductive analyses of key ethical terms, such as Frank Jackson (1998; 2012) and Michael Smith (1994). While Jackson is confident about the possibility of fully reducing moral vocabulary to purely descriptive vocabulary by means of conceptual analysis, Smith thinks that such analyses must be pursued but ultimately face what he calls a "permutation problem."

9 Non-reductive realists of a naturalistic persuasion include the so-called Cornell realists (Richard Boyd 1988; David Brink 1989; Nicholas Sturgeon 1985) as well as Peter Railton (1986; 2006). Among the Cornell realists, Nicholas Sturgeon (1985: 239) explicitly claims that his naturalistic realism, the doctrine that moral facts are nothing but natural facts, does not commit him to the possibility of a semantic reduction of moral concepts and propositions, which he in fact rejects.

10 Jackson (1998: 119) formulates this relation in this way: (S) For all worlds w and w*, if w and w* are exactly alike descriptively, then they are exactly alike ethically. But critics find problems with this thesis. For example, Timothy Williamson (2001: 627) argues that the reduction of the moral to the descriptive requires a stronger supervenience thesis along the lines 'For all worlds w and w* and individuals i and i*, *if i in w and i* in w** are exactly alike descriptively, then they are exactly alike ethically.' For more on this, see Nuccetelli (2019).

11 Cf. Jackson, Pettit, and Smith (2000: 83). For more on the relation between supervenience and entailment, see Chapter 8.

12 Jackson thinks that Hare bolstered the OQA by noting that the argument's point

> is not *that* it always makes sense to ask what I ought to do no matter how much descriptive information I have, but *why* it always make sense. To accept an ethical account of some situation is per se to take up an essentially directed attitude towards it, whereas accepting a descriptive account of it can never be in itself the taking up of a directed attitude towards it.
>
> (Jackson 1998: 153, our emphasis)

13 W. K. Frankena (1963: 99–100) argues that the OQA seems to work in *Principia* only because Moore ascribes to his naturalistic competitors analyses that plainly fail to capture what speakers ordinarily intend when they say that a thing is good. But the naturalistic "equivalents" of goodness that he selected

do not do justice to what his opponents mean. Surely, questions such as "Is what we desire on reflection good?" and "Is what we approve when we take an impersonal point of view right?" do not seem open. See also Sturgeon (2003) for a non-reductive naturalist reply along similar lines.

14 Other critics who agree on the invalidity of the OQA include Baldwin (1990), Feldman (2019), Pigden (2007; 2019), and Nuccetelli and Seay (2007; 2012).

15 Besides Jackson and Smith, other critics who take the paradox of analysis to represent a serious problem facing Moore's conception of analysis include Beaney (2014), Darwall, Gibbard, and Railton (1992) and Langford (1942). In the camp that minimizes the problem for Moore are Hurka (2014); Katz (2004); and Nuccetelli and Seay (2007).

16 Jackson (1998: 152) claims that once the relevant equivalences between the ethical vocabulary and the purely descriptive vocabulary has been established, the appearance of contradiction in asserting, say, 'A is an act of promise keeping but is not right' is merely pragmatic – something akin to commanding 'Shut the door, but do not shut it.' However, an appeal to pragmatics along these lines might seem plausible for injunctions, but not for assertions such as 'Pleasure is not always good' given Jackson's cognitivist reading of them.

17 Of course, these rivals on non-naturalism rejected Moore's positive ontological and semantical conclusions from his OQA, such as his claim that goodness is a simple, indefinable, *sui generis* ethical property. But this reaction of his fellow travelers need not concern us here.

SUGGESTED READING

Baldwin, Thomas, "The Open Question Argument," in *The Routledge Companion to Ethics*, John Skorupski ed., London: Routledge, 2010, pp. 286–296. Reconstructs the OQA and replies to objections to this argument by semantical varieties of naturalistic realism. Also argues that, since Moore took some natural properties to be ought-implying, he was committed to rejecting Hume's point that no moral conclusion follows deductively from exclusively descriptive premises.

Ball, S. W., "Reductionism in Ethics and Science: A Contemporary Look at G E. Moore's Open Question Argument," *American Philosophical Quarterly* 25 (1988): 197–213. Qualified defense of the OQA against the objection that it begs the question and is thus invalid. Argues that the OQA rests on linguistic evidence against reductive naturalism in ethics. When applied *seriatum* to a sufficient number of naturalistic analyses, the argument accumulates evidence against those theories and for Moore's conclusion.

Durrant, R. G., "Identity of Properties and the Definition of 'Good'," *Australasian Journal of Philosophy* 48(3) (1970): 360–361. Charges that Moore's ontological conclusion from the OQA fails to take into account the distinction of sense and reference that Frege offered to solve what he regarded as a puzzle of cognitive value: viz., the problem of explaining why identity statements such as 'x = x' and 'x = y' have different cognitive value. After all, one of these identities is trivial while the other is significant. Moore might have assumed a Millean, referentialist semantics for the term 'good,' a claim that seems supported by the fact that he often calls concepts "objects before the mind." (In fact, Moore might not have been alone in assuming a semantics of that kind for moral concepts, since Russell's *Elements of Ethics* (1987/1910) – a book inspired by *Principia Ethica* – seems to assume that too.)

Hare, R. M., "'Naturalism'," Chapter 5 in *The Language of Morals*, Oxford: Clarendon Press, 1952, pp. 79–93. Vindicates a version of the OQA according to which its strength consists in showing that naturalistic theories in ethics leave out the essential prescriptive or commendatory force of moral judgments. In this way, Hare explains why Moore gets his result from the OQA for any attempt to reduce Goodness to a purely descriptive concept. Hare's explanation of why the OQA would block any such attempt is, roughly, that sincerely accepting a moral judgment *ipso facto* amounts to taking a pro- or con-attitude toward what the judgment is about. No such attitude is associated with sincerely making a descriptive judgment.

Harman, Gilbert, *The Nature of Morality*, New York: Oxford University Press, 1977. Argues that Moore's OQA faces a *reductio* since an argument along the same lines can be deployed to "prove" evidently false propositions such as that water is not H_2O. Harman considers his objection fatal for all versions of the OQA. This result leaves open the possibility that either of two rival doctrines, ethical naturalism and ethical nihilism, could be true. Since each of these doctrines can accommodate the "sensible" naturalist thesis "that *all* facts are facts of nature" (p. 17), for Harman, the hard question facing naturalists in ethics is whether to endorse ethical nihilism or ethical naturalism (broadly construed as to include relativism).

Moore, G. E., Chapters 1–4 of *Principia Ethica*, Cambridge: Cambridge University Press, rev. ed., Thomas Baldwin ed., 1993/1903. These chapters offer the two formulations of the OQA discussed here as the barren tautology and the debatable equivalence formulations. They also feature Moore's discussion of a large number of doctrines he regarded as refuted by the OQA. We'll have more to say about his list of "culprits" in Chapter 6.

Nuccetelli, Susana and Gary Seay, "What's Right with the Open Question Argument?" in Susana Nuccetelli and Gary Seay eds., *Themes from G. E. Moore: New Essays in Epistemology and Ethics*, Oxford: Oxford University Press, 2007, pp. 261–282. Looks closely at Moore's OQA, defending an understanding of the argument along the lines we proposed in this chapter. Argues that, thus understood, the OQA succeeds in placing the burden of proof on proponents of reductive naturalistic analyses of ethical vocabulary.

Pigden, Charles R., "Identifying Goodness," *Australasian Journal of Philosophy* 90(1) (2012): 93–109. Takes the OQA reconstructed in Pigden (2007) to be valid while arguing that the direct-reference theory objection to the OQA is not credible because it rests on some implausible assumptions about the semantics of moral terms.

Putnam, Hilary, *Reason, Truth and History*, Cambridge: Cambridge University Press, 1981, pp. 205–211. Crucial reading for the direct-reference theory's critique of the OQA, charging that Moore mistakenly drew from it a conclusion about the non-identity of moral and natural properties. He neglected to consider that the identity at stake in a reductive naturalistic analysis might be like the identity in the reference of certain natural kind terms: viz., a synthetic, necessary identity knowable only *a posteriori*.

Stratton-Lake, Philip. "Intuitionism in Ethics," 2014, in *Stanford Encyclopedia of Philosophy*, Edward N. Zalta ed., 2003/2014, https://plato.stanford.edu/entries/intuitionism-ethics/ In the course of outlining the classical non-naturalists' moral epistemology and metaphysics, Stratton-Lake vindicates a version of the OQA that is consistent with our reconstruction in this chapter. See also Nuccetelli and Seay (2007; 2012).

Sturgeon, Nicholas, "Ethical Naturalism," in *The Oxford Handbook of Ethical Theory*, D. Copp ed., Oxford: Oxford University Press, 2006, pp. 91–121. Outlines the ethical naturalists' chief objection to the OQA (viz., that it is possible that two predicates expressing different concepts denote the same ethical property) while also charging that Moore's conclusion from the argument amounts to a hasty generalization.

6

THE NATURALISTIC FALLACY

With Gary Seay

6.1 RECONSTRUCTING MOORE'S NATURALISTIC FALLACY CHARGE

Under the label 'naturalistic fallacy' the early Moore made at least three related charges against certain types of ethical principles and inferences that he ascribed to naturalistic ethics as well as to metaphysical ethics.[1] Of the three charges, two involve a mistake in the analysis of an ethical term, and one a mistake in inference. Moore's account of these mistakes occurs prominently in the first chapter of *Principia Ethica* (*PE*: §10, §§12–14), where the naturalistic fallacy figures as a pattern of mistake committed by any ethical theory that flouts one of the following principles whose truth Moore based on reason alone:

1. 'Good' expresses the sole ethical term that admits of no reductive analysis at all.

DOI: 10.4324/9780429275975-6

2. No ethical term admits of a reductive analysis in purely naturalistic or metaphysical terms.
3. No moral proposition follows from non-moral propositions alone.

A charitable reading of principles 1 and 2 requires putting Moore's conflation of concepts and properties in *Principia* at work to his advantage by interpreting the analysis at issue in them as involving bans on certain semantical analyses of *concepts*, rather than on metaphysical analyses of properties. (Non-naturalism as well as its rival, ethical naturalism, both take key ethical concepts to denote ethical properties.)[2] On the other hand, principle 3 boils down to the Humean rule banning any attempt to deduce an ethical or "ought" conclusion from purely descriptive or "is" premises alone. Although there is some debate about whether Moore vindicated this rule, in Chapter 3 we provided some evidence that he did. Flouting either of these three principles amounts, in Moore's view, to committing the naturalistic fallacy. If we are right, an ethical theory may commit the naturalistic fallacy in either of these three ways:

> NF1 – By attempting an analysis of Goodness, and thereby flouting principle 1 above.
>
> NF2 – By attempting a reductive analysis of an ethical concept into some purely descriptive concept or concepts, and thereby flouting principle 2 above.
>
> NF3 – By attempting an inference to an ethical conclusion from some purely descriptive premises alone, and thereby flouting principle 3 above.

Each of these uses of the naturalistic fallacy, which we'll now take up in turn, appear in *Principia*. Of the three, NF1 stands out as the weakest. For, thus understood, the naturalistic-fallacy charge comes with the baggage of *monism* about the simple concepts of ethics. Shared by Moore and Sidgwick, monism is a type of conceptual minimalism holding that there is just one key ethical concept that is "too elementary to admit of any formal definition" (Sidgwick 1967/1874: 32) and amounts to the simple ethical component of any other ethical concept. Yet Sidgwick postulated for that role the deontic concept expressed by 'ought' and Moore the value concept expressed by the term 'good' in its primary ethical use. In later ethical writings, however, Moore had replaced the monism of *Principia* with a dualism featuring both Good and Right as the sole simple ethical concepts. This suggests that Moorean non-naturalism stands to lose nothing of importance with the rejection of NF1. Furthermore, the OQA falls short of supporting the Goodness-centered monism that fuels this construal of the naturalistic fallacy. In addition, Moore was not fully invested in defending such a thesis, as shown by the fact that he did not charge Sidgwick with having committed the naturalistic fallacy, even when Sidgwick had flouted principle 1 above by attempting to analyze Good partly in terms of Ought.

MOORE ON SIDGWICK AND THE NATURALISTIC FALLACY

Sidgwick (1967/1874: 25, 34) held that Good and Bad are analyzable in terms of what an ideally rational agent ought to desire or be averse to in a circumstance, respectively. We'll have more to say about Sidgwick's attempted analysis of Good in Chapter 10. For now, note that in *Principia*, Moore wrote not merely that Sidgwick avoided the naturalistic fallacy, but that he was the first ethical writer to identify the fallacy. In Moore's words, "so far as I know, there is only one ethical writer, Prof. Henry Sidgwick, who has clearly recognized and stated this fact [that Goodness is indefinable]" (*PE*: §14, 69). Might Moore have been ignorant of Sidgwick's Ought-centered semantical minimalism? And in light of his attempted reductive definition of Good partly in terms of Ought, why did Moore exempt him from the commission of the naturalistic fallacy? Let's take up in turn each of these questions.

In our view, ascribing to Sidgwick a Goodness-centered conceptual minimalism amounts to an oversight about which not much should be made in light of the fact that, a few lines later in the same Chapter 1 of *Principia* Moore correctly ascribed to Sidgwick the thesis that Ought is the sole indefinable, unanalyzable, ethical concept. Of more interest to us is his exempting Sidgwick's analysis of Good from the commission of the naturalistic fallacy.

After all, the Moore of *Principia Ethica* would say that any flouting of something like the principle 1 above is an instance of the naturalistic fallacy. More precisely, it is an instance of our NF1 above. But Moore can solve this puzzle if he embraces one of the following options:

1. Abandon principle 1 and the associated, naturalistic-fallacy charge NF1.
2. Say that Sidgwick had offered a paraphrase but not an analysis of good, something akin to Moore's own paraphrases in terms of Intrinsic Value, What Ought to Exist, and What Ought to Be Promoted.
3. Admit that he made a mistake in exempting Sidgwick from having committed the naturalistic fallacy.

In our view, (3) is not really an option for Moore, since the claim that Sidgwick committed the naturalistic fallacy would be implausible. Now in Chapter 10, we argue that Sidgwick's definition of Goodness falls short of amounting to a reductive analysis of this concept. If so, then (2) is a live option for Moore. (2) can also be combined with option (1), which Moore in fact took in his incomplete preface for the second edition of *Principia*, where he denied that the relevant passage of *Principia* "actually means by 'committing the naturalistic fallacy' merely 'identifying G ['good'] with some predicate other than G." He then went on to restrict the scope of the fallacy to the problem facing any attempt at a reductive analysis of a key ethical term in non-ethical terms, whether these be naturalistic or metaphysical.[3] That is, the naturalistic fallacy boils down to the NF2 above, which results from flouting anti-reductionist principle 2.

THE NATURALISTIC-FALLACY CHARGE AGAINST HEDONISM

But the naturalistic fallacy has often been cast as a Humean is-ought problem. On this construal, it boils down to the NF3 above. Although the NF3 concerns a mistake in inference and the NF2 a mistake in definition or analysis, these mistakes are related. After all, any reductive analysis of an ethical concept in terms of purely descriptive concepts would sanction inferences that violate Hume's rule. Say, if Goodness means 'What maximizes pleasure,' then from 'x is pleasure-maximizing' one could logically infer 'x is good.' Nonetheless, the NF3 (hereafter, Hume's rule) points to a problem of validity affecting certain kinds of logical derivation, while the NF2 (hereafter, simply 'the naturalistic fallacy' or 'the default naturalistic fallacy' when the context requires it) points to a problem of cogency affecting either naturalistic or metaphysical definitions of ethical vocabulary.[4]

To illustrate how these problems may affect a naturalistic ethical theory, let's consider some arguments for hedonism, beginning with

HEDONISM I
P   Most people desire pleasure.
C   *Therefore*, pleasure is good.

Although HEDONISM I might appear to face Hume's problem, in fact it doesn't when charitably read as involving a missing ethical premise. For it then runs this way:

HEDONISM II
P0   What most people desire is good.
P1   Most people desire pleasure.
C   *Therefore*, pleasure is good.

Provided there is no equivocation affecting the occurrences of 'good' in the premise and conclusion, Hedonism II is obviously valid and thus immune to objection by invoking Hume's rule. It also escapes the naturalistic-fallacy charge when premise P0 is read as stating a synthetic identity. After all, hedonists might argue that this identity is comparable to some identities of reference often noted between pairs of natural kind concepts such as water/H_2O and heat/molecular motion.

Suppose now the hedonist naturalists read premise 0 of Hedonism II as claiming that the concepts flanking the identity in their principle are synonymous. The argument for hedonism now runs as follows:

HEDONISM III

Po   The predicates 'good' and 'what most people desire' are meaning equivalent.

P1   Most people desire pleasure.

C   *Therefore*, pleasure is good.

Since in the context of a properly construed OQA, P0 is *a priori* debatable, and Hedonism III is unsound. Although the argument passes the is-ought test (i.e., it is valid), its P0 exemplifies a pattern of mistake in definition that occurs when, in the context of a rational deliberation, an audience sufficiently competent with the predicates involved may be skeptical about their meaning equivalence. Given that the grounds for P0 are *a priori*, a critical audience sympathetic to the OQA* can have *a priori* doubts about this premise. Furthermore, since other semantical analyses of this sort may also face an objection along these lines, we can infer that their *a priori* openness to doubt seems not an accidental feature of a particular audience and a particular reductive naturalistic or metaphysical definition of an ethical concept. Rather, such definitions seemingly exemplify a regular pattern of mistake committed by certain reductive naturalism of a semantical kind.

If we are right, then there is dialectical space for Moore to meet the objection that the default naturalistic fallacy amounts to no fallacy at all. He could reply that although it is not one of the so-called formal fallacies, it captures a problem of cogency facing definition, one that is akin to the problem facing any valid argument that amounts to a *petitio principii*, a complex question, or any other fallacy of presumption. Thus understood, the naturalistic fallacy is a species of a more general *definist fallacy*, which occurs when, in the context of a deliberation about some contested identity of properties, their identity is said to rest on the semantic equivalence of the concepts involved.[5] It is committed, for instance, by any reductive materialists who argue that pain is C-fibers firing, simply because 'being in pain' just means 'having one's C-fibers firing;' or by epistemic externalists who claim that 'belief x is justified' just means 'x is the outcome of a reliable belief-forming mechanism.' Of course, in each case, the hypothetical theorist cannot settle by definition a philosophical question that is in fact debatable.

In short, charging a moral theory with the commission of a definist fallacy amounts to saying that it begs the question against rivals – *unless* of course they have already discharged their burden of proof by producing reasons as compelling as those of any skeptical opponents. In ethics, since a properly construed OQA creates a dialectical context for skepticism about the reductive programs of semantical naturalists, charging that they commit the naturalistic fallacy amounts to saying that initially those programs have the burden of proof. If they cannot discharge it, they would beg the question against Moore.

Yet, if there is a reading in which Moore's naturalistic fallacy objection has some force, why do critics like Frankena (1939) think that Moore's objection amounts to a *petitio*? We submit that these critics have notoriously evaluated it in isolation from its dialectical context, and as a result have failed to recognize its force. Rather than focusing on the reductive programs of semantical naturalism in ethics, they have focused solely on reductive programs of metaphysical naturalism that are resistant to OQA reasoning in the ways suggested in Chapter 5.

6.2   HAS ANYONE COMMITTED THE NATURALISTIC FALLACY?

Let's now turn to a different line of questioning facing Moore's naturalistic fallacy charge: Which ethical doctrines, if any, have pursued reductive programs in ethics of the sort that might commit the fallacy? For a great part of the twentieth century, not very many – a phenomenon perhaps explicable at least in part by the popularity of Moore's charge against such programs. As we have seen, a charitable reading of the naturalistic fallacy takes it to consist in a dialectical fallacy committed chiefly by semantical reductive programs of what Moore called 'naturalistic' and 'metaphysical' ethics. Obviously, if no significant program of either kind was ever a live option, his charge would amount to a straw man. But in *Principia Ethica*, he claimed to have found the naturalistic fallacy in the work of almost every philosopher in the history of Western ethics. His list includes Aristotle (§106, 225), the Stoics

(§27, 93), Spinoza (§67, 164), Kant (§67, 164), Rousseau (§27, 93), Bentham (§14, 69), Mill (§40, 118), Spencer (§31, 101), and Green (§84, 189). True, Moore appears to have an inflated conception of who is vulnerable to his naturalistic-fallacy charge, and often his reasons for including someone in his list are too abridged and confused. But in what follows we review some doctrines available at his time that did in fact countenance the possibility of either deducing ethical conclusions from exclusively descriptive premises, analyzing key ethical terms in exclusively naturalistic or metaphysical terms, or both.

ARISTOTLE, RALPH BARTON PERRY, AND BARUCH SPINOZA

According to Moore's reading of *Nicomachean Ethics* in Chapter 5 of *Principia Ethica*, Aristotle's virtue ethics amounts to a variety of ethical naturalism vulnerable to the naturalistic fallacy charge (*PE*: §106, 225 ff.). In his view, Aristotle committed the fallacy by claiming that the highest intrinsic value consists in the exercise of a contemplative life, something in turn achievable by means of the exercise of the practical virtues to which he assigned lesser intrinsic value. Moore points out that these virtues, as defined by Aristotle, are habitual dispositions to perform certain actions. He failed to realize about the concept of a virtue that we must add a moral component to, such as that the action in question is one's duty. Moore thought of its moral component as concerning the performance of one's duty. Since Duty itself is a complex concept, analyzable in consequentialist terms as the act or omission that in a circumstance maximizes Goodness, Aristotle's virtues have only "external rightness" in the sense that they are not ultimate ends. And they lack a moral component.

On a different, "non-teleological" interpretation, Aristotle's virtue ethics also comes out as vulnerable to the naturalistic fallacy charge. Frankena and Granrose (1974: 370–371) offer a perspicuous interpretation, according to which Aristotle's ethics amounts to a form of naturalistic realism that reductively defines 'good' in non-ethical terms in this way:

'Good' = 'that which we all aim at.'

If adequate, this definition provides the Aristotelian theorists with a tool for deducing ethical conclusions from purely descriptive premises. For once they have identified, say, *happiness* as *what we all aim at*, they could deduce the goodness or badness of a thing or trait of character merely by empirical investigation of its tendency to promote or hinder happiness. On this reading of Aristotle's ethics, the justification of evaluative judgment rests on both *a priori* and *a posteriori* premises and is therefore inferential. For it proceeds in steps involving the following:

1. An *a priori* analysis of 'good' in terms of 'that what we all aim at.'
2. An empirical investigation that yields *happiness* as *what we all aim at*.
3. An empirical investigation to determine how a certain thing or trait of character scores in the promotion of happiness.

From (1) and (2), the Aristotelian theorists can infer that a certain thing or trait of character is good, bad, or neutral. The result would depend on how that thing or trait fares in promoting or hindering happiness. But Moore's OQA appears to block the naturalistic definition of 'good' in (1), thereby blocking any inference of the value of things or traits of character that relies on such definitions.

For another ethical theory that attempts a naturalistic definition of a key ethical term Moore could have looked at the ethical subjectivism of one of his contemporaries, Ralph Barton Perry. Perry attempted to reduce intrinsic value to a psychological, and therefore purely descriptive, term. In *General Theory of Value* (1926), he wrote:

> [t]hat which is an object of interest is *eo ipso* invested with value. Any object, whatever it be, acquires value when any interest, whatever it be, is taken in it; just as anything whatsoever becomes a target when anyone whosoever aims at it ...

> (ibid.: 139)

Throughout Perry's book, a key moral term 'value' appears as a semantical equivalent of a psychological term "whatever an agent has taken an interest in."[6] This renders his theory a fully-fledged version of the simple ethical subjectivism targeted by the simple OQA that we discussed in Chapter 5. Perhaps in search of a more objective ethical criterion, in a later book, *Realms of Value* (1954), he turned to an inter-subjectivist principle that defines 'good' in terms of 'harmonious happiness.' Either way, Perry's naturalistic conception of intrinsic value does not fit within the realist ethical doctrines discussed in Chapter 5 because even when he countenanced moral properties, he took them to be ontologically contingent on psychological states (interests, happiness) which may vary across agents and cultures. As a result, his conception of value falls within ethical relativism, a competitor of ethical realism. Perry acknowledged the relativist import of his subjectivism, but argued that it did not amount to extreme relativism (1926: 150–151).[7]

It is however a form of *naturalistic* ethics that Perry traced to the ethical theory of Baruch Spinoza. Moore might disagree but nonetheless charge Spinoza with having committed the naturalistic fallacy "when he tells us that we are more or less perfect, in proportion as we are more or less closely united with Absolute Substance by the 'intellectual love' of God" (*PE*: §67, 164). In addition, Moore charged Kant with a similar mistake for having thought of the Kingdom of Ends as the ideal. Be that as it may, Moore regarded Spinoza's *Ethics* as an example of *metaphysical* ethics vulnerable to the naturalistic fallacy charge. By contrast, as Perry read Spinoza, he was proposing a subjectivist form of ethical naturalism according to which to say that a thing is good is to say that we strive for, wish for, or desire that thing.[8] However, Spinoza's claim is consistent not only with subjectivism but also with ethical constructivism and even nihilism. For it does not require Spinoza to say that intrinsic value is a property of anything at all. Spinoza could have been claiming instead that a certain psychological state (or states) simply *causes us to believe* that that a thing has value, regardless of whether the ascription of value is false or even lacks a truth-value. In sum, Spinoza might have held a principle of metaphysical ethics (Moore's interpretation), a subjectivist principle of naturalistic ethics (Perry's interpretation), or something else. In any of these interpretations, if he advanced his principle as a reductive definition, whether naturalistic or metaphysical, his theory seems vulnerable to Moore's naturalistic fallacy charge.

JEREMY BENTHAM AND J. S. MILL

In his *Introduction to the Principles of Morals and Legislation* (1988/1789), Jeremy Bentham advanced the utilitarian principle that actions are right insofar as they maximize pleasure or minimize pain for all those affected by them. Sidgwick read this principle as a *synthetic* ethical proposition, not as a definition of what it is for an action to be right. However, even if Bentham's principle is a synthetic proposition and he uses the term 'right' to denote "what is good as a means, whether or not it is also good as an end," according to Moore, there is room to charge him with the naturalistic fallacy because "the reasons which he actually gives for his ethical proposition are fallacious ones so far as they consist in a definition of 'right'" (*PE*: §14, 69/70).

Since Bentham wrote that right action *means* action in accordance with the principle of utility (1988/1789, Chapter 1, §10), Moore's less charitable reading appears to rest on textual evidence. But Bentham might have used the language of meaning and definition simply to express his naturalistic view of moral properties. After all, like Moore himself, Bentham did not draw a clear distinction between claims about moral properties and about concepts.

Moore was less tentative about charging John Stuart Mill with the commission of the naturalistic fallacy (*PE*: §§40–41, 117/120). His central objection concerns Mill's "proof" of hedonism, which as offered in *Utilitarianism* runs as follows:

> The only proof capable of being given that an object is visible is that people actually see it. The only proof that a sound is audible is that people hear it; and so forth for the other sources of experience. In this manner, I apprehend, the sole evidence it is possible to produce that anything is desirable is that people actually desire it.
>
> (Mill 1979/1863: 34)

Under the most direct interpretation of this passage, Mill seems to be making at least an attempt to deduce a moral conclusion (viz., that pleasure is desirable) from a purely descriptive premise (viz., that people desire pleasure), and therefore he commits NF3, the naturalistic fallacy facing arguments that have an is-ought problem.

If in addition he is attempting to reduce 'desirable' to 'desired,' he would be committing the NF2, the naturalistic fallacy facing any reductive analysis of an ethical term into a purely descriptive term. Either way, he seems vulnerable to one or the other version of Moore's naturalistic fallacy that we found defensible.

However, there are other possible readings of Mill's "proof." According to Henry West (1997; 2017), Mill was aware that no apodictic proof of hedonism could be offered. In this passage, he intends to argue that the truth of hedonism is self-evident in the sense of being directly justified, with no appeal to evidence or reasons necessary. Mary Warnock (1960: 28–33) would concur, since on her reading, when Mill wrote "the only evidence that pleasure is desirable is that people do desire it," he was not arguing that "from the fact that people desire pleasure it follows that pleasure is good." Rather, he was arguing that the fact that people desire pleasure suggests that they already regard pleasure as self-evidently good on its own. If so, Mill's controversial passage in fact invokes the intuitive nature of pleasure as an intrinsic value, and does not differ greatly from what Moore said in *Principia Ethica* about things that have intrinsic goodness. If Warnock's defense of his proof is persuasive, then the above passage does not commit the naturalistic fallacy. It simply emphasizes that, with regard to ultimate ends, their value must be something that is already evident without proof. For people can accept an appeal to a certain ultimate end as a *reason* for pursuing some intermediate goals only if the intrinsic value of that ultimate end is self-evidently good. However, like West's defense, hers also conflicts with the standard construal of self-evidence under which propositions such as 'Pleasure is the sole good' hardly qualify. More plausible candidates include mathematical propositions, propositions that are true by the meanings of their terms alone, and possibly first-person judgments about one's own psychological states.

But the Warnock-West is not the only line of reply to the above critique of Mill's "proof". Another line draws attention to the fact that Mill's argument neither states nor presupposes the self-evidence of hedonism – or that 'desirable' and 'desired' mean the same (Mulgan, 2007; Sayre-McCord 2001). Rather, his "proof" is best construed as a non-deductive argument holding that the fact that pleasure is commonly desired counts as *evidence* of its being desirable. Emphasizing Mill's empiricism, this line of reply renders his talk of "proof" a metaphor since it contends that at no point did he attempt an apodictic proof of his proposition. On this reading, Mill intended a non-deductive argument running along these lines:

HEDONISM IV

    Po What most people desire is likely to be desirable.

    P   Most people desire pleasure.

    Therefore,

    C   Likely pleasure is desirable.

But Hedonism IV has a number of fatal problems. For one thing, the fact that most people desire pleasure (or anything else) seems an exceedingly weak reason for holding that, on reflection, pleasure (or something else) is the only thing desirable as an ultimate end. That is, since, for classical utilitarians, pleasure is the sole intrinsic value and all other values are instrumental, Mill is committed to a far more ambitious conclusion – namely,

    C* Likely pleasure is the sole intrinsically desirable value.

Hedonism IV has no tendency to support C*. Furthermore, this version of Mill's argument would need robust scientific data to the effect that most people desire pleasure as the sole valuable end.

Finally, note that in addition to charging Mill's 'proof' with the naturalistic fallacy, Moore's critique opens the way for charging it with the commission of other fallacies. For one thing, it relies on equivocation and a weak analogy when it compares the normative term 'desirable' with the non-normative terms 'visible' and 'audible.' Second, its universalist conclusion that the general happiness is an intrinsic good for the *aggregate of persons* rests on nothing more than a fallacy of composition.

HERBERT SPENCER

By the turn of the twentieth century the first wave of evolutionary accounts of morality seemed widely attractive. This was especially true of Herbert Spencer's ethics, a type of "evolutionistic ethics" with which Moore took issue in *Principia Ethica* (*PE*: §§28–34, 96/106). According to Moore, Spencer equivocated between two ethical doctrines: hedonistic ethics and some non-hedonistic form of evolutionary ethics. Of these two, here we are concerned only with Spencerian evolutionary ethics, which Moore summarized as follows:

> Spencerian Evolutionary Ethics – "[T]he view that we need only to consider the tendency of evolution in order to discover the direction in which we ought to go."[9]

Moore was not the first to object to a view of this sort. Among some notable objectors preceding him were Henry Sidgwick and Thomas H. Huxley. According to Sidgwick's objection, not only is evolutionary ethics unable to contribute a criterion for distinguishing true moral principles from false ones, but this kind of ethical theory entails a self-defeating global skepticism that "would end destroying its premises" (1876: 54). T. H. Huxley likewise questioned the value of evolutionary ethics by contending that knowledge of the origins of morality cannot "furnish any better reason why what we call good is preferable to what we call evil than we had before" (1894: 132). Furthermore, it is a fallacy to reason that

> because, on the whole, animals and plants have advanced in perfection of organization by means of the struggle for existence and the consequent 'survival of the fittest'; therefore men in society, men as ethical beings, must look to the same process to help them toward perfection.
>
> (ibid.)

Moore would agree that evolution "has very little" to say to ethics when it comes to offering an adequate criterion of right conduct or helping to solve any major disagreement among the doctrines of philosophical ethics (*PE*: §34, 109). At the same time, like each of these predecessors, Moore recognized the value of Darwin's theory of evolution in biology but remained skeptical about its value in ethics, beyond providing "some help in discovering what it is *possible* to attain and what are the means to its attainment" (ibid.: §34, 108). He was careful to draw a line between Spencer's evolutionary ethics and Darwin's theory of evolution, noting that

> Spencer, for example, constantly uses more evolved as equivalent to higher. But it is to be noted that this forms no part of Darwin's scientific theory. That theory will explain, equally well, how by an alteration in the environment (the gradual cooling of the earth, for example), quite a different species from man, a species which we think infinitely lower, might survive us. The survival of the fittest does not mean, as one might suppose, the survival of what is fittest to fulfil a good purpose—best adapted to a good end: at the last, it means merely the survival of the fittest to survive; and the value of the scientific theory, and it is a theory of great value, just consists in shewing what are the causes which produce certain biological effects. Whether these effects are good or bad, it cannot pretend to judge.
>
> (ibid.: §30, 99)

Yet while Moore made sure to announce his endorsement of Darwin's theory in biology (carefully omitting any reference to Darwin's speculations about the evolutionary genealogy of moral and religious beliefs in *The Descent of Man*), he voiced deep disagreement with Spencer's take on the relation between evolution and ethics. Moore objected to Spencer's association of the ethical predicate 'better' as applied to conduct with the evolutionistic predicate 'more evolved.'

However interpreted, that association commits the naturalistic fallacy, either by taking these predicates to be semantically equivalent, or by attempting to infer 'x is better conduct' from 'x is more evolved conduct.'[10] If Spencer attempted to produce a reductive analysis of 'better,' he seems susceptible to what we have described above as the default naturalistic fallacy. And if he attempted the inference that Moore ascribed to him, he faces the version of the fallacy that amounts to Hume's problem. Either way, fueling Spencer's commission of the naturalistic fallacy is a principle that we may call 'evolutionistic ethical progressivism' and cast in Moore's terms,

Evolutionistic Ethical Progressivism – The principle that "[c]onduct is better in proportion as it is more evolved" (*PE*: §32, 102).

According to Moore, Spencer held "that the more evolved is better simply because it is more evolved," an argument consistent with "the leading moral ideas" of naturalistic hedonism that Spencer also embraced. Moore took those leading ideas to be (1) that life is good or bad in proportion to the amount of agreeable feeling or pleasantness that it produces, and (2) "that the more pleasant is better, simply because it is more pleasant." In Chapter 3 of *Principia*, he offered a number of reasons against the principle underwriting these claims of evolutionistic ethical progressivism. Among them, one is a dilemma facing that principle. For evolutionistic ethical progressivism is either an analytic or a synthetic proposition. If Spencer says that it is an analytic proposition (i.e., a proposition that is true given the meaning of the predicates 'better' and 'more evolved' alone), then his principle is defeated by the OQA. If he says that it is a synthetic proposition (i.e., a proposition whose truth may be revealed only by empirical investigation), then his principle is in need of support by appeal to evidence. Sidgwick, Huxley, and Moore would agree that it cannot have such support because Darwin's theory of natural selection has little bearing on ethics. So, on our reading of this argument against evolutionary ethics, it amounts to a dilemma running like this:

1. Given Spencer's principle of evolutionistic ethical progressivism, morally better conduct is conduct that is more evolved.
2. Spencer's principle is either an analytic or a synthetic proposition.
3. If Spencer's principle is an analytic proposition, then the OQA can show it to be false.
4. If Spencer's principle is a synthetic proposition, it requires evidential support.
5. No evidence supporting Spencer's principle seems forth coming.
6. *Therefore*, Spencer's principle is likely either false or unsupported by the available evidence.

Conclusion 3 of the first horn of the dilemma hinges on an OQA invoking the plausible semantical intuition that the relevant question ('Granted, conduct x is more evolved, but is it good?') is open. On the other hand, if what Spencer had in mind was an inference from conduct that is more evolved to conduct that is morally better, Moore could invoke Hume's problem to argue that the inference is invalid. Regarding the support for premise 5 in the other horn of the dilemma, Moore has plausibly argued that there is "no evidence for supposing Nature to be on the side of the Good" (*PE*: §34, 108). Additional support may come from a widely held empiricist tradition in epistemology according to which, perhaps with a few exceptions, knowledge of synthetic propositions must be based on evidence or inference from evidence.

To these reasons Moore added that Spencer's evolutionary progressivism relies on questionable empirical assumptions about the course of evolution such as that Darwin's laws invariably warrant further development, environmental circumstances will always promote such development, and the fight for survival will always favor organisms that are more evolved (ibid.: §34, 109). Had the circumstances been different, organisms simpler than the present ones might instead have survived. Moore also insightfully noted that Spencer's association of evolution with progress is itself a normative judgment that "we certainly cannot use it as a datum from which to infer details" (ibid.: §34, 107).

NOTES

1   Moore had some reservations about naming the mistakes in ethical theories he had in mind 'naturalistic fallacy'. But in the end, he kept the label, writing

> I do not care about the name, what I do care about is the fallacy. It does not matter what we call it, provided we recognize it when we meet with it. It is to be met with in almost every book in Ethics; and yet it is not recognized: and that is why it is necessary to multiply illustrations of it, and convenient to give it a name.
>
> (*PE*: §12, 65/66)

2   On the reading we are suggesting, Moore accepts the fact that the term 'good' denotes a natural property but holds that it expresses an irreducible ethical concept. Proposed by Robert Shaver (2007: 291) among others, this interpretation faces the problems discussed in Chapter 4. But in the present context, it allows a charitable reconstruction of the naturalistic fallacy charge.

3   In Moore's words, "the only predicates with which people do, in fact, con-
fuse G are both analyzable and natural or metaphysical" (P2: 18–19). Thus
restricted, this is what we are calling here 'the default naturalistic fallacy.'

4   In separating the no-ought-from-is rule and Moore's naturalistic-fallacy
charge we follow a tradition among his critics traceable at least to Frankena
(1939), White (1958), and Sylvester (1990). But see Williams (1985) and Ridge
(2012) for a different take on this issue.

5   The label 'definist fallacy' here is inspired by William Frankena (1939), who,
unlike us, used it for reductive definitions of properties. As he conceived the
fallacy, it consists in the mistake of either attempting a definition of one property in terms of some entirely different property, or conflating two different
properties, or identifying one property with another. Frankena exempts from
the commission of the fallacy naturalists who try to provide a definition of a
key ethical *term*. In his view, in associating goodness with what's productive
of pleasure the hedonists need not be confusing two properties, but merely
saying that there are two different ways of naming the same property.

6   More precisely, Perry submitted as a "general definition of value" the claim
that the predicates 'an interest is taken in x' and 'x is valuable' mean the same
(1926: 140). Thus, his account of value seems definitional owing to the language he uses to state it.

7   True, Perry's general metaphysics aligned with an American school of
early-twentieth-century realism. Furthermore, critics such as Mark van
Roojen (2015) allow for subjectivism to count as a "minimal realism." Clearly
relativism counts as a kind of moral naturalism, but its consistency with realism is a different matter. See, for instance, Harman (1996; 2012).

8   It is unclear whether Spinoza held the naturalistic position ascribed to him by
Perry, who based his interpretation on this passage of Spinoza's *Ethics* (Part
II, Prop. 9):

> In no case do we strive for, wish for, long for, or desire anything because
> we deem it to be good, but on the other hand we deem a thing to be good,
> because we strive for it, wish for it, or desire it.

In a footnote, Perry states:

> It is, of course, possible to desire a thing because it is good, where its
> goodness consists in its being desired by other subjects, or by some other
> interest of the same subject. But in the last analysis good springs from
> desire and not desire from good.

> (p. 138, cited in Perry 1926)

9   Moore (*PE*: §34, 106). See also §29: 96.

10   Moore (*PE*: §31, 100/101). More precisely, Spencer commits the naturalistic fallacy NF3 by inferring that a conduct is ethically higher or better from
its being more evolved (ibid.: 100). Moore compared such an inference with
attempting to deduce that a thing is good from the fact that it is natural—or
that it is bad from the fact that it is unnatural (ibid.: §28, 96/97). But Spencer
also commits the default naturalistic fallacy (NF2 in this chapter) by attempting to equate the predicates 'more evolved' and 'higher' or 'better.' Moore

argued that, although it may be true that if one of these predicates applies to a thing, the other may apply too, they are different predicates. After all, to assert one is *not* to assert the other (ibid.: §32, 101).

SUGGESTED READING

Brink, David O., *Mill's Progressive Principles*, Oxford: Clarendon Press, 2013. Chapter 5 defends Mill's proof from standard objections, including Moore's objections in *Principia Ethica*. Brink presents Mill as a "methodological naturalist" who is using "proof" to refer to an inductive argument. He neither confused desirable with desired nor drew a weak analogy with audible and visible but argued instead that reflection on actual desires provides the "best" defeasible evidence of what's desirable, just as visual experiences provide the best defeasible evidence of what is visible (p. 122).

Curneo, Terence, "Ethical Nonnaturalism," in *The International Encyclopedia of Ethics*, Hugh LaFollette ed., 2013, pp. 3641–3652. DOI: 10.1002/9781444367072.wbiee134. Addresses the weaknesses of some assumptions that Moore made in formulating his naturalistic-fallacy charge. Although the article provides an overall good discussion of those assumptions, it contains some inaccurate references to *Principia Ethica*.

FitzPatrick, William J., "Open Question Arguments and the Irreducibility of Ethical Normativity," in Neil Sinclair ed., *The Naturalistic Fallacy*, Cambridge: Cambridge University Press, 2019, pp. 138–161. Elaborates on an interpretation of Moore's naturalistic fallacy along the normativity lines emphasized in Frankena (1942) and Darwall (2007). Accordingly, FitzPatrick vindicates dismissing the naturalistic fallacy charge as amounting to an ontological problem for naturalistic, reductive analysis of ethical properties and facts. Moore's charge, though clouded by his dubious assumptions about synonymy and properties, points to the irreducibility of the normative.

Frankena, William, "The Naturalistic Fallacy," *Mind* 48 (1939): 464–477. Classic objection to Moore's notion of a naturalistic fallacy, which Frankena considers at best a species in ethics of a more general "definist fallacy" that may affect certain analyses of properties. Moore begs the question against the naturalists in ethics by first declaring that goodness is an indefinable quality and then charging them with the fallacy. The ethical naturalists see two terms that have the same extension, where Moore see two properties different in kind.

Huxley, Thomas H., *Evolution and Ethics*, London: Macmillan and Co., 1894. [References to selection, pp. 111–150 in Thompson (1995).] Early formulation of a fallacy problem facing evolutionary ethics. Huxley distinguishes knowledge of the evolutionary genealogy of any belief that a thing is good from an explanation of why *what we think is good is preferable to what we think is evil*.

Lewy, Casimir, "G. E. Moore on the Naturalistic Fallacy," in *Studies in the Philosophy of Thought and Action*, P. F. Strawson ed., London: Oxford University Press, 1968, pp. 134–146. For many years, this article was the source of Moore's afterthoughts about the naturalistic fallacy as offered in an incomplete preface of *Principia*'s second edition of 1922. Still a useful reading for the view that Moore's naturalistic fallacy charge begs the question against naturalistic ethics.

Moore, G. E., Chapters 1–4 of *Principia Ethica*, Cambridge: Cambridge University Press, rev. ed., Thomas Baldwin ed., 1993/1903. Best account of the sort of ethical doctrines and inferences that Moore charged with the commission of the naturalistic fallacy. See especially §§10–13 of Chapter 1.

Moore, G. E., "Preface," in Moore, *Principia Ethica*, Cambridge: Cambridge University Press, rev. ed., Thomas Baldwin ed., 1993/1903, pp. 1–32. Written for *Principia Ethica*'s second edition of 1922, this Preface was not published during Moore's lifetime. Moore makes clear that in *Principia Ethica* the expression 'naturalistic fallacy' does not refer to a formal fallacy.

Pigden, Charles R., "No-Ought-From-Is, the Naturalistic Fallacy and the Fact/Value Distinction: The History of a Mistake," in Neil Sinclair ed., *The Naturalistic Fallacy*, Cambridge: Cambridge University Press, 2019, pp. 73–95. Useful historical and evaluative study of the relation between the naturalistic fallacy, the is-ought problem, and the autonomy-of-ethics thesis. Of three kinds of autonomy discussed in the literature (ontological, semantical, and logical), Pigden argues that Moore's naturalistic fallacy concerns only semantical autonomy or the irreducibility of moral vocabulary to purely naturalistic or metaphysical vocabulary.

Ruse, Michael, "Evolution and the Naturalistic Fallacy," in Neil Sinclair ed., *The Naturalistic Fallacy*, Cambridge: Cambridge University Press, 2019, pp. 96–116. Considers the development of sociobiology a turning point in the vindication of evolutionary ethics, including the Spencerian variety discussed in this chapter. For Ruse, the naturalistic fallacy is not a fallacy and Hume's problem is not a problem. Evidence from the evolution of morality supports anti-realist and non-cognitivist views in ethics. An early reply to Moore alone these lines can be found in Ruse (1986).

Sayre-McCord, Geoffrey, "Mill's 'Proof'' of the Principle of Utility: A More than Half-Hearted Defense," *Social Philosophy & Policy* 18(2) (2001): 330–360. Argues that Moore misinterprets Mill, whose "proof" of hedonism does not say that 'desired' and 'desirable' mean the same. Yet Sayre-McCord neglects to account for Mill's attempt to draw an analogy between the evaluative term 'desirable' and the purely descriptive terms 'audible' and 'visible.'

Sinclair, Neil, ed., *The Naturalistic Fallacy*, Cambridge: Cambridge University Press, 2019. The most up-to-date collection of articles on the naturalistic fallacy. Its twelve essays focus on different aspects of Moore's charge and their implications. They range from introductory or historical articles to studies of some plausible replies to his charge from quarters such as relativism, non-cognitivism, evolutionary ethics, and analytical descriptivism.

Warnock, Mary, *Ethics Since 1900*, London: Oxford University Press, 1960, pp. 28–33. On Warnock's reading of Mill, Moore's objection is a strawman argument. For Mill attempted no apodictic "proof" of hedonism since he held that ultimate ends must be *self-evident* in order for people to accept them as a reason for pursuing some intermediate goal. He rather held that the fact that people desire pleasure is evidence that they already regard pleasure as a good and in need of no proof. So, Mill was actually saying, about the intuitive nature of pleasure as an end, something very much like what Moore himself said about the things that have intrinsic value. See also West (2017).

7

MORAL KNOWLEDGE

7.1 NATURAL/NON-NATURAL: AN EPISTEMOLOGICAL CRITERION

In *Principia Ethica*, Moore was particularly concerned with the natural/non-natural distinction of properties, which he drew along the metaphysical and epistemological criteria outlined in a few passages such as this:

> What, then, is to be understood by "metaphysical"? I use the term ... in opposition to "natural." I call those philosophers preeminently "metaphysical" who have recognised most clearly that not everything which is *is* a 'natural object.' 'Metaphysicians' have, therefore, the great merit of insisting that our *knowledge is not confined to the things which we can touch and see and feel.* They have always been much occupied, not only with that other class of natural objects which consists in mental facts, but also with the class of objects or properties of objects, which certainly *do not exist in time, are not therefore parts of Nature, and which, in fact, do not exist at all.*

DOI: 10.4324/9780429275975-7

> To this class, as I have said, belongs what we mean by the adjective 'good.' It is not goodness, but only the things or qualities which are good, which can exist in time—can have duration, and begin and cease to exist—can be objects of perception. But the most prominent members of this class are perhaps numbers. It is quite certain that two natural objects may exist; but it is equally *certain that two itself does not exist and never can*. Two and two are four. But that does not mean that either two or four exists. Yet it certainly means something. *Two is somehow, although it does not exist.*[1]

Consistent with Moore's claims here is another passage of *Principia* (§26: 92/93) where he added epistemological-*cum*-methodological criteria for the natural/non-natural distinction: of properties of these two kinds, it is only the natural properties that are the subject matter of the natural and social sciences, including psychology. Putting all these criteria together, Moore's distinction looks like Table 7.1.

The Moore of later ethical writings did not invoke this set of criteria to draw the natural/non-natural distinction. By the 1920s, he had abandoned criteria 1(b) and 1(c) but continued to regard versions of 1(a), 2, and 3 as providing the best approximation to the natural/non-natural distinction of properties.[2] He also had little to say about how that distinction applies to moral judgment. Yet given his moral semantics, to qualify for being a moral judgment, any such judgment must feature at least one moral property that is reducible to goodness itself or its counterpart evil (unless of course the judgment features at least one of these simple moral properties instead). Statements such as 'Pleasure is good' and 'Pain is bad' are ambiguous moral judgments since they may express either judgments of practical ethics or moral principles if read as stating that pleasure is the sole good and pain the sole bad. In this chapter and Chapter 8, I take for granted this view of moral judgment in order to have a closer look at Moore's epistemological and metaphysical criteria for the natural/non-natural distinction as formulated in *Principia Ethica*. I first consider how his epistemological-cum-methodological criteria fit within moral intuitionism and the problems they might raise for an intuitionist moral epistemology. After

Table 7.1 Moore's criteria for the natural/non-natural distinction

Criteria	Natural property	Non-natural property
	Any property that either is simple and meets conditions 1 through 3 below, or is complex and analyzable into other properties that meet those conditions	Any property that is either simple and meets conditions 1 through 3 below, or is complex and analyzable into at least one simple property that meets those conditions
1 Metaphysical criteria (*PE*: §26, §66)	(a) Natural properties are either simple essential "parts" of any of the things (objects, states, or events) that have them, or complexes featuring only properties reducible to some such simple properties (b) Natural properties can exist by themselves in time, independent of the things that have them (c) Natural properties have both being and existence	(a) Non-natural properties are inessential properties of any of the things that have them. But if a thing has a non-natural property, it does so *in virtue of* some of its natural properties (b) Non-natural properties cannot exist by themselves in time (c) Non-natural properties have being but lack existence
2 Epistemological criterion (*PE*: §66)	A property that is such that renders any informative belief about it the exclusive subject of empirical justification by either perception or introspection alone, or inference from perception or introspection	A property that is such that renders any belief about it the exclusive subject of *a priori* justification by either rational intuition alone, or a combination of rational intuition and empirical justification
3 Methodological criterion (*PE*: §26)	Natural properties are the proper subject matter of the natural or social sciences, including psychology	Non-natural properties are the proper subject matter of ethics or the formal sciences

considering what intuitionists can say to solve those problems, in Chapter 8, I turn to *Principia*'s metaphysical criteria 1(a) through 1(c).

BEING THE SUBJECT MATTER OF THE SCIENCES OR OF ETHICS

Condition 3 in the above summary of Moore's criteria distinguishes natural and non-natural properties according to whether they are respectively the subject matter of the natural and social sciences or of ethics. Condition 2 sorts them according to whether the relevant properties are knowable by empirical means or rational intuition. Both types of condition figure prominently in Moore's attempts to draw that distinction in §26 and §66 of *Principia*. Condition 3 concerns the method by which properties of either kind can be studied, condition 2 the nature of epistemic justification for beliefs involving the relevant properties. Although both criteria are ultimately epistemological, owing to their emphases, we may call them 'methodological' and 'epistemological' respectively. Given the methodological criterion, perhaps the best known of the two, unlike non-natural properties, natural properties are "parts of Nature" and constitute the proper subject-matter of the natural and social sciences, including psychology. Criterion 2 adds that, unlike natural properties, non-natural properties can be the objects of neither perception nor introspection. Each criterion, however, faces problems.

Let us consider the methodological criterion first: since the expression 'natural' somehow figures in the definition of a natural property, the criterion is blatantly circular. To Moore's credit, he did not regard this criterion as providing necessary and sufficient conditions for a property to be either natural or non-natural; rather, he took it to provide an intuitive grasp of the relevant distinction (P2: 13). Furthermore, he was aware of the difficulties facing attempts at sharpening the criterion. For suppose we say the following:

> A property is natural just in case it plays a role in our scientific laws or explanations.

This criterion seems too broad and too narrow. For on the one hand, it may sanction as natural some properties that are not natural, such as phlogiston and luminiferous ether, which at some point played a role in what is deemed scientific explanations of fire and the propagation of light respectively. On the other hand, this criterion leaves out properties that are natural but their naturalness is unknown to us. After all, science is still in the making and no one knows yet what properties will figure in the laws or explanations of mature science. To accommodate this objection, Moore might amend his criterion to read as follows:

> A property is natural just in case it might figure in the laws and explanations of finished science.

Thus formulated, the methodological criterion turns out to be too vague and therefore useless. In addition, it faces a relevance problem. For, if non-natural is any property that fails to be natural in the sense of the methodological criterion, a great number of properties would be classified as non-natural, many of which are irrelevant to ethics and to ethical non-naturalism. Counted as non-natural would be key properties of ethics together with key properties of a vast number of other normative domains (e.g., the domains of rationality, mathematics, modality, logic, and epistemology). Most crucially, in the group would also be key properties of domains that are not primarily normative, such as metaphysics and the supernatural properties of theology. But as noted by some critics (Cuneo 2013; Dancy 2006; Ridge 2003/2014), non-naturalists do not use the term 'non-natural' to denote these types of properties.

ORTHODOX VERSUS MODEST MORAL INTUITIONISM

Let us now turn to epistemological criterion 2 for the distinction between natural and non-natural properties. From what Moore wrote concerning this criterion and his scarce, but significant, observations about the role of intuition in moral knowledge, we can reconstruct his moral intuitionism as well as infer how he would react to some common objections facing it. Given criterion 2, of the two kinds of property in it, qualifying for empirical justification are only the natural properties (*PE*: §26, §66). Their justification rests on evidence from either sense perception (e.g., the yellowness and circularity of a ball) or introspection (e.g., the painfulness of one's current, conscious toothache).[3] True generalizations ascribing a simple non-natural property to, say, experiences of pain or pleasure, are basic moral beliefs, or as Moore sometimes puts it, they amount to "intuitions" that are justified directly, with no need to appeal to evidence, introspection, or inference. Moore's rationalist account of the justification of basic moral beliefs is inspired by Sidgwick's, according to which the justification of certain moral propositions rests entirely on self-evidence (1967/1874: 338–342). Both Moore and Sidgwick believed that in the case of basic moral propositions, evidence cannot be legitimately demanded or provided. But neither can reasons, since such propositions admit of no proof (or disproof) simply because any attempted proof would have premises that are less acceptable than the conclusion of any alleged proof.

However, unlike Sidgwick, Moore did not have much to say about the role of intuition in the justification of key moral judgments and principles.[4] Even so, it is clear from the first pages of *Principia Ethica* that he rejected any association of his intuitionism with an orthodox intuitionism presupposing the existence of a quasi-perceptual moral faculty that could justify any basic moral belief. In its Preface, after first identifying what he considered the two major questions of ethics ("What kind of things ought to exist for their own sakes?" and "What kind of actions ought we to perform?"), he made clear that his intuitionism was modest. For example, in the following passage,

> It becomes plain that, for answers to the first question ['What kind of things ought to exist for their own sakes?'], *no relevant evidence whatever can be adduced: from no other truth, except themselves alone, can it be inferred that they are either true or false*. We can guard against error only by taking care, that, when we try to answer a question of this kind, we have before our minds that question only, and not some other or others; but that there is great danger of such errors of confusion I have tried to shew, and also what are the chief precautions by the use of

which we may guard against them. As for the second question ['What kind of actions ought we to perform?'], it becomes equally plain, that *any answer to it is capable of proof or disproof*—that, indeed, so many different considerations are relevant to its truth or falsehood, as to make the attainment of probability very difficult, and the attainment of certainty impossible. Nevertheless the kind of evidence, which is both necessary and alone relevant to such proof and disproof, is capable of exact definition. *Such evidence must contain propositions of two kinds and of two kinds only: it must consist, in the first place, of truths with regard to the results of the action in question—of causal truths—but it must also contain ethical truths of our first or self-evident class.*

("Preface," *PE*: 33–34; my emphasis)

Thus, for Moore, questions of intrinsic value, but not of right conduct, are accessible by moral intuition alone, which in this case amounts to a species of general intellectual grasping of truths that are *a priori* or self-evident but synthetic. Only such truths about intrinsic value are eligible for being 'intuitions' but not in the standard sense of this term, something he indicated by writing:

In order to express the fact that ethical propositions of my first class are incapable of proof or disproof, I have sometimes followed Sidgwick's usage in calling them "Intuitions." But I beg that it may be noticed that I am not an "Intuitionist," in the ordinary sense of the term. Sidgwick himself seems never to have been clearly aware of the immense importance of the difference which distinguishes his Intuitionism from the common doctrine, which has generally been called by that name. The Intuitionist proper is distinguished by maintaining that propositions of my second class—propositions which assert that a certain action is right or a duty—are incapable of proof or disproof by any enquiry into the results of such actions. I, on the contrary, am no less anxious to maintain that propositions of this kind are not "Intuitions," than to maintain that propositions of my first class are Intuitions.

(ibid.: 36)

For prime candidates of such intuitions Moore need look no further than certain almost universally accepted truths such as that pain is bad.⁵ Of course, intuitions can misfire and yield as "true" beliefs that are in fact false. Moore can accommodate this result, since there is textual evidence that he did not invoke any of the epistemic immunities standardly associated with (but not entailed by) self-evidence, such as indubitability, incorrigibility, and infallibility. Against both the infallibility of moral intuitions and the orthodox view that such intuitions are deliverances of a quasi-perceptual faculty, he told his readers the following:

> [W]hen I call such propositions "Intuitions," I mean merely to assert that they are incapable of proof; I imply nothing whatever as to the manner or origin of our cognition of them. Still less do I imply (as most Intuitionists have done) that any proposition whatever is true, because we cognise it in a particular way or by the exercise of any particular faculty: I hold, on the contrary, that in every way in which it is possible to cognise a true proposition, it is also possible to cognise a false one.⁶

With these remarks in view, we can reconstruct Moore's moral epistemology as a modest rationalist intuitionism according to which some ascriptions of intrinsic value or disvalue are self-evident: they enjoy a kind of direct epistemic justification based on reflection alone. Beliefs in mathematical or logical necessary truths best exemplify this type of epistemic justification. For Moore, moral knowledge is simply another kind of *a priori* knowledge of necessary truths. True generalizations ascribing intrinsic value to certain psychological states (e.g., the admiration of a beautiful object) and certain wholes (e.g., the admiration of a beautiful object that actually exists) require only careful reflection for being justified and amounting to knowledge. Moore made no appeal to a quasi-perceptual faculty of moral intuition. In fact, he would agree with current critics of orthodox intuitionism in holding that there is empirical evidence of neither the existence nor the workings of a faculty of that kind.⁷

As noted by some present-day non-naturalists, whose moral epistemology is consistent with Moore's and therefore also at odds with orthodox intuitionism, their recognition of the *a priori* status of some basic moral judgments does not commit them to the existence of any such faculty (Cox 1970; Huemer 2005; Parfit 2011; Shafer-Landau 2003). This line of defense of the epistemology of non-naturalism typically rests on some companion-of-guilt reasoning whereby the epistemic status of basic moral beliefs is held to be analogous to that of basic normative beliefs in some more established areas of *a priori* knowledge, such as logic, mathematics, epistemology, and modality. Accordingly, for example, on the non-naturalist perspective of Derek Parfit, propositions such as *that the conclusion of a valid argument with true premises must be true* are not about any natural fact to be apprehended by empirical means – as neither is the proposition *that if a figure has exactly three internal angles, then it must have three sides*. In his view, these analogs of moral belief support the thesis that

> among the facts of the world are facts of what is rational and what is not. A person of normal mental powers can discern these facts. Judgments of rationality are thus straightforward apprehensions of fact, not through sense perception but through a mental faculty analogous to sense perception.
>
> (Parfit 2011: 488)

There is some reason to believe that here Parfit does not have in mind a quasi-perceptual faculty, since the normative examples he has proposed are true in every possible world. That is, they could not express contingent truths knowable by perceptual means.

Arguably, Moore's intuitionism is as modest as Parfit's, even when Moore sometimes used the language of perception when assessing the epistemic status of certain propositions. Or when he wrote that such an assessment requires "carefully distinguishing exactly what the thing is about which we ask the question, and then *looking to see* whether it has or has not the unique predicate 'good'" (*PE*: §134, 271; my emphasis) – or that the judgment assigning intrinsic value to a thing involves a "feeling." Nevertheless, the evidence from the passages of *Principia Ethica* reviewed here suggests that this language is metaphorical. Further evidence for placing Moore in the modest intuitionist camp stems from the fact that he never claimed to know with certainty any simple ethical proposition and gave no *definite* list of them (Cox

1970: 269). In addition, in his "Reply to My Critics" (p. 588), he expressed agreement with C. D. Broad on matters of moral epistemology and metaphysics. In "Is 'Goodness' a Name of a Simple Non-Natural Quality?" Broad outlined an unquestionably modest type of moral intuitionism, according to which some simple moral truths are metaphysically necessary but synthetic and *a priori*. He rejects the thought that they enjoy any Kantian analyticity on the compelling grounds that, if propositions such as that pain is bad were analytic, the concept *badness* must somehow be contained in the natural concept *pain*. Since this claim seems preposterous, he concluded that necessary propositions of this sort must be instances of the synthetic *a priori*.

Moore gave abundant evidence of a similar view not only in *Principia* but also in *The Elements of Ethics*. In this early manuscript, judgments such as 'That this or that is good' and 'That this or that is bad' are taken to express propositions that

> are all of them, in Kant's words, synthetic and must rest in the end
> upon some propositions which must be simply accepted or rejected,
> which cannot be logically deduced from any other proposition ... the
> fundamental principle of Ethics must be self-evident.[8]

Such ordinary judgments follow from certain moral generalizations that are basic or underivative. However, the non-naturalists need not rule out the possibility that some unsubstantive ethical judgments express analytic truths.[9]

Finally, note that on Moore's moral epistemology, the generally accepted rules of common morality have an epistemic status analogous to that of scientific predictions. Although Moore said that we must follow them strictly, he did not consider them self-evident truths knowable by intuition. Rather, they are generalizations from assessments of the effects of individual actions and on occasion might be false. But if we follow them, we are more likely to do our duty on each particular occasion than if we act according to our own calculation of options available to us in a circumstance and their actual results. The action-guiding force of generally used rules of common morality hinges on the fact that decision-making based on them is more likely to conduce to a greater sum of intrinsic value than if it is left to each of us alone. Moore regarded individual decision-making as unreliable owing to the complexity involved in the calculation of alternatives available to us and the effects of our actions as well as our biases. Moreover, the question of whether an action is right or wrong and to what degree depends on *all* of its results through time (*E*: 7, 68–69). Although time may add new contributory causes that somewhat dilute the initial causes of certain effects, it does not erase those causes. In addition, we humans have biases that might lead us to minimize bad results for others or pursue actions that favor our preferences. Such limitations render us prone to mistakes in determining either all the alternatives open to us in a situation, the effects of our actions, or both.

In *Principia Ethica*, Moore regarded qualifying rules of common morality as prescribing acts and omissions that are good as means and illustrated this claim with an analysis of the instrumental value of the effect of acting according to the negative command 'Do not murder' (*PE*: §95, 205/207). At no point did Moore write that agents must follow this rule because murder is intrinsically bad. Given his value-based consequentialist theory of normative ethics, discussed in Chapter 11, he could not actually say that a *painless* murder is intrinsically bad. Instead, he said that 'Do not murder,' like other generally accepted rules of common-sense morality, prescribes an omission whose effect is likely to be *instrumentally best* to the maximization of intrinsic value. "If we are told 'do not murder' is a duty," wrote Moore, "we are told that the action, whatever it may be, which is called murder, will under no circumstances cause so much good to exist in the Universe as its avoidance" (*PE*: §95, 206).

However, Moore was aware that on some occasions this command, like any other rule of common morality, might prescribe what is actually and objectively wrong. On those occasions 'Do not murder' would fail as a means to achieve the maximization of intrinsic value. Yet this is not a problem for Moore since, in his view, the commonly used rules of common morality are generally effective, though fallible, guides to right conduct. Acting in accordance with these rules is better as a means to maximal value than acting in accordance with an individual's own calculations of available alternatives and results, given their epistemic limitations discussed above. In the case of murder, its instrumental badness stems from the following facts:

1. Murder is inconsistent with the general human desire to go on living.
2. A widespread practice of murder would be a distraction that would derail many people's efforts to attain positive intrinsic goods, such as pleasure, knowledge, and above all, enjoyment of personal love and appreciation of beauty.

That is, a widespread practice of murder would have a negative impact on social stability and thus on people's ability to maximize intrinsic goods. We can assume that Moore would offer *mutatis mutandis* analogous accounts of the instrumental value of the effects of acting in conformity with other commonly used rules of common morality concerning actions or attitudes such as lying, industriousness, promise keeping, and respect for private property (his examples, *PE*: §95, 206/207).

7.2 AGAINST MORAL INTUITIONISM: THE CAUSAL AND THE RELIABILITY OBJECTIONS

THE CAUSAL OBJECTION

Of two major problems facing moral intuitionism, one is the so-called causal objection, modeled on Hartry Field's objection to Platonist rationalism in mathematics (2016: 494 ff.). It charges that an intuitionist moral ontology entails an implausible moral epistemology because non-natural properties can stand in no causal relation to any observable effect. If unrelated to anything observable, how could non-naturalists claim that at least some beliefs about non-natural properties are justified or even true? If some ethical beliefs turned out to be true, that would seem an incredible coincidence. In short, the causal objection runs: Non-natural properties and facts are causally inert, *therefore*, there is no way of knowing about these properties and facts.

Of the several versions of this causal objection, the first to be considered here has been labeled "explanatory superfluity objection" (FitzPatrick 2015). It begins by noting that non-natural moral properties and facts can play no role in scientific laws and explanations, or in any account of the reliability of our moral-belief-forming mechanism. Moral properties and facts are superfluous in these ways if, as Moore claimed, they are supervenient properties. After all, such supervenient properties can have no causal effects on the natural world. This in turn entails that there is no way of knowing or justifying belief about moral properties and facts. If some ethical truths happen to be true, given non-naturalism, that would be a cosmic coincidence.

However, non-naturalists have room for a number of replies to this causal objection. For one thing, even if the objection is compelling, it could at most saddle intuitionism with epistemic moral skepticism (Enoch 2011; Shafer-Landau 2012). Non-naturalism might still be true. Furthermore, non-naturalists may offer one or more of these lines of response:

1. Invoke a companion-of-guilt argument to the effect that moral beliefs are not epistemologically worse off than mathematical or logical beliefs (*PE*: §66, 161/162).
2. Argue that evolution has unintentionally designed our basic moral beliefs in ways conducive to their truth (Parfit 2011).
3. Appeal to a sort of pre-established harmony between a basic moral belief and the moral truth (Enoch 2011; Skarsaune 2010).
4. Contend that, although moral facts are not explanatory, unlike theological facts, they are not inconsistent with philosophical naturalism (Shafer-Landau 2006; 2007).

We have already examined option (1) and have something to say about options (2) and (3) in Section 7.3, after a quick look at (4) – an option that involves the complex metaphysical question of whether non-naturalism and a plausible general thesis of philosophical naturalism are compatible. Moore may be interpreted as holding that they are compatible. For given the general metaphysical picture that he outlines in "What Is Philosophy?" (WIP), the universe contains only natural phenomena of two irreducible kinds: material objects and mental events. He acknowledges moral properties by writing "it is certainly one of the most important facts about the universe that there are in it these distinctions of good and bad, right and wrong" (WIP: 26–27). But he grants them only a metaphysically derivative or supervenient status. Only natural phenomena exist in a strong sense. As a result, Moore's moral ontology is in some sense consistent with the philosophical naturalist thesis that all there is *is* the natural world. He can say, with Shafer-Landau, that unlike theological properties and facts, non-natural properties and facts need not conflict with scientific accounts of the natural world.

THE RELIABILITY OBJECTION

Let us now turn to the reliability objection (Dreier 2012; Gibbard 1990: 154; Smith 1994: 38) according to which moral intuitionism is committed to what I have called 'orthodox intuitionism' – i.e., a doctrine that invokes a quasi-perceptual psychological faculty to justify moral beliefs. Since, unlike perception, such a faculty would function in ways we do not fully understand, the reliability objection charges that, given moral intuitionism, there is no good reason for thinking that our moral beliefs are either true, justified, or both. Our discussion of orthodox intuitionism in the previous section suggests a credible line of reply to the reliability objection, namely, to point out that non-naturalism does not commit to orthodox intuitionism. As already noted, Moore does so in the Preface and the main text of *Principia* (especially in §13). Among present-day non-naturalists, more elaborated replies are not difficult to find. For example, on Philip Stratton-Lake's interpretation of moral intuitionism, this doctrine does not claim that a non-natural moral property like goodness or rightness is "observable" by the senses, still less that it is known through some "faculty of moral intuition" (2002b: 7). Rather, it claims that acquaintance with such properties arises in the course of moral reflection. It is only then that ethical properties become "present to the mind," as Moore would put it. Furthermore, although some intuitionists may postulate a moral sense that functions specifically to cognize moral truths, most of them classify the faculty that delivers such results as a general faculty that yields *a priori* knowledge also in other normative domains, such as mathematics, logic, modality, and so on.[10] That is, they too reject orthodox intuitionism. Furthermore, their replies to orthodox intuitionism put the burden of argument on the objector, who must now show that non-naturalism commits to such an implausible moral epistemology. A starting point for them might be to explore the disanalogy in degree of disagreement that seems evident when we compare the moral domain with domains such as mathematics and logic. However, Moore and other non-naturalists have contested that moral disagreement is a widespread phenomenon.[11]

7.3   EVOLUTIONARY DEBUNKING ARGUMENTS

Moore's objections to Spencerian evolutionary ethics in *Principia Ethica*, discussed here in Chapter 6, might have played a role in the eclipse of evolutionary ethics during most of the twentieth century (Pinker 2003; Ruse 2019). However, since the mid-1970s the interest in the bearings of evolution on ethics has been steadily on the rise, in part owing to some breakthroughs in the evolutionary accounts of the psychology of social animals. In the late twentieth century, with the emergence of sociobiology, a strong response to Moore came from a second wave of evolutionary theorists in ethics holding that his "naturalistic fallacy" amounts to no fallacy and Hume's problem to no problem.[12] To this response, unlike Moore's mysterious speculative ethics, evolutionary ethics can provide the only account of morality worth having (Ruse 1986: 234). More recently, the evolutionary genealogy of moral belief has led to questioning the moral ontology and epistemology of non-naturalism. For, if there were any non-natural moral truths, given the evolutionary genealogy of moral belief, non-naturalists in general would have no way to tell which moral beliefs track the moral truths. As a result, they seem to fall prey to an "evolutionary debunking argument."

   Although the evolutionary debunking argument amounts to a challenge to any moral realists, if compelling, it would be more damaging for Moore and the other non-naturalists because of their reliance on intuition for the epistemic justification of moral belief. This challenge rests on the premise that, plausibly, evolution has selected moral and religious beliefs because of their Darwinian advantages, in a manner completely independent of whether they track the truth. This fact appears to support the following objection:

> Evolutionary forces have played a tremendous role in shaping the content of human evaluative attitudes. The challenge for realist theories of value is to explain the relation between these evolutionary influences on our evaluative attitudes, on the one hand, and the independent evaluative truths that realism posits, on the other. Realism, I argue, can give no satisfactory account of this relation.[13]

Evolutionary theorists in ethics seem now in a position to claim that their challenge rests neither on a reductive naturalistic definition of a key ethical concept, nor on an inference about what we ought to do from a premise entirely about the course of evolution. As a result, it seems immune to a rejoinder invoking either the naturalistic fallacy or the Is-Ought problem discussed in Chapter 6. Rather, if compelling, the evolutionary debunking argument has anti-realist, debunking implications that would particularly affect non-naturalism. Recall that the Moore of *Principia Ethica* holds that there are some response-independent ethical truths accessible by rational intuition alone and offers no compelling explanation of how our moral intuitions sometimes just happen to capture the ethical truths. As a result, if they turn out to be true, it would be a massive coincidence. He appears to be committed to skepticism in moral epistemology – a result that, though not fatal, would be quite damaging. By contrast, naturalistic moral realists might have more resources to meet this objection, since given their ontology, moral properties and facts reduce to natural properties and facts. If so, then moral beliefs would have causal effects amenable to empirical investigation and these realists avoid any version of the causal objection (Sturgeon 2006).

But Moore can follow Derek Parfit (2011: 520–521) and defend his confidence in the deliverances of rational intuition by claiming that moral belief is not an exception: without appeal to rational intuition, there would be no way to account for knowledge of truths in any normative domain at all. Moreover, the evolutionary debunking argument tacitly rests on unsound reasoning of this kind,

1. You don't know that 2 + 2 = 4 unless you know how your belief is causally related to its truth.
2. *Therefore*, you don't know that 2 + 2 = 4.

Parfit calls this argument "*2 + 2 = 4*" and claims that it is as unsound as the evolutionary debunking argument. Why? Because its premise (1) amounts to an instance of an unsophisticated epistemic externalism that not even the epistemic externalists would accept. Once the unsoundness of the evolutionary debunkers' reasoning is exposed, there seems to be no problem in holding that moral beliefs might be justified by appeal to the same general belief-producing mechanism of other *a priori* beliefs.

This defense of the intuitionist epistemology rehearses a companion-of-guilt argument that can be found in Moore. Although it does not remove the problem posed by the evolutionary debunkers, it challenges them to explain how their argument does not lead to skepticism in other normative domains. In fact, as noted by Michael Huemer (2016: 2006), the evolutionary debunkers may be raising for moral knowledge a problem faced by any form of *a priori* knowledge. Parfit (2011: 494) adds to this defense of non-naturalism the more dubious claim that evolutionary debunkers need sound reasons against the hypothesis that moral truths, like other normative truths, may have resulted from the unintentional design of evolution. In addition, the evolutionary debunkers face an empirical challenge based on Huemer's (2016: 1994) robust data from the social sciences and evolutionary theory to the conclusion that their account of the role of evolutionary pressures in shaping our moral beliefs is vastly inflated. Given that data, it appears that some recent changes towards more liberal moral beliefs could not have occurred owing to the lengthy time-frame required by natural selection to induce the relevant changes in the gene pool. For example, changes in moral beliefs leading to, say, the abolition of Jim Crow laws in the American South in the 1960s occurred too recently to have been a result of evolutionary pressures.

Finally, Moore and other non-naturalists may develop a line of reply suggested by Sidgwick (1876), which points to the self-defeating character of an appeal to Darwinian evolution in ethics. After all, when natural selection is invoked in a debunking argument against moral realism, consistency requires that the debunkers run a similar argument against the epistemic justification of beliefs of other kinds. Thus, debunkers cannot avoid a self-defeating global skepticism. For, if evolutionary forces have shaped completely the contents of our moral beliefs, then there is no compelling argument to the effect that even perceptual beliefs can avoid becoming prey to evolutionary debunking arguments. Some debunkers have tried to insulate beliefs of this kind by holding that they track the truth because there is an evolutionary advantage in this. But as some critics point out (Parfit 2011: 511 ff.; Stich 1990: 63), natural selection primarily cares about survival fitness and reproductive success, not about truth. After all, an unreliable belief-forming mechanism might be able to produce beliefs that can better contribute to the survival of a species than a reliable one that may be too expensive in terms of time, effort, and hardware.[14] Therefore, Moore could dismiss the evolutionary debunkers on the ground that they are committed to an implausible global skepticism that destroys epistemic justification even for belief in Darwinian evolution.

NOTES

1 Moore (*PE*: §66, 161/162). In this passage Moore rehearses the metaphysical and epistemological criteria he offered previously in a manuscript of 1898, *The Elements of Ethics* (p. 44).

2 This change of mind is clear in two of Moore's writings of 1922: an unfinished preface that he drafted for the second edition of *Principia* (P2) and his essay "The Conception of Intrinsic Value" (CIV).

3 That Moore included introspection in perceptual knowledge follows from his willingness to accept Broad's (1933–1934) account of the natural/non-natural distinction (RC: 588).

4 Some critics have interpreted Moore's scarce references to his moral intuitionism as a sign of his inability to defend that moral epistemology (Gibbard 1990; Warnock 1967). But it is also possible that Moore was deferring to Sidgwick's defense (1967/1874: 338–342).

5 In *Ethics*, Moore also held that the principle of utilitarianism is self-evident and synthetic, thus changing his mind about the analytic status ascribed to it in *Principia*. As mentioned before, he credited Russell with having shown him that, if construed as an analytic truth, his own utilitarianism would face an objection from the Open Question Argument.

6 Moore, "Preface" (*PE*: 36). Moore makes similar remarks in *Elements of Ethics*, p. 50.

7 There is some consensus that a strong quasi-perceptual model of moral intuitionism seems implausible (Dreier 2012; Smith 1994: 21–25). Present-day endorsements of that model, though rare, seem nonetheless available. On my reading, Audi's (2012) "non-pictorial" perceptual model of moral intuition is a well-argued instance of it.

8 Moore (*EE*: 106). See also Russell (1987/1910: 20) and Broad (1933–1934: 266 ff.).

9 Parfit is among the non-naturalists who entertain the possibility of *a priori* knowledge of such analytic, but unsubstantive ethical truths. For example, 'Punishing someone for a crime not committed could not be just' (Parfit 2011: 490).

10 For a strong defense of a modest intuitionism along these lines, see Huemer (2016: 1986) and Parfit (2011: 488).

11 Moore rules out pervasive ethical disagreement, construed as disagreement about what is good in itself. There is widespread disagreement only about the "causal" or empirical (and therefore non-ethical) question of what produces best effects (*PE*: §17, 77). Present-day non-naturalists who also minimize the pervasiveness of ethical disagreement include Huemer (2016), Wedgwood (2014), and Shafer-Landau (2004: 107–109).

12 Prompting the revival of evolutionary ethics have been works such as Wilson (1975) and Ruse and Wilson (1986). For recent appeals to evolutionary ethics in debunking arguments against moral realism, especially non-naturalism, see Street (2006) and Joyce (2006).

13 Street (2006: 109). Richard Joyce (2006: 181–182) argues for a similar anti-realist conclusion by means of this thought experiment. first, suppose we know that there is a pill causing whoever takes it to believe that Napoleon was defeated at Waterloo. We further know that after taking the pill, users forget its effect on belief immediately. In this scenario, Joyce contends, we lack warrant for our true belief that Napoleon was defeated at Waterloo. He takes this thought experiment to show that given moral realism, especially of the intuitionist variety, we cannot rule out that evolution has had a similar effect on the contents of our moral beliefs, which would therefore lack warrant. For, we would have the moral beliefs we do regardless of whether they are true or false.

14 To adapt an illustration of this point from Stich (1990: 59–63), compare two traditional societies: in society 1, people *falsely* believe that all mushrooms nearby are poisonous and don't eat them. As a result, they survive. In society 2, people *truly* believe that there are some edible mushrooms nearby, but eat some poisonous mushrooms by mistake and become extinct.

SUGGESTED READING

Audi, Robert, "Intuitionism, Pluralism, and the Foundations of Ethics," in *Moral Knowledge*, Walter Sinnott-Armstrong and Mark Timmons eds., Oxford: Oxford University Press, 1996, pp. 101–136. An outline of the strengths and weaknesses of intuitionism, especially W. D. Ross's version. Good source for the study of this moral epistemology, even if somewhat dated since it predates evolutionary debunking arguments as well as objections to intuitionism from experimental philosophy. Argues that reflective equilibrium can help extend and systematize the inputs of intuitions.

Audi, Robert, "Can Normativity Be Naturalized?" in *Ethical Naturalism: Current Debates*, Susana Nuccetelli and Gary Seay eds., Cambridge: Cambridge University Press, 2012, pp. 169–193. A rare defense of what seems an orthodox form of moral intuitionism. Contends that non-reductive realism can invoke the epistemic authority of perception and hold that moral properties are epistemically accessible through a kind of "non-pictorial" moral perception. Moral facts thus become epistemically available from descriptively accessible facts. Audi thinks that our psychological constitution determines that we cannot have certain perceptual experiences (say, of an act of stealing) without having a "phenomenal" perception of wrongdoing. While the phenomenal elements of seeing something are representational, those of moral perception are not.

Dreier, Jamie, "Quasi-Realism and the Problem of Unexplained Coincidence," *Analytic Philosophy* 53(3) (2012): 269–287. Argues that not only do moral realists but also quasi-realists (Blackburn 1984; Gibbard 1990; 2003) face the challenge of a massive-coincidence problem because they too engage in "realist talk." This problem does not arise for perceptual beliefs because their justification can appeal to a reliable, well-understood belief-forming mechanism of sense perception.

Enoch, David, "Epistemology," in *Taking Morality Seriously*, Oxford: Oxford University Press, 2011, pp. 151–184. Replies to evolutionary debunking arguments by holding that at most they generate a skeptical problem for non-naturalism. To solve it, Enoch proposes a third-factor or pre-established-harmony theory, according to which the belief that survival is good counts as an excellent candidate for being true, shaped by evolution, and the ground for inferring other moral truths.

FitzPatrick, W., "Debunking Evolutionary Debunking of Ethical Realism," *Philosophical Studies* 172(4) (2015): 883–904. Contends that, of two understandings of evolutionary debunking arguments, one fails to raise any special problem for realism, the other relies on explanatory claims about moral beliefs that lack scientific support.

Huemer, Michael, "A Liberal Realist Answer to Debunking Skeptics: The Empirical Case for Realism," *Philosophical Studies* 173 (2016): 1983–2010. Replies to evolutionary debunking arguments against moral intuitionism by arguing that their proponents cannot explain the spread of liberalism on moral issues involving war, murder, torture, execution, slavery, democratization, and decolonization. The spread of liberalism took place too rapidly to admit explanation in evolutionary terms.

Hurka, Thomas, "Soames on Ethics," paper presented at APA Pacific Division Author-Meets-Critics Session on Scott Soames's *Philosophical Analysis in the Twentieth Century*, Portland, OR, March 24, 2006, https://thomashurka.com/writings/papers-in-progress/ *Contra* Soames (2003), Hurka argues that the Moore of *Principia* did appeal to pre-theoretical intuitions about the deontic status of ethical judgments to substantiate his ethical doctrines. He did not have a top-down method whereby these judgments are justified by abstract generalizations of philosophical theory. In addition, Moore's principles for the justification of ethical judgments were not more abstract than those implicit in Soames's "restricted generalities" (i.e., his proposed self-evident truths about the good). For another rejoinder to Soames's objection to the moral epistemology in *Principia Ethica*, see McGrath and Kelly (2015).

Joyce, Richard, *The Evolution of Morality*, Cambridge, MA: MIT Press, 2006. An early version of the evolutionary debunking argument invoking the premise that natural selection would push us to entertain beliefs that are advantageous for reproduction and survival, regardless of whether they are true. If our moral beliefs do not track the truth, there is no reason to think that they are true or justified.

Parfit, Derek, "Rationalism," in *On What Matters*, vol. 1, Oxford: Oxford University Press, 2011, pp. 511–542. Defends an intuitionist epistemology consistent with Moore's, while arguing that evolutionary arguments against non-naturalism face various counterexamples to a crucial premise: viz., that the content of our moral beliefs is shaped completely by natural selection. Although evolution may have played an initial role in the shaping of moral beliefs, these later developed independently of evolution. In the case of the belief that pain is bad, evolution selects the motivation to avoid pain but not the content of the belief.

Shafer-Landau, Russ, "Evolutionary Debunking, Moral Realism and Moral Knowledge," *Journal of Ethics and Social Philosophy* 7(1) (2012): 1–37. Contends that an evolutionary debunking argument at most engenders a moral skepticism problem for realists, which they can solve by invoking the 'natural reply': viz., hold that some moral beliefs are immune to evolutionary pressures. But to take off from the ground, this "promising" reply needs some conceptual constraints on what can qualify as beliefs of that sort.

Sinnott-Armstrong, Walter, "Moral Intuitionism Meets Empirical Psychology," in *Metaethics after Moore*, T. Horgan and M. Timmons eds., Oxford: Clarendon Press, 2006, pp. 339–365. Emphasizes a negative legacy of the publication of *Principia Ethica* in moral epistemology consisting in the setting of the stage for the neglect in ethics of data from the sciences during most of the next sixty years. Following Moore, many moral philosophers continued to neglect theories of general and applied normative ethics until the 1970s and 1980s.

Smith, Michael, "Non-Naturalism and Epistemology," in *The Moral Problem*, Oxford: Blackwell, 1994, pp. 21–24. A clear statement of what Smith considers the non-naturalists' epistemological debt: viz., they need to explain the widespread belief that an object has a certain moral property M in virtue of some of its natural properties N. They are committed to saying that in any specific case, intuition involves a perceptual apprehension of the co-instantiation of N and M. Yet they cannot explain why, first, the supervenience of any M on an N looks like an *a priori* truth, instead of the *a posteriori* conclusion of an inductive argument; and, second, it seems implausible that moral knowledge is a species of causal knowledge.

Soames, Scott, "The Mixed Legacy and Lost Opportunities of Moore's Ethics," in *Philosophical Analysis in the Twentieth Century*, vol. 1, Princeton, NJ: Princeton University Press, 2003, pp. 242–260. Offers a critical introduction to *Principia Ethica*, arguing that Moore in this book mistakenly departed from his innovative, commonsense approach in epistemology. He arrived at some counterintuitive conclusions about the good such as that aesthetic enjoyments and friendships are the ideal by means of a top-down process of ethical reasoning that begins with very broad generalizations considered self-evident and subsumes more specific judgments under them. But he should have first invoked "restricted generalities" such as 'Anyone who habitually tortures children for the pleasure of watching them suffer and die is a bad person,' 'Keeping one's promises is prima facie right,' etc. (pp. 68–69). These self-evident platitudes would have offered him some strong, pre-philosophical certainties similar to the beginning points he successfully invoked in epistemology.

Stratton-Lake, Philip, "Introduction," in *Ethical Intuitionism: Re-evaluations*, Oxford: Clarendon Press, 2002, pp. 1–28. An assessment of the prospect for intuitionism and its non-cognitivist rivals that is optimistic about the former and pessimistic about the latter. Although as objected in Frankena (1939), non-naturalists cannot show that moral properties are graspable by either sense perception or a faculty of moral intuition, they need not show either. After all, as Moore often puts it, acquaintance with moral properties arises when they become present to the mind in the course of our thinking about what we experience.

Stratton-Lake, Philip, ed., *Ethical Intuitionism: Re-evaluations*, Oxford: Clarendon Press, 2002. A collection of essays on moral intuitionism that take up a variety of problems facing what once was a dominant moral epistemology. They show that moral intuitionism has little do to with the strawman sometimes offered against it.

Street, Sharon, "A Darwinian Dilemma for Realist Theories of Value," *Philosophical Studies* 127 (2006): 109–166. Challenges moral realists, especially non-naturalists, to explain the relation between the objective moral truths and the evolutionary influences that shaped moral beliefs. If they opt for denying those influences, then their doctrine conflicts with our best science. If they opt for accepting those influences, then they must say that either our moral beliefs most likely do not track the moral truths, or that by a mysterious massive coincidence they do. Either way, moral realism is untenable.

Wedgwood, Ralph, "Moral Disagreement among Philosophers," in Michael Bergmann and Patrick Kain eds., *Challenges to Moral and Religious Belief: Disagreement and Evolution*, Oxford: Oxford University Press, 2014, pp. 23–39. Argues that non-skeptical moral realism can accommodate disagreement among peers in ethics, which in any case has a reduced scope. There is mostly agreement about "middle-level truths" (the rightness of promise-keeping, truth telling, etc.) and about prudential reason (to avoid pain, look after one's health and financial security, staying alive, etc.). Disagreements arise at the level of ethical theory, but the same happens in other areas of philosophy where epistemic justification rests on reflective equilibrium.

Zimmerman, Aaron, "The Skeptic and the Intuitionist," in *Moral Epistemology*, London: Routledge, 2010, pp. 73–106. Good discussion of the skeptical challenge facing empiricist and rationalist forms of moral intuitionism. Rationalists like Moore owe us a plausible account of his analogy between moral knowledge and mathematical knowledge. Without that account, there is no reason to accept their claim that the process of reflection that might justify certain moral beliefs is analogous to the process that justifies certain non-inferential mathematical truths.

8

MORAL PROPERTIES AND TRUTHS

8.1 NATURAL/NON-NATURAL: A METAPHYSICAL CRITERION

A defining feature of metaphysical non-naturalism is captured by one of Moore's three metaphysical criteria for the natural/non-natural distinction of properties introduced in Table 7.1, namely,

1(a)	Natural properties are either simple essential "parts" of any of the things (objects, states, or events) that have them, or complexes featuring only properties reducible to some such simple properties	Non-natural properties are inessential properties of any of the things that have them. But if a thing has a non-natural property, it does so *in virtue of* some of its natural properties

DOI: 10.4324/9780429275975-8

Following Moore, let's understand the term 'thing' in 1(a) broadly, as a shorthand for either an object, act, attitude, state, or event. Given criterion 1(a), non-natural properties are derivative or supervenient on the natural properties of a thing, in the sense that they are necessarily metaphysically determined by some of its natural properties. This supervenience thesis is my focus in the present chapter, together with the other two metaphysical criteria for the natural/non-natural distinction of properties in *Principia* according to which,

| 1(b) | Natural properties can exist by themselves in time, independent of the things that have them | Non-natural properties cannot exist by themselves in time |
| 1(c) | Natural properties have both being and existence | Non-natural properties have being but lack existence |

None of these three criteria has gone without a challenge. On the one hand, criterion 1(a) seems vulnerable to a mysterious-supervenience objection because non-naturalism appears unable to account for the necessary metaphysical dependence of ethical properties on natural properties.[1] On the other, criteria 1(b) and 1(c) seem to render non-naturalism vulnerable to an extravagant-ontology objection. To these criteria I turn next.

BEING, EXISTING, AND EXISTING-IN-TIME

Charitably construed, *Principia Ethica*'s criteria 1(b) and 1(c) amount to the early Moore's attempt at deflating a moral metaphysics that looks non-parsimonious and 'extravagant' because it countenances some ontologically queer non-natural properties and truths.[2] His deflationism pioneered a series of analogous attempts by present-day non-naturalists who adopt a 'relaxed' attitude toward the ontological implications of non-naturalism. They claim that non-natural properties and truths fit within philosophical naturalism, the general metaphysical doctrine that all there *is* is the world as studied by science.[3] Critics sympathetic to the extravagant-ontology objection reject that claim.

Note, however, that including the Moore of later ethical writings, not all non-naturalists appear committed to a moral ontology shaped by criteria 1(b) and 1(c). For example, C. D. Broad was among the classical non-naturalists who took issue with these criteria for the natural/non-natural distinction of properties. On Broad's view, only epistemological criteria are available for drawing that distinction and *no* natural property could possibly meet Moore's metaphysical criteria. Broad wrote:

> I do not believe for a moment that a penny is a whole of which brownness and roundness are parts, nor do I believe that the brownness or the roundness of a penny could each exist in time all by itself. Hence I should have to count brownness, roundness, pleasantness, etc., as non-natural characteristics if I accepted Professor Moore's account of the distinction. Yet he certainly counts them as natural characteristics.
>
> (1933–1934: 361–362)

Clearly, Broad's first objection here concerns the phrasing, not the substance, of criterion 1(a) for the natural/non-natural distinction. After all, he agreed with Moore that any non-natural properties of a thing would necessarily depend on some of its intrinsic natural properties. In fact, their agreement is evident in Broad's friendly amendment to Moore's characterizaion of the natural properties of a thing as those properties that would make incomplete any description of that thing which omits one or more of them (CIV: 273). Broad qualified this characterization by adding that it applies unless the omitted properties are presupposed by some of the other properties in the description (1970: 352). In Broad's own example, a description of a thing might omit its being colored but would still be complete if it included its being red.

With these qualifications, Broad was in a position to accept *Principia*'s criterion 1(a) (that ethical properties necessarily depend on natural properties), even when he objected to Moore's phrasing of it on the grounds that it presupposes an implausible conception of material objects as aggregates of their essential natural properties. This reaction is consistent with Broad's rejection of criteria 1(b) and 1(c) (that of properties of these two kinds, it is only that natural properties can exist by themselves in time and have both being and existence). As we saw, he questioned 1(b) on the grounds that, *contra* Moore, no one could possibly imagine the existence in time of natural properties *by themselves*, completely independent of any object. What would it be for the brownness and the roundness of a penny to so exist without the penny? Moore attempted to support 1(b) by merely asking "Can we imagine 'good' as existing by itself in time, and not merely as a property of some natural object?" (*PE*: §26, 93). But not all who would agree with him in a 'No' answer would further accept the moral metaphysics of non-naturalism, including sympathizers of rival theories such as ethical naturalism, the error theory, and non-cognitivism. Moore simply begged the question with criterion 1(b).

However, there is a more charitable reading of 1(b), which starts out by placing it in the context of the other two metaphysical criteria Moore proposed for the natural/non-natural distinction of properties. On this reading, given 1(a), certain natural properties of a thing *constitute* that thing, and therefore, any description that omitted a property of that sort would be incomplete unless the property is presupposed by some other intrinsic property mentioned in the description. Moreover, acccording to a plausible commonsense realist doctrine that Moore at some point famously defended (DCS, PEW), the constitutive natural properties of perceptual objects are properties of such objects that exist in either space, time, or both (this charitable reconstruction ignores his further claim that they exist by themselves, independently of any object that have them). In this context, Moore can claim that non-natural properties are, but do not exist in the same way that natural properties exist. Like mathematical properties, their being is derivative in the sense that if a thing has any such property, it has it in virtue of some of its intrinsic natural properties, and a complete description of that thing need not list that derivative property.

In other words, if I am right, there is room for Moore to argue that the ethical properties of a thing lack existence in the strong sense, which is the sort of existence natural properties plausibly have. Among present-day non-naturalists, Derek Parfit (2011) offers reasons to this effect. But Moore himself did not attempt to do so except by invoking an analogy between ethical properties and mathematical properties (*PE*: §66, 161–162). In fact, in an incomplete preface for the second edition of *Principia*, he wrote that some of this book's metaphysical criteria for the natural/ non-natural distinction of properties are "utterly preposterous" (P2: 13). Perhaps he was alluding to 1(b) or 1(c), the two criteria from *Principia* discussed in this section.

SUPERVENING ON NATURAL PROPERTIES

Let's now consider the more plausible criterion 1(a), which amounts to an early casting of the relation of supervenience now commonly held to obtain between the ethical and the natural or descriptive. According to this criterion, of the natural and the non-natural properties of an object, it is only some of its natural properties that are essential to it and necessarily determine its non-natural properties. Unlike non-natural properties,

> [natural properties] are, in fact, rather parts of which the object is made up than mere predicates which attach to it. If they were all taken away, no object would be left, not even a bare substance: for they are in themselves substantial and give to the object all the substance that it has.
>
> (*PE*: §26, 93)

Putting aside a seemingly controversial understanding of natural objects as aggregates of their intrinsic natural properties, considered their "parts" in this quote, the claim here is that natural properties are constitutive of objects in a way that ethical properties (among other non-natural properties) never are. Moore further held that an object's natural properties necessarily determine any ethical properties the object might have. If so, no two objects can be exactly alike in their essential natural properties but differ in their ethical properties. Given this claim, if a mental state of pain is ethically bad, then any mental state exactly like that one must also be ethically bad and to the same degree. Or as Moore put it, when a thing has intrinsic value or disvalue "if true of one instance of the thing in question [it] is necessarily true of all" (ibid.: §18, 78). Conversely, "that a thing may retain its value, while losing some of its [essential natural] qualities, is utterly untrue" (ibid.: §123, 255).

Evidence that Moore held this thesis, even when he did not refer to the relevant relation as 'supervenience,' also comes from later ethical writings.[4] Although in *Principia Ethica* the relation tends to focus on intrinsic value, since other ethical properties are analyzable, at least in part, in terms of it, we can assume that in his view other key ethical properties supervene on natural properties too. He was committed to thinking, for example, that the degrees of duty cannot vary so that an agent may have a duty in a circumstance while another lack it or have it to a lesser degree in the same circumstance.[5] This way of thinking about the supervenience of key moral properties on natural properties recurs in a 1922 article where Moore rules out again the metaphysical possibility "that of two exactly similar things one should possess it [intrinsic value] and the other not, or that one should possess it in one degree, and the other in a different one" (CIV: 261). The modality at work here amounts to an unconditional metaphysical impossibility across possible worlds.

Of course, since Moore stated his thesis in the early twentieth century, theorizing about supervenience has come a long way, with philosophy benefitting from great advances in modal semantics, philosophy of mind, and other areas. But arguably, Moore would endorse some of the current construals of the relation of supervenience between the ethical or more generally the normative, on one hand, and the purely descriptive or natural, on the other. If so, he might go along with current slogans loosely describing it as an asymmetrical relation of covariance such as:

- Any actions, things, states, or events that are descriptively exactly alike must be normatively alike.
- Once God fixed (metaphorically speaking) all the natural properties and facts, the normative properties and facts necessarily followed.
- There is no difference in normative properties or truths without a difference in natural properties or facts.
- Indiscernibility in natural properties or facts entails indiscernibility in normative properties or facts.

But for a more precise statement of the supervenience of ethical properties on descriptive properties, Moore would need to look at something like the following:

> Strong Supervenience of the Ethical on the Descriptive (SSED) – The thesis that, necessarily, for any worlds w and w^* and things a and a^*, if a has in w the same purely descriptive properties that a^* has in w^*, then a has in w the same ethical properties that a^* has in w^*.

This thesis, modeled on a thesis of supervenience advanced by Jaegwon Kim (1993; 1998) to account for the relation between the mental and the physical, seems to capture the necessary metaphysical dependence of ethical properties on natural properties that Moore had in mind. Furthermore, with some plausible assumptions of modal logic, SSED mirrors some claims that he actually made, as evident in the quote above from his key (1922) article "The Conception of Instrinsic Value." Since SSED entails that all worlds that are descriptively alike necessarily would be ethically alike, Moore would have to agree on the global supervenience of the ethical on the descriptive, a thesis that amounts to the following:

> Global Supervenience of the Ethical on the Descriptive (GSED) – The thesis that any two worlds that are indiscernible with respect to their purely descriptive properties are indiscernible with respect to their ethical properties.[6]

Textual evidence from later writings such as the passage cited above strongly suggests that Moore construed the asymmetrical relation of supervenience of ethical properties on natural properties in ways consistent with SSED, and therefore with GSED. That something along these theses were his 'official view' of the relevant relation is also plain in passages from his "Reply to My Critics" where he agrees with Broad on the necessary metaphysical dependence of an object's intrinsic value on some of its intrinsic natural properties:

> I have always supposed that it did so depend, in the sense that, if a thing is good (in my sense), then that it is so follows from the fact that it possesses certain natural intrinsic properties, which are such that

from the fact that it is good it does not follow conversely that it has those properties.[7]

8.2 OBJECTIONS TO METAPHYSICAL NON-NATURALISM

THE SUPERVENIENCE PROBLEM

Moore's non-naturalism presupposes that ethical properties and natural properties are utterly distinct in kind. As I discuss in this section, some think that there is a problem for this doctrine, not because it claims that properties of these two kinds stand in a supervenience relation, but because it cannot explain why that relation obtains. On Geoffrey Warnock's early version of this line of objection, Moore must deny the possibility of any relation holding between the ethical and the natural. In the absence of any such relation, non-natural properties and facts would "float free," completely unrelated to natural properties and facts. That is, morality would have no anchor in the natural world. Warnock puts the problem for Moore in this way:

> [F]or Moore, there is no reason why what is good is good – that it is good is not only a distinguishable, but a totally isolated, fact about it, not just different from, but unrelated to, anything else. But if so, then it seems that morality is not only not reducible to, or identifiable with, any ordinary features of the world or of human beings; it seems to stand in absolutely no relation to any such features, and to be, in the strictest sense, entirely inexplicable. The picture presented is that of a realm of ethical qualities, *sui generis* and indefinable, *floating, as it were, quite free* from anything else whatever, but cropping up here and there, quite contingently and for no reason, in bare conjunction with more ordinary features of the everyday world.
>
> (1967: 14, my emphasis)

But there is textual evidence that Moore neither held nor was committed to saying that morality floats free, completely unrelated to the natural world. For one thing, if our discussion in the previous section is on the right track, he consistently claimed that there is a relation of metaphysical determination holding from natural properties and facts to ethical properties and truths. This supervenience doctrine is consistent with the minimal philosophical naturalism that Moore advanced in various writings. As mentioned earlier, for instance in "What Is Philosophy?," he defended a dualist general ontology, according to which there are only two fundamental kinds of entity in the world: material objects and mental states. Either way, the world consists of *natural* entities since, arguably, mental states are natural entities. This ontological naturalism is consistent with the claim that, besides such *fundamental* natural entities, there are also some *derivative* ethical properties and facts. It follows that he was not committed to the view that ethical properties must be floating free of the natural world and the Warnock objection fails.

Yet that line of objection contains an element that anticipates more recent formulations of the supervenience problem facing Moore's non-naturalism (McPherson 2012; Ridge 2003/2014; 2012; Smith 1994: 22–23); namely, that Moore and the other classical non-naturalists must leave unexplained the relation of supervenience they postulate between the ethical and the natural. They must do so because on their ontology the descriptive and the normative are distinct in kind. Since they must consider ethical supevenience a mystery, they find themselves in a position akin to that of the emergentists of the 1920s and 1940s in the philosophy of mind, who were committed to regarding the supervenience of the mental on the material or even the physical as a brute fact, a claim actually made by Broad in his 1924 emergentist "solution" to the mind/body problem. True, by distinguishing fundamental and derivative properties and vindicating mind/body supervenience, the emergentists need to renounce neither philosophical naturalism (the view that all there *is* is the natural world) nor materialism and physicalism (the views that all there *is* is the material or the physical world respectively). But like the non-naturalists about ethical properties, the emergentists about mental properties can only invoke a relevant supervenience relation without being able to explain why it obtains. This is because supervenience itself stands in need of an explanation and the emergentists about the mind/body relation lack the resources available to some non-emergentists who can further appeal to other relations such as identity, causal dependence, or non-reductive dependence to provide an explanation of mind/body supervenience. Since these rivals of emergentism can do so, that gives their doctrines a theoretical advantage over emergentism (Kim 1998).

Yet, since emergentism's inability to explain the relevant relation hardly counts as a fatal blow, perhaps the ethical non-naturalists should regard their moral metaphysics as analogous to emergentism about the mind/body relation. In fact, that they should do so has been recommended by Roger Crisp (2012) as a way of reaching a compromise with at least some of their rivals, such as the non-reductive naturalistic realists in ethics. Might Crisp's recommendation solve the supervenience problem facing non-naturalism? Not entirely, since if the non-naturalists become ethical emergentists, like the mind/body emergentists, they would commit to understanding the supervenience of the ethical on the natural as an inexplicable, brute fact. While the non-reductive naturalists in ethics can invoke, for example, a relation of non-reductive dependence, and thus explain the supervenience of the ethical on the natural, the non-naturalists who follow Crisp's recommendation cannot. Or they can postulate the existence of certain ethical/descriptive identities that are necessary but *a posteriori*. No such account is available to non-naturalists, who must construe their supervenience thesis as a synthetic truth that is knowable a priori. The non-naturalists cannot say that the supervenience of the ethical on the natural is an analytic truth because they accept Hume's rule that no ethical conclusion may follow from entirely descriptive premises. If the supervenience of the ethical on the natural were analytic, ethical conclusions would follow from purely descriptive premises (Blackburn 1984: 182–190; 1993: 130 ff.). Moore agreed with Kant in thinking that '7 + 5 = 12,' 'Every event has a cause,' and many other such necessary truths are synthetic, and saw no problem in ascribing a similar epistemic status to his thesis about the metaphysical relation between the ethical and the natural. Of course, the emergentists in the philosophy of mind might claim a similar status for their supervenience thesis. But either response would fall short of removing the impression in favor of some rivals who can explain why there is a relation of supervenience between two domains that differ in kind.

THE EXTRAVAGANT-ONTOLOGY PROBLEM

Let's now consider whether Moore scores better in resolving another problem facing his moral metaphysics. What we may call the 'extravagant-ontology' objection charges that non-naturalism conflicts with philosophical naturalism owing to its countenancing non-natural, and therefore ontologically 'queer' ethical properties and truths. These entities would be queer if they could not fit in a naturalistic picture of what there is. In reply to this objection, Moore and other mainstream non-naturalists might take one or more of the replies suggested on their behalf by Robert Shaver (2007: 287 ff.), according to which they should say that

1. Non-naturalism does not explicitly argue for any extravagant ontology.
2. The standard reasons for classical non-naturalism do not entail any extravagant ontology.
3. Non-naturalism, whether classical or present-day, need not entail any extravagant ontology.

Is the ontology of Principia Ethica extravagant?

A quick look at Moore's arguments in *Principia Ethica* suggests that Shaver's reply 1 is true: for the reasons rehearsed above in connection with our discussion of the natural/non-natural distinction of properties, Moore did not explicitly defend an extravagant ontology simply because, except for some vague remarks, he offered no systematic account of the ontological status of non-natural properties and truths. Furthermore, in the first four chapters of the book, he aimed chiefly at presenting a negative doctrine about what ethical notions and judgments *do not mean* rather than a positive theory about what they do mean.

However, even if true, this line of reply misses the point of the extravagant-ontology objection. That Moore (or any of the other classical non-naturalists) did not provide a positive account of ethical properties and truths does not seem enough to rid him of the objection. After all, we rightly hold a philosopher's feet to the fire if her ontology conflicts with the plausible outlook of general philosophical naturalism. We find just such a problem making trouble, for example, for Plato, when he postulates timelessly exist-ing "ideas" or "forms," for Descartes, when he fails to explain how a completely immaterial mind could interact with a material body, and for Locke, when he neglects to say what it is to be a myste-rious substrate of attributes which is only a "something, I know not what." Why, then, not require of Moore and his fellow non-naturalists that they produce a compelling account of what it is for a property or fact to be "non-natural?" Thus, Shaver's reply 1 falls short of meeting the extravagant-moral-ontology objection.

Does the Open Question Argument entail an extravagant ontology?

More weighty than reply 1 would be reply 2 if it turned out to be compelling, for it claims that the standard reasons for classical non-naturalism do not entail an extravagant ontology. Thus, in the case of Moore, we need to revisit his chief reason for non-naturalism, the Open Question Argument (OQA) examined in Chapter 5. From this argument Moore concluded that the term 'good' in its primary ethical use captures a non-natural or *sui gen-eris* concept and property, neither of which reduces to the concepts and properties captured by other terms, especially any naturalistic term. In drawing these conclusions, he assumed that

1. The term 'good' denotes a mind- and language-independent ethical property.
2. If 'good' and some purely descriptive term differ in meaning, then they must denote distinct properties.

In twentieth-century metaethics, much effort has been focused on pointing out the problems with these assumptions. Realist cogni-tivist assumption (1) begs the question against anti-realists and non-cognitivists, each of whom drew from the OQA a conclusion opposite to Moore's: the error theorists accepted the cognitivist part but rejected the realist part, taking the OQA to suggest that if there were any such ethical properties, they could not reduce to any natural property and therefore would be ontologically queer. Since there are no ethical properties, no ethical judgment can be true except for negative judgments of the sort 'Abortion is not morally wrong' (e.g., Mackie 1977: 50–51). In the hands of the prescriptivists and other non-cognitivists of the mid-twentieth century, Moore's OQA acquired a new twist. These theorists rejected (1) and (2) but seemed committed to holding that no ethical term can express a purely descriptive concept since moral language is not in the business of describing facts but rather has a conative function. That is what makes moral judgment characteristically action guiding, a feature absent in purely descriptive language or thought (e.g., Ayer 1952/1936: 103–106; Hare 1952: 82–86; Kerner 1966: 16). To critics of either kind, Moore's *further* conclusion from the OQA is unsupported by the argument and *does* amount to an extravagant ontology. But the fact that alternative conclusions from the OQA are possible shows that at least this chief argument of a classical non-naturalist need not entail an extravagant ontology. After all, the OQA is compatible with error theoretic and non-cognitivist conclusions even when Moore mistakenly took it to support his own non-naturalism.

Does non-naturalism entail an extravagant ontology?

The most ambitious line of reply that Shaver offers to non-naturalists, whether classical or current, requires them to show that their moral metaphysics does not entail an extravagant ontology. Non-naturalists do not regard their own moral ontology as a kind of supernaturalism and generally attempt to deflate any implications of their non-naturalism seemingly incompatible with philosophical naturalism. As I maintained earlier, Moore himself regarded his non-naturalism in ethics as consistent with a metaphysical naturalistic dualism of material objects and mental states (WIP: 26). Yet Moore might not be in a position to explain why the relation of supervenience between the ethical and the descriptive obtains and he needs to appeal to this relation to anchor ethical properties and truths in the natural world. In fact, his appeal to this relation can be read as one of many attempts by non-naturalists to accommodate their moral ontology within a philosophical naturalistic picture of the world. In this section I consider whether either of the two other attempts, both by present-day non-naturalists, entails an extravagant moral ontology. First, I have a quick look at the 'relaxed' non-naturalism of Derek Parfit, then I turn to the 'non-relaxed' non-naturalism of Terence Cuneo and Russ Shafer-Landau.

Like the Moore of *Principia Ethica*, the Parfit of *On What Matters* thinks that non-natural normative properties and truths metaphysically depend on some features of the natural world. Also like Moore, he rejects the correspondence theory of truth for ethical judgments and holds that simple normative propositions, such as that pain is bad, are true in a robust yet non-correspondence sense. To support this claim, Parfit offers an analogy between morality and other domains where it makes sense to say that some propositions are true but do not correspond to facts that admit of any representation at all. In mathematics, for example, the proposition that there is an infinite number of prime numbers seems true without corresponding to any fact. As this analogy illustrates, again like Moore, Parfit reasons along the lines of a companion-of-guilt argument that invokes less contested normative domains (usually, math and logic) for the purpose of deflating the ontology of non-naturalism.

But, most important, Parfit's central response to the extravagant-ontology objection, sounding downright Moorean, is to contend that normative properties "are" in the sense of having being but do not exist in time and space. In fact, they do not exist at all yet their existence is not required for some of the propositions in which they occur to qualify as true in a robust sense. When they happen to be true, this fact has no *ontological implications* because only propositions about natural facts can have implications of that kind (Parfit 2011, vol. 2: 464–487).

Parfit calls this deflationist type of non-naturalism "non-metaphysical cognitivism" and regards it as a brand of non-naturalism that is crucially defined by the following thesis:

> There are some claims that are irreducibly normative in the reason-involving sense, and are in the strongest sense true. But these truths have no ontological implications. For such claims to be true, these reason-involving properties need not exist either as natural properties in the spatio-temporal world, or in some non-spatio-temporal part of reality.
> (ibid.: vol. 2: 486)

To support the claim that we can have knowledge of basic normative truths of this sort, Parfit (ibid., vol. 2: 490–494) advances a moral epistemology parallel to Moore's rationalist intuitionism discussed in Chapter 7. Thus, now we can focus on the chief problem facing his non-metaphysical cognitivism. As noted earlier in the case of Moore's moral metaphysics, Parfit needs to say a lot more about the ontological status of key ethical truths and properties to eliminate the appearance that his non-metaphysical cognitivism posits mysterious entities that "are" but have no metaphysical implications. Otherwise neither Parfit nor Moore can succeed in ridding their non-naturalism of the extravagant-metaphysics objection. After all, fictional objects in some sense "are" without existing so that their "being" has no ontological implications. And surely fictional claims such as 'David Copperfield lived in London' in some non-correspondence way are true. But as suggested by their analogies between morality and the mathematical and logical domains, neither Parfit nor Moore is a fictionalist willing to say that moral judgments are true in a way relevantly analogous to the truth of 'David Copperfield lived in London.' Both of them ascribe to some key entities of ethics, math, and logic a mind- and language-independent sense of "being." In other ways, they are realists whose rejection of fictionalism in ethics and math is quite clear, for example, in Parfit's reply to the fictionalism of Hartry Field (2011, vol. 2: 492–494).

Now, surely it is far from commonly agreed in science that certain mathematical or logical properties are but do not exist, and certain propositions involving them are true but correspond to no facts. As a consequence, present-day-relaxed as well as classical-relaxed non-naturalism do seem to countenance a moral ontology that conflicts with what is amenable to discovery by science. That is, relaxed non-naturalism appears to entail an extravagant ontology.

Let's now consider the "non-relaxed" non-naturalism of Cuneo and Shafer-Landau (2014). By contrast with Moore and Parfit, these non-naturalists acknowledge that true moral judgments do have certain metaphysical implications. At the same time, like their fellow realists of a naturalistic persuasion, they accept that *ethical facts* are reducible to natural facts. But, unlike these realists, they vindicate a non-naturalist moral ontology construed as the doctrine that some key *moral judgments* are irreducible to purely descriptive judgments. This is so even if it turned out that no ethical properties can be reduced to natural properties. Naturalistic reductions of ethical properties do not matter in responding to the extravagant-ontology objection: according to Cuneo and Shafer-Landau (ibid.: 405 ff.), all that non-naturalists need to say concerns ethical truths.

Central to how Cuneo and Shafer-Landau would respond to the extravagant-ontology objection facing non-naturalism is their claim that certain true ethical judgments, the so-called moral fixed points, are not only true but capture propositions that are necessary for having morality at all. For example, the proposition *that it is pro tanto wrong to engage in the recreational killing of a fellow person*. Cuneo and Shafer-Landau maintain not only that this and other moral fixed points are true "in virtue of the essences of their constituent concepts," but also that this claim does not commit them to the analyticity of any of the propositions they deem eligible for having the status of moral fixed point (of which there might be many).

In fact, Cuneo and Shafer-Landau explicitly reject the analyticity of the moral fixed points while insisting that the account of concepts that they invoke to account for truth of any eligible propositions is "traditional." But within a traditional account of concepts, these are a type of mental content that have predicates as their linguistic counterparts. Now recall that Cuneo and Shafer-Landau take the moral fixed points to be true *by virtue of the moral concepts* that are their building blocks or essential constituents. If so, *contra* their explicit rejection of analyticity, their account does in fact commit them to the analyticity of the moral fixed points. For, after all, analyticity as standardly construed consists precisely in the doctrine that some propositions are true by the meanings of their building blocks. Grasping the truth of an analytic proposition depends entirely on being competent with the meanings or concepts involved. If analytic, the propositions eligible for the moral fixed points would be immune to revision on any grounds, empirical or *a priori*. It would be self-contradictory to deny a moral fixed point since denying, say, the propositions expressed by the judgment 'It is *pro tanto* wrong to engage in the recreational killing of a fellow person' would be analogous to denying the propositions expressed by '2 + 2 = 4' or 'A sister is a female sibling.' Thus, Cuneo and

Shafer-Landau's non-relaxed response to the extravagant-ontology objection faces the problem of presupposing the analyticity of the moral fixed points.[8] For it in fact rests on a standard view of concepts, which renders the moral fixed points analytically true or true by their meanings alone. After Quine's (1951) critique of the analytic/synthetic distinction, any vindication of analytic truths seems incompatible with philosophical naturalism. The moral fixed point theorists begged the question against that tradition. As a result, they failed to show that non-naturalism can fit within a philosophical naturalistic view of the world.

Nevertheless, suppose the moral fixed point theorists are saying instead that the conceptual truths of ethics rest on an *a priori* belief such as that *if* there are moral truths, *then* the moral fixed points are among them. According to this construal, the moral fixed point thesis would fall short of entailing that there are any moral truths or that the existence of such truths has *no* extravagant ontological implications. After all, analogous appeals to such conceptual truths might be made to argue that, say, God exists. Our hypothetical fixed-point theorist would start out by claiming that it is a conceptual truth that God is necessarily good, from which it follows that God exists since his goodness entails his existence. However, the conceptual truth (if there is one) is that *if* God exists, then he is necessarily good, from which *that God exists* does not follow. Similarly, in the case of moral propositions an appeal to conceptual truths can be of no help in getting ontological non-naturalism off the ground.[9]

Furthermore, the moral fixed-point theorists are committed to the implausible claim that anyone who rejects a moral fixed point – say, the error theorist – suffers from conceptual deficiency. Cuneo and Shafer-Landau (2014: 412) in fact draw this conclusion in the case of error theorist J. L. Mackie. That cannot be right, since not solely the error theorists but many people who seemingly master moral vocabulary may deny without self-contradiction any of Cuneo and Shafer-Landau's moral fixed points, including *that it is pro tanto wrong to engage in the recreational killing of a fellow person*. Or consider the proposition *that pain is bad*: although it comes out as true according to a great number of normative theories, whether pain is bad amounts to a fact that calls for a legitimate justification instead of an appeal to the essence of the concepts involved. Providing justification for such judgments is precisely one of the factors that motivate theories of value and right conduct.

For these reasons, I think that the classical as well as the present-day non-naturalists would be worse off by invoking the moral fixed points strategy in an attempt to show that their moral ontology is compatible with either philosophical naturalism, non-reductive ethical naturalism, or both. They should instead prefer the strategy of Moore and Parfit, even when their relaxed non-naturalism fails to meet the objection that non-naturalism entails an extravagant ontology.

NOTES

1 The best primary sources for Moore's claim that moral properties necessarily depend on natural properties are "The Conception of Intrinsic Value" (1922: 259 ff.) and "A Reply to My Critics" (1942b: 585 ff.). But passages that vindicate this thesis can also be found in *Principia Ethica* (§18, 78; §123, 255), an incomplete preface written for *Principia*'s second edition (P2: 13), and "Is Goodness a Quality?" (1932: 130–131).

2 There are several early formulations of the charge that non-naturalism is committed to an extravagant ontology of moral properties and facts. Among them are Ayer (1954: 242); Nowell-Smith (1954: 41); Stevenson (1937: 30; 1944: 108–109), and Warnock (1967: 14).

3 The 'relaxed' non-naturalists attempt to minimize the ontological implications of non-natural entities, whether these be moral properties, moral propositions, or both. Among them are Parfit (2011), Scanlon (2014), and Kramer (2009). By contrast, the non-relaxed non-naturalists do nothing to minimize such implications. In fact, they embrace them. In this group we may count Cuneo and Shafer-Landau (2014), Enoch (2011), and FitzPatrick (2008).

4 See especially Moore's P2, RC, and CIV.

5 The impossibility of this scenario is consistent with Moore's value invariabilism – the view that a part preserves its value as it travels from whole to whole, which I discuss in Chapter 11.

6 The assumptions needed for SSED to entail GSED are the widely accepted systems of modal logic S4 and S5. But not all non-naturalists accept these systems. For example, Ralph Wedgwood (2007: 211) rejects S5 in an attempt to solve the supervenience problem for non-naturalism by means of blocking that entailment. See Ridge (2012) for an objection to Wedgwood's strategy and Sturgeon (2009) for a total rejection of the supervenience of the ethical on the non-moral.

7   Moore (RC: 588). Although Moore insists that his sense of 'follows from' is 'deductive entailment' (RC: 607), charitably construed, the relevant expression in this passage refers to metaphysical depence or supervenience. Thus read, Moore's contentions are consistent with his defense of the autonomy of ethics (but cf. Dreier 2006 and Baldwin 2010). He also writes:

> It is true, indeed, that I should never have thought of suggesting that goodness was 'non-natural,' unless I had supposed that it was 'derivative' in the sense that, whenever a thing is good (in the sense in question) its goodness (in Mr. Broad's sense) depends on the presence of certain non-ethical characteristics' possessed by the thing in question ...

8   Relaxed non-naturalists may concede that some moral truths are analytic but hold that such cases involve non-substantive propositions such as, in Parfit's example, that *punishing someone for a crime not committed could not be just* (2011, vol. 2: 490).

9   I'd like to thank Charles Pigden for suggesting to me an objection to moral fixed point theorists which I take to run along these lines.

SUGGESTED READING

Cox, H. H., "Warnock on Moore," *Mind* 79 (1970), 265–267. A strong rebuttal of Warnock's charge that given non-naturalism, ethical properties would "float free," in the sense that they would be completely unrelated to natural properties.

Crisp, Roger, "Naturalism: Feel the Width," in Susana Nuccetelli and Gary Seay eds., *Ethical Naturalism: Current Debates*, Cambridge: Cambridge University Press, 2012, pp. 58–69. Proposes a compromise between non-reductive naturalistic realism and non-naturalism provided non-naturalism in ethics is understood as analogous to emergentism in philosophy of mind. Either of these doctrines can say that there is identity between the moral and the natural at the level of properties but informational difference at the level concepts.

Cuneo, Terence and Russ Shafer-Landau, "The Moral Fixed Points: New Directions for Nonnaturalism," *Philosophical Studies* 171 (2014): 399–443. An attempt to deflate the ontological-extravagance problem facing non-naturalism by holding that some moral truths (the "moral fixed points") are pre-conditions for having morality at all. It aims at showing that non-naturalism about moral truths is consistent with both non-reductive ethical naturalism and philosophical naturalism.

Dreier, Jamie, "Was Moore a Moorean?" in Terence Horgan and Mark Timmons eds., *Metaethics after Moore*, Oxford: Clarendon Press, 2006, pp. 191–207. Argues that Moore's remarks on supervenience in "A Reply to My Critics" must be reinterpreted in order to avoid inconsistency with his thesis that ethical terms admit no reduction into purely descriptive terms. On this interpretation, Moorean non-naturalism is an ancestor of expressivism.

FitzPatrick, William J., "Ethical Non-Naturalism and Normative Properties," in Michael Brady ed., *New Waves in Metaethics*, Basingstoke: Palgrave

Macmillan, 2011, pp. 7–35. A "non-relaxed" non-naturalist approach to normative properties and facts according to which these are neither equivalent nor reducible to any properties and facts that are the proper subject of scientific inquiry. For FitzPatrick, non-naturalism is a doctrine primarily about moral ontology and only derivatively about moral semantics. He responds to a number of critics of non-naturalism, who reject the non-naturalists' ontology, semantics, and epistemology – from realists to non-cognitivists including quasi-realist expressivists.

Horgan, Terence, "From Supervenience to Superdupervenience: Meeting the Demands of a Material World," *Mind* 102(408) (1993): 555–586. Contends that the notion of supervenience cannot denote merely a conceptual/semantic constraint on our use of language, as argued in Hare (1952). Rather, it must denote an ontological relation that is explanatory, something that Moore's conception of goodness as a supervenient non-natural property fails to do. For this reason, Moorean non-naturalism conflicts with physicalism and metaphysical naturalism.

McPherson, Tristram, "Ethical Non-Naturalism and the Metaphysics of Supervenience," in *Oxford Studies in Metaethics* 7, R. Shafer-Landau ed., Oxford: Oxford University Press, 2012, pp. 205–234. Points out some major difficulties non-naturalists would face if they were to embrace the inexplicability of the supervenience of the ethical on the natural. See also McPherson (2015) and cf. Crisp (2012).

Moore, G. E., "The Conception of Intrinsic Value," in *Philosophical Studies*, London: Routledge & Kegan Paul, 1922, pp. 253–275. *Locus classicus* for the Moorean doctrine that intrinsic value supervenes on some intrinsic natural properties of the thing that has it. The article elaborates on the notion of 'intrinsic natural property' and provides some reasons for thinking that 'good' in its primary ethical sense expresses an intrinsic value but not an intrinsic property.

Parfit, Derek, *On What Matters*, vol. 2, Oxford: Oxford University Press, 2011. Present-day defense of a relaxed non-naturalism akin to Moore's. Parfit considers this doctrine a *non-realist* type of cognitivism whose truths lack ontological implications. Among his arguments for it, the Triviality Objection is similar to Moore's barren-tautology formulation of the Open Question Argument. Like Moore, Parfit also defends non-naturalism from an appeal to moral disagreement by contending that under ideal conditions there would instead be widespread agreement.

Ridge, Michael, "Supervenience and the Nature of Normativity," in Susana Nuccetelli and Gary Seay eds., *Ethical Naturalism: Current Debates*, Cambridge: Cambridge University Press, 2012, pp. 144–168. Argues that non-naturalism, whether in its classical or present-day forms, cannot account for the widely accepted relation of supervenience of the normative on the natural. For Ridge, standard replies to the mysterious-supervenience objection fail, including "companion-of-guilt" arguments of the sort offered by Moore.

Shaver, Robert, "Non-naturalism," in Susana Nuccetelli and Gary Seay eds., *Themes from G. E. Moore: New Essays in Epistemology and Ethics*, Oxford:

Oxford University Press, 2007, pp. 283–306. Good overview of standard objections facing not only Moore but also other classical non-naturalists, including that their ontology and epistemology are extravagant.

Warnock, G. J. *Contemporary Moral Philosophy*, New York: St. Martin's Press, 1967. Early source for the objection that, given Moore's non-naturalism, moral properties must bear no relevant relation to natural properties. It should be read together with Cox's (1970) reply.

9

INTRINSIC VALUE

For the Moore of *Principia*, not only is the Open Question Argument his chief reason against naturalistic and metaphysical ethics, it is also his chief reason for the claim that intrinsic goodness has certain key attributes that set it apart from both other moral properties and from natural and metaphysical properties. Here I take a closer look at those attributes of intrinsic goodness, together with some of the controversies that this conception of this key ethical property continues to generate.

9.1 THE ATTRIBUTES OF MOOREAN GOODNESS

NON-NATURALNESS, IRREDUCIBILITY, SIMPLENESS, AND UNIQUENESS

Moore outlined his early conception of 'good' mostly in Chapter 1 of *Principia Ethica*, where this predicate is said to capture an ethical concept and property that are non-natural,

DOI: 10.4324/9780429275975-9

simple, indefinable, unanalyzable, unique, intrinsic, and non-relational. The ascription of these attributes occurs in connection with Moore's attempt to spell out the semantics of 'good.' On his account, 'good' is an ambiguous term of ordinary discourse that nonetheless has a primary ethical use in which it expresses the concept of intrinsic value (*PE*: §§2–10, 53/62; IGQ: 89–90). This predicate occurs with its primary ethical sense in, for example, the hedonist principle 'Pleasure is good,' where it has the grammatical function of an adjective. When 'good' has the grammatical function of a noun, as in 'the good' or 'that which is good,' it expresses instead one or another of several concepts and properties of practical ethics.

In the process of identifying the primary ethical use of 'good', Moore ascribed to this predicate some attributes that render it irreducible to any other ethical predicate. At the same time, he contended that 'good' enters into the reductive analyses of other ethical terms, which somehow inherit from it their admitting of no reductive analysis in non-ethical terms, whether these be naturalistic or metaphysical terms.[1] In his view, what renders ethical vocabulary irreducible to non-ethical vocabulary is the *sui generis* or non-natural character of 'good' and its converse 'evil,' either of which is a component of other ethical terms.

But what is the argument for this doctrine? As mentioned earlier, in *Principia Ethica*, the OQA amounts to Moore's chief reason for both the non-naturalness and the irreducibility of 'good.' But while his irreducibility claim gained some traction in ethics (especially with its vindication by non-cognitivists and some other theorists), his non-naturalness claim did not. As many of Moore's fellow travelers noted, the non-naturalness of 'good,' and, by extension, of other ethical terms, fails to follow on from the OQA. By contrast with Moore, having a broadly naturalistic philosophical outlook, these critics refused to accept in their moral semantics and ontology that ethical concepts and properties are *sui generis* – or of a kind unlike anything else in the world.

The simpleness and uniqueness of 'good' are attributes independently related to its irreducibility. Simpleness consists in what we would call today the 'basicness' or 'underivativeness' of some concepts and properties. If simple, 'good' would be indefinable and unanalyzable, given that, as Moore put it, it would have no parts.[2] Although the idea of a concept or a property as having or lacking *parts* appears counterintuitive, under a charitable interpretation it amounts to this more plausible view:

> A concept or property is simple just in case it is unstructured.

On Moore's account, simple predicates express simple concepts and may denote simple properties (if anything at all) while complex predicates are semantically and logically structured from simple predicates. Of the two, only predicates that are simple may have definitional priority. Moore later became more tentative about the simpleness of 'good.' In 1932, he wrote:

> In *Principia* I asserted and proposed to prove that 'good' ... was indefinable. But all the supposed proofs were certainly fallacious; they entirely failed to prove that 'worth having for its own sake' [i.e., 'good'] is indefinable. And I think perhaps it is definable: I do not know. But I also think that very likely it *is* indefinable.
>
> (IGQ: 98)

Either way, 'good' would express a concept and denote a property of ethics that is *sui generis* or unique in the sense of differing in kind from the two other types of entity that are, so to speak, part of the furniture of the universe according to the Moore of "What Is Philosophy?" (1–25): material objects and mental events.

INTRINSICALITY AND NON-RELATIONALITY

In addition, the early Moore ascribes to the concept and property captured by the term 'good' the qualifiers 'intrinsic' and 'nonrelational.' In what follows, let's consider how he applies these terms of art to the property of goodness, which he often calls 'intrinsic value.' On Moore's construal,[3] 'intrinsic,' 'relational,' and their counterparts mean roughly the following:

> Intrinsic/Extrinsic Property: A property is intrinsic or internal just in case its possession does not presuppose the existence of anything other than the thing that has it. If it does, then the property is extrinsic or external.

> Relational/Non-Relational Property: A property is relational just in case whether a thing has it depends on its standing on a certain relation to one or more things other than itself. Any property a thing may have all by itself is non-relational.

Intrinsic properties are necessary properties of a thing (i.e., an object, state, or event) that have them in the sense that if a thing A has a certain intrinsic property P, then any other thing B that's exactly identical to A would also have P. Conversely, if given two identical things, one has a property and the other lacks it, that property is extrinsic. To illustrate these pairs, first consider the statement 'This nail has a cylindrical plate.' Being a cylindrical plate counts as an intrinsic property because whether the nail has it presupposes the existence of nothing other than the nail itself. In addition, it is a non-relational property since the nail can have it all by itself. But being lightweight would be an extrinsic property of the nail since it presupposes the existence of gravity – as would its being rusted, which presupposes the existence of oxygen and water or moisture in the air. By contrast, 'This nail is attached to a surface' invokes a relational property of the nail because the nail has it only when connected in a certain way to a surface.

In later writings Moore revisited *Principia Ethica*'s claim that goodness is an intrinsic non-relational property. In his "Conception of Intrinsic Value" (CIV: 260), he listed among ethical properties with these attributes not only goodness but also beauty, rightness, and their converses. Consistent with our definition above, he wrote that 'intrinsic' as applied to any of these properties means "merely that the question of whether a thing possesses it, and in what degree it possesses it, depends solely on the intrinsic nature of the thing in question."[4] And in his *Ethics* (1912: 65) he maintained "'x is intrinsically good' means 'it would be a good thing that x should exist, even if x existed quite alone, without any further accompaniments or effects whatever'." About twenty years later, in "Is Goodness a Quality?" Moore offered the following alternative definition:

> 'Being intrinsically good' = 'Being worth having for its own sake.'

On this alternative definition, 'intrinsically good' and 'ultimately good' mean the same. Yet the letter of the proposed definition raises some problems for Moore. For one thing, it might commit him to saying that goodness is in fact an extrinsic property since it appears to presuppose the existence of someone for whom something is worth having as an end. But he can respond to this objection by saying about the expression 'being worth having for its own sake' that, if it presupposes an agent at all, it is merely a *hypothetical* agent. We'll have more to say about this line of response to the objection in Section 9.2.

Another problem, this time one that Moore himself noticed (RC: 555), is that the above *analysans* invokes an experience that is worth having for its own sake. Although if something is worth having for its own sake, that implies that it is good, the implication does not hold in the other direction. In Moore's view, it is simply false that if something is intrinsically good, then it must be an experience worth having for its own sake. Unlike other classical non-naturalists like Sidgwick, Moore did not restrict the kinds of thing that can be intrinsically good to states of consciousness – as *Principia*'s two-unexperienced worlds thought experiment, discussed here in Chapter 11, demonstrates.

We may now consider one of Moore's own examples of intrinsic-/extrinsic-property distinction. In objecting to C. D. Broad's view that pleasantness is an intrinsic natural property, Moore wrote:

> I personally find the experience of tasting caviare pleasant; but I believe that some people do not find it pleasant; and I see no reason to suppose that an experience of mine, which was tasting caviare, might not be exactly like an experience of another person, which was testing caviare, and yet that my experience might be pleasant to me, while his exactly similar experience was not pleasant to him. If so, the property which I assert to belong to my experience ... cannot be an intrinsic property of that experience ... But now contrast with another use of 'pleasant.' Suppose that on a particular occasion I am not only tasting caviare but also find it pleasant ... [T]his is ... an experience of *feeling pleased with the taste* ... If we use 'pleasant' in this second sense, as I think we often do, then pleasantness is an intrinsic property of any

experience which is pleasant, since it is obvious that no experience which did not contain pleasure could be exactly like one which did.

(RC: 588–589)

Given Moore's detailed discussion in this passage, 'pleasantness' as ascribed to an experience of eating caviar equivocates between an extrinsic and an intrinsic interpretation. Narrowly construed, this term denotes an extrinsic property since any two individuals might have exactly the same experience of eating the same thing and one may feel it pleasant and the other may not. Broadly construed (what Moore's calls the 'inclusive' interpretation), the experience itself contains some pleasantness – it is the intrinsic property of being an experience of feeling pleased with the taste of caviar. Now it is metaphysically impossible in Moore's view that an individual is in a psychological state that has this property and the psychological state of her exact doppelganger lacks it.

Now if goodness is an intrinsic property, it follows that many of the predicates that naturalistic philosophers in ethics regard as denoting ethical properties fall short of doing so. Among them are of course the predicates of evolutionary ethics, with which Moore took issue in *Principia* and in "The Conception of Intrinsic Value." Of 'better fitted for survival,' he argued that it cannot mean what's best adapted to a good end: "it means merely 'the survival of the fittest to survive'" (*PE*: §30, 99). If so, it cannot denote an intrinsic property even when at first it might appear otherwise. In sentences such as 'Creatures A are better fitted for survival than creatures B,' the property of being better fitted for survival does not qualify as intrinsic because whether creatures A or B have it does not depend entirely on the intrinsic nature of those creatures but rather on things outside their intrinsic nature, such as their circumstances and the actual laws of nature. Had these been different creatures, B might have been favored by natural selection (CIV: 255–256).

At the same time, being better fitted for survival also illustrates a property that is relational since it requires that those of whom it is predicated stand in a certain relation to other creatures that exist or have existed. Compare the property of *eating caviar with Vladimir Putin in Moscow*: for an individual to have it, it requires that she be in a certain relation with Vladimir Putin and Moscow.

In *Principia*, Moore took intrinsic goodness to be a non-relational property, something that sometimes he meant by simply writing that 'good' denotes a *quality*. Aware of the misunderstanding that this idiosyncratic use of the term 'quality' had generated, he later clarified that by 'quality,' "I meant merely that the character of being worth having for its own sake [i.e., being good] was a character and not a relational property" (IGQ: 97).

But not everyone agreed that goodness is a non-relational property. If two of the critics to be considered in Section 9.2, are right, C. D. Broad and Peter Geach, the term 'good' in its primary ethical sense may abbreviate some relational expression such as 'better than' or 'good of its kind.' Accordingly, if 'good' denotes a property at all (Geach is skeptical about this), it denotes a relational property. However, in due course, I show that these objections are quite different and Moore can accommodate one while rejecting the other.

Finally, let's introduce a question, the relevance of which will also become clear in our discussion of a different criticism: Can Moorean goodness be a normative property and metaphysically depend on some of the intrinsic properties of the thing that has it? On Moore's account, it can, since some of the intrinsic natural properties of a thing might imply obligations for agents to act or believe in certain ways. For example, if an experience contains a feeling of admiration for a beautiful object, this might imply that an agent ought to promote it; if it contains some pain, she ought to avoid it, and so on. Although Moore's account thus appears consistent with the view that goodness is a normative property, the critics to be considered next disagree.

9.2 CHALLENGES TO MOOREAN GOODNESS

Do the attributes of Moorean goodness make up a consistent set? Which of them, if any, could this conception of goodness lose and remain a distinct type on non-naturalism in metaethics? In *Ethics*, Moore himself revised his claim about the simpleness and uniqueness of 'good,' replacing his early monism with a pluralism, according to which 'right' too in its primary ethical use captures a simple, unique concept and property of ethics. In later ethical writings, he said that "it was a pure mistake to lay so much stress as I did upon the question of whether it [goodness] is or not" a simple property (P2: 6). If complex, then goodness would be analyzable in part in terms of some other ethical property. In this section I take up the arguments of C. D. Broad and Peter Geach against Moore's view that 'good' names a simple non-relational property. But first I consider an objection to the set of properties he ascribed to goodness launched by W. K. Frankena (1942) and more recently recast by Stephen Darwall (2007). If compelling, this objection entails that the ought-centered non-naturalism of Sidgwick better captures the normative aspect of morality than the goodness-centered non-naturalism of Moore.

THE FRANKENA-DARWALL DILEMMA

In *Principia*, Moore conceived of moral goodness as having, in addition to the features discussed above, a certain normative force. Its normativity is evident in a number of paraphrases he used to refer to goodness such as 'what ought to exist,' 'what ought to be real,' and 'what ought to be for its own sake.'[5] In 1942, W. K. Frankena objected that Moorean goodness cannot be a normative property and also have some of the other features that Moore attributed to it, especially simpleness, unanalyzability, intrinsicality, and non-relationality. More recently, Stephen Darwall (2007) has recast Frankena's objection along lines compatible with the following dilemma facing Moore:

1. Either goodness is a normative property or it isn't.
2. Given Moore's non-naturalism, goodness is a simple, unanalyzable, intrinsic, non-relational, normative property.
3. But if goodness is a normative property, then it is analyzable in terms of what is to be promoted.
4. If goodness is analyzable in terms of what is to be promoted, then goodness is a complex, extrinsic, relational property.
5. *Therefore*, if goodness is a normative property, then Moore's non-naturalism is false.
6. If goodness is not a normative property, then goodness is a natural property.

7. If goodness is a natural property, then Moore's non-naturalism is false.
8. *Therefore*, if goodness is not a normative property, Moore's non-naturalism is false.
9. *Therefore*, either way Moore's non-naturalism is false.

Since this dilemma seems valid, if its premises were well supported, it would amount to a *reductio* of Moore's non-naturalism. Given Moore's general ontology, he would likely accept the reasoning in the second horn, and therefore be committed to offer a compelling challenge to one or more of the premises in the first horn. But this horn starts with a necessary truth (premise 1), followed by a statement of the attributes that Moore ascribed to goodness in *Principia Ethica*. Thus, Moore must question either premise 3, premise 4, or both. Moore in fact questioned such premises in a 1942 reply to Frankena that we'll consider shortly, after taking a quick look at the best reason for premise 3, the claim that if goodness is a normative property, then it is analyzable in terms of moral obligation. This would have the consequence that it is not a value property but a deontic property instead that has ontological priority. If Moore were to deny the normativity of goodness, then he must "leave open whether there is any reason to desire or take any attitude toward or action regarding it" (Darwall 2007: 192). So, either Moore's non-naturalism collapses into Sidgwick's ought-first non-naturalism (first horn of the dilemma), or it is not an ethical theory (second horn of the dilemma). Since the second option is unpalatable for Moore, he has no choice but to accept Sidgwick's non-naturalism, which regards 'good' as complex and analyzable in terms of 'ought.' Since Sidgwick understood goodness roughly as what ought to be desired by an agent whose psychology is ideal, he was better positioned to account for the reason-providing force of ethical terms as well as for the reasoning at work in ordinary moral appraisals, where the moral obligation of agents determines ascriptions of blame or praise. Furthermore, on Darwall's critique (ibid.), by analyzing goodness in terms of ought, Sidgwick was able to defend consequentialism "as an explicitly normative doctrine and not as an empty tautology."

True, in *Principia Ethica*, Moore defined 'right' partly in terms of 'what maximizes goodness.' For example, he wrote: "The assertion 'I am morally bound to perform this action' is identical with the assertion 'This action will produce the greatest amount of good in the Universe'" (*PE*: §20, 82). Nevertheless, Darwall's critique neglects to take into account that by the time Moore published *Ethics*, he had changed his view about analyzability of 'right.' Although he now held his consequentialist principle to be self-evident and thus *a priori* true, he regarded it as a *synthetic a priori* truth.

In any case, since an ought-first type of non-naturalism conflicts with the views of the early Moore, he needs a compelling reply to the following premises of the Frankena-Darwall dilemma:

3. If goodness is a normative property, then it is analyzable in terms of what is to be promoted.
4. If goodness is analyzable in terms of what is to be promoted, then goodness is a complex, extrinsic, relational property.

To support something like premise 3, Frankena argued that Moore is committed to the normativity of goodness in order to distinguish this property from intrinsic natural properties of things, such as yellowness or circularity. That Moore understood this commitment is clear in his numerous references to goodness as what *ought* to exist, must be promoted, etc. But now, if goodness is something that ought to exist or must be promoted whenever possible, then there is an obligation to bring it about that is *someone's obligation*. Some agents ought to bring it about whenever possible. This suggests that

> [i]ntrinsic goodness can have a normative character as such only if it essentially or analytically involves a reference to an agent on whom something is actually or hypothetically enjoined, that is, only if it is not a simple, intrinsic quality.
>
> (Frankena 1942: 99)

That is, Moore's goodness is a relational extrinsic property analyzable in terms of ought. Moore ignored the implications of his own commitment to the normativity of goodness.

Yet the reasons for premises 3 and 4 rest on a debatable interpretation of Moore's language in *Principia* as well as a neglect of a plausible distinction between ought-to-be and ought-to-do obligations. First, note that in *Principia* expressions such as 'what ought to exist' figure as *paraphrases* rather than as analyses of intrinsic value. Second, in reply to the alleged collapse of his non-naturalism into Sidgwick's, Moore can invoke C. D. Broad's (1964) observation that, while ought-to-dos in fact create on agents a categorical obligation for action or attitude, ought-to-bes lack that implication. This is evident in examples such as 'A sugar cube ought to be soluble in liquid,' or 'Arsenic ought to be poisonous.' Since arguably a sugar cube would be soluble even if liquid did not exist, or arsenic poisonous even if nothing else but arsenic existed, being soluble in liquid and being poisonous seem intrinsic properties in the sense discussed in Section 9.1 because neither of these properties presupposes the existence of anything other than the thing that has it (viz., the sugar cube, arsenic). And this is so whether or not the property in question is relational, which it may turn out to be. Moore can now insist that paraphrasing goodness as what ought to exist need not presuppose the existence of any real agent, but rather a hypothetical agent: someone, if any one at all who if it existed, ought to bring goodness about whenever possible. In fact, Moore himself had exemplified this line of reply with the following thought experiment:

> To say of anything, A, that it is "intrinsically" good is equivalent to saying that, if any agent were a Creator before the existence of any world, whose power was so limited that the only alternatives in his power were those of (1) creating a world which consisted solely of A or (2) causing it to be the case that there should never be any world at all, then, if he knew for certain that this was the only choice open to him and knew exactly what A would be like, it would be his duty to choose alternative (1), provided only he was not convinced that it would be wrong for him to choose that alternative.
>
> (RC: 600)

Furthermore, in "External and Internal Relations," Moore explained how a property may be both relational *and* intrinsic.

If so, if goodness were a property of a state that ought to be promoted whenever possible, this would at most entail that goodness involves a relation between the state that has it and an agent. But since the state may have the property even if no agent ever existed, goodness would be an intrinsic property of that state. On this account, Moore gives up only the claim that goodness is non-relational. Frankena would need an independent reason for the claim that goodness, if normative, must be an extrinsic property. This suggests that the first horn of the Frankena-Darwall dilemma is unsound owing to the fact that its premises 3 and 4 are debatable.

THE BROAD AND THE GEACH OBJECTIONS

Let's now consider two independent objections by Broad and Geach to the effect that the term 'good' as used in *Principia Ethica* does not denote a simple, non-relational property. Broad's objection amounts to a friendly amendment that leaves the core of Moore's non-naturalism untouched, while Geach's objection attempts to refute that central doctrine of Moorean moral metaphysics. In this section I argue that while Moore cannot easily resist Broad's amendment, there is room for him to reject Geach's challenge altogether.

In *Principia Ethica*, Moore contended that whenever a property or state of affairs is good or bad as an end, its goodness or badness cannot metaphysically depend on any relation that thing might bear with something else, including feelings of approbation, desires, beliefs or circumstances. But not all the classical non-naturalists accepted this conception of ultimate value and disvalue. Among the skeptics, Broad (1933–1934: 259) early objected that for all Moore has said in *Principia*, the term 'good' might instead be an abbreviation of an expression like "better than the average member of its proximate species." If so, then the term stands for a complex, relational property. Given this alternative account, to say, for example, that a state of admiration of a beautiful object is ultimately good amounts to saying that it is better than some other states of a comparable kind, such as the states of admiration of an ugly object and of indifference to a beautiful object. Moore cannot reject this amendment to his conception of intrinsic value by appealing to the OQA, his chief argument for that conception in *Principia*. After all, the OQA falls short of ruling out that goodness is a complex relational property. Indeed, it falls short of categorically ruling out that it might turn out to be a natural property since, as Broad pointed out (ibid.: 259–260), there might be some alternative adequate analyses of goodness, including naturalistic analyses, that Moore neglected to target with his OQA.

Nevertheless, as we saw in Chapter 5, Moore may reply that although the OQA, an argument that proceeds by cases, falls short of ruling out *all* naturalistic analyses, it renders them implausible. An appeal to reasoning along the lines of this argument has force against reductive naturalistic analysis of key ethical terms but is weaker against a reductive analysis of 'good' in some other *ethical* terms.

The possibility of such analysis is consistent with Moore's relaxed attitude toward the analysis of 'good' in terms of 'ought' offered by Sidgwick, which as we saw in *Principia* is exempted from the commission of the naturalistic fallacy. Broad's claim that 'better than' is definitionally prior to 'good' (a pioneer of a non-naturalist, fitting-attitude approach) is quite congenial to Sidgwick's attempted analysis of 'good.' On Broad's version, 'x is intrinsically good' turns out to be equivalent in meaning and denotation to 'x is something which it would be right or fitting to desire as an end.' Yet, as I argue in connection with my discussion of Moore on moral obligation (Section 10.1 in Chapter 10), a reductive ethical analysis of value in terms of obligation involves an obligation concerning *attitude*. Obligations of this sort lack the full deontic status of any obligations concerning an *act or omission*. Something along similar lines could be said of Broad's attempted analysis of 'good' in terms of 'right' or 'fitting.' Any such attempt at a reductive analysis of an ethical term raises questions about whether its *analysans* is really deontic or evaluative, and the "analysis" itself amounts to an analysis instead of a statement of some synthetic necessary connection.

In any case, Broad's objection to the simpleness and non-relationality of Moorean goodness must not be conflated with Geach's objection, which, if well supported, would have far more devastating consequences for Moore's moral metaphysics. After all, given this objection, Moorean non-naturalism rests on altogether mistaken assumptions about the logical and grammatical function of the term 'good.' To show this, Geach first draws attention to a distinction between adjectives of two classes depending on their grammatical and logical function: some are predicative adjectives, others are attributive. No adjective falling in one of these classes can also fall in the other. For example, 'red' as in the phrase 'a red book' falls in the predicative class, while 'small' as in the phrase 'a small flea' falls in the attributive class. Attributive adjectives have their meaning relative to a kind: a small flea and a small elephant are small relative to the set of fleas and elephants respectively. Another key difference between these classes of adjective is that only predicative adjectives allow an inference from 'x is an AB' to 'x is an A' and 'x is a B.' Given that 'red' is predicative, from 'x is a red book' it follows 'x is red' and 'x is a book.' By contrast, given that 'small' is attributive, from 'Dumbo is a small elephant,' it does not follow 'Dumbo is small' and 'Dumbo is an elephant.' Similarly, from 'Mary is an expectant mother,' it does not follow 'Mary is expectant' and 'Mary is a mother.'

According to Geach, as used in *Principia Ethica*, 'good' amounts to non-sense: it is a term of art that defies ordinary use and has neither meaning nor denotation because Moore failed to understand its grammar and logical function. Properly construed, 'good' in its primary ethical use is short for 'good of a kind' and therefore has an exclusively attributive, grammatical function. As used by Moore, this ethical term turns out to be a-grammatical – something comparable to Chomsky's "green ideas ...". Here is how Geach (1956: 34) puts the objection:

> [T]here is no such thing as being just good or bad, there is only being a good or bad so-and-so. (If I say that something is a good or bad thing, either 'thing' is a mere proxy for a more descriptive noun to be supplied from the context; or else I am trying to use 'good' or 'bad' predicatively, and its being grammatically attributive is a mere disguise. The latter attempt is, on my thesis, illegitimate.)

The clear implication of this line of objection to Moore's use of 'good' is that it does not name any property at all, and *a fortiori* any property with the features he ascribed to it such as non-naturalness, simpleness, etc. But Geach is no nihilist: on his neo-Aristotelian view, 'good' does pick out a property, in fact, it picks out a purely natural property. It suits that view that 'good' – together with its counterpart 'bad' – be an attributive adjective that would have the exclusive function of a noun modifier, something comparable to occurrences of 'good' in phrases such as 'a good knife' or 'a good hygrometer.' These phrases presuppose some objective facts about the relevant class that can help establish what is to count as a good or bad knife, a good or bad hygrometer, and so on. In the moral case, the neo-Aristotelian agenda of Geach aims at extracting from nature some objective requirements for what it is to be a good (or evil) human being, human act, etc.

Thus read in its theoretical context, Geach's objection raises some problems. For one thing, it is unlikely that the standard to determine what is to count as a good or an evil human being, human act, etc. can be extracted from nature. No matter how many requirements neo-Aristotelians like Geach think they can objectively extract from nature, at some point moral intuitions must come into play: they are needed to determine whether actions of a certain sort are, say, conducive to human flourishing and therefore admit the modifier 'good.' Or they hinder or destroy human flourishing and therefore admit the modifier 'bad.' At this point, their view becomes vulnerable to a properly construed OQA. After all, for instance, rape might have helped our ancestors flourish, but it is an open question whether its practice was morally good. No matter how many descriptive details evolutionary psychology tells us about this practice among our hominid ancestors, more than invoking, say, the selfish gene, is needed to determine whether any of our ancestor rapists was a good or an evil human being. And no matter how much medical science is able to tell us today about fetal mental development, more is needed to determine whether a woman's elective termination of a pregnancy is a good or bad human act. This objection may also be cast as a knowledge problem facing neo-Aristotelians (Pigden 2012) owing to the availability of numerous counterexamples suggesting that knowledge of nature can never tell whether a human being or an act is good or evil.

Now what about Geach's objection that Moore's predicative uses of the term 'good' and even its occurrences as a noun in *Principia Ethica* amount to non-sense? There is abundant evidence from popular culture, and thus from ordinary discourse, supporting the legitimacy of such uses. It comes from some commonly available headlines in the news media such as, "Is Artificial Intelligence Good or Evil?" (*IBTimes*, February 14, 2019). Furthermore, headlines such as "Now, Too Much of a Good Thing Is Bad" (*Economic Times*, May 29, 2017) suggest that there is no reason in the offing to agree with Geach's claim that 'good' cannot have a wide general scope as in 'a good thing' but must always have a specific scope as in 'a good knife' or 'a good elephant.'[6] The availability of such counterexamples suggests that when used as an adjective, 'good' might modify generics the generality of which varies greatly and also functions either way: sometimes predicatively, other times attributively. Geach has provided no good grounds for thinking that in its primary ethical use, 'good' cannot have the predicative grammatical role that is predominant in *Principia Ethica*.

In sum, if as Broad objected (1933–1934: 259), 'good' in its primary ethical sense is always an abbreviation for 'good of its kind' and this term means 'better than the average member of its proximate species,' then the property that this ethical term actually denotes would be relational. But Moore might accommodate this result without having to abandon some of the most crucial attributes he ascribed to goodness, such as its intrinsicality and nonnaturalness. A more radical challenge facing his account of this key ethical property comes from Peter Geach, which would entail that what Moore takes to be the primary ethical use of 'good' in fact amounts to nonsense and denotes nothing at all. But for the reasons provided above, this objection now is out of the way.

NOTES

1   In *Principia Ethica*, by 'definition' or 'analysis' (hereafter, simply 'analysis') Moore meant *reductive analysis*. In any analysis of this sort, the *analysandum* (i.e., the expression to be analyzed, standardly placed on the left-hand side of the analysis) and the *analysans* (i.e., the expression that gives the analysis,

standardly placed on its right-hand side) are semantically equivalent but the *analysandum* does not occur in the *analysans*. To illustrate reductive analysis of complex concepts by decomposition, Moore later offered some ordinary examples such as the analysis of 'x is a brother of y' in terms of 'x is male and x & y had a common parent' (*LP*: 156–157).

2   Moore (*PE*: §§7–9, 59/61). Hereafter I use 'definition' and 'analysis' interchangeably.

3   Primary sources relevant to Moore's use of 'intrinsic,' 'relational,' and their counterparts are his articles "External and Internal Relations" (1919–1920), "The Conception of Intrinsic Value" (1922), and "Is Goodness a Quality?". His aims in these articles were, respectively, raising an objection to Francis Herbert Bradley's thesis that all relations are internal; unpacking *Principia*'s notion that the moral supervenes on the natural (see Chapter 8); and objecting to H. W. B. Joseph's view that goodness is not quality.

4   Moore went on to say:

> I can only vaguely express the kind of difference I feel there to be by saying that intrinsic properties seem to describe the intrinsic nature of what possesses them in a sense in which predicates of value never do. If you could enumerate all the intrinsic properties a given thing possessed, you would have given a complete description of it, and would not need to mention any predicates of value it possessed; whereas no description of a given thing could be complete which omitted any intrinsic property.
>
> (CIV: 273)

5   For example, in *PE*: §134, Moore contrasts 'good' in the sense of "what ought to be for its own sake" with "what ought to be for the sake of its results." See also §69 and §70 of *Principia Ethica*.

6   Other counterexamples to Geach's claim based on ordinary uses of 'good' include Hurka's appeal to Martha Stewart's TV catchphrase "It's a good thing" (2011a: 39). In addition, Hurka points to the biblical book of Genesis, which of course is read by millions of people who do not find passages such as "having created light, He [God] saw the light, that it was good" odd at all, or think that the term 'good' as used in the book should have a relativized, attributive reading.

SUGGESTED READING

Broad, C. D., "Is 'Goodness' a Name of a Simple Non-Natural Quality?" *Proceedings of the Aristotelian Society* 34 (1933–1934): 249–268. Argues that although intrinsic goodness is a non-natural property, its simpleness amounts to an unsettled matter. Also a good source for Moore's criteria for the natural/ non-natural distinction of properties.

Broad, C. D., "G. E. Moore's Latest Published Views on Ethics," *Mind* 70(280) (1961): 435–457. Comprehensive discussion of the chief objections facing

Moore's ethical theory, with an excellent discussion of what I have called above 'the Frankena-Darwall dilemma.'

Darwall, Stephen, "How Is Moorean Value Related to Reasons for Attitudes?" in Susana Nuccetelli and Gary Seay eds., *Themes from G. E. Moore: New Essays in Epistemology and Ethics*, Oxford: Oxford University Press, 2007, pp. 183–202. Reconstructs Frankena's (1942) objection to Moore's view of intrinsic value as a dilemma roughly along the lines offered in this chapter, charging that it delivers a fatal blow to his brand of non-naturalism (as opposed to Sidgwick's). Yet Darwall contends that all non-naturalists failed to take into account the distinctive moral demand that is at issue in moral appraisal.

Frankena, William K., "Obligation and Value in the Ethics of G. E. Moore," in Paul Arthur Schilpp ed., *The Philosophy of G. E. Moore*, Lasalle, IL: Open Court, 1942, pp. 93–110. Points to some inconsistencies in Moore's conception of goodness, objecting that this property cannot be normative and at the same time simple, unanalyzable, intrinsic, and non-relational. If as Moore said goodness is "what ought to exist for its own sake," then it is a normative property. But it lacks some of the other attributes he mentioned such as being simple, unanalyzable, intrinsic, and non-relational. As a property analyzable in terms of, say, what ought to be brought about whenever possible, goodness presupposes the existence of some agents. On the other hand, if Moore had in mind a non-normative property, then goodness is analyzable in terms of some natural properties, such as being a state of contentment or of pleasure.

Geach, Peter T., "Good and Evil," *Analysis* 17 (1956): 33–42. A classical logical-*cum*-grammatical objection to Moore's non-naturalism focused on his use of 'good' in *Principia Ethica*. Argues that nothing is good (or bad) period since a thing is a good (or a bad) *something*. If so, then being a good (or a bad) person, human action, etc. would turn out to be akin to being a good (or a bad) knife, car, etc. in that they all count as naturalistic predicates.

Moore, G. E., "Is Goodness a Quality?" *Proceedings of the Aristotelian Society*, Suppl. vol. 11, 1932: 116–131. [References to reprint pp. 89–105 in Moore 1959.] A further reflection on *Principia Ethica*'s claim that in its primary ethical use the ambiguous term 'good' denotes an intrinsic quality. Moore discounts some objections facing his previous characterization of 'intrinsic' property, and paraphrases 'intrinsic goodness' as 'being worth having for its own sake.' Seemingly fueling Frankena's objection, this paraphrase was rejected in "A Reply to My Critics".

Moore, G. E., "A Reply to My Critics," 1942b, in Paul Arthur Schilpp ed., *The Philosophy of G. E. Moore*, Lasalle, IL: Open Court, 1942, pp. 533–677. Moore's replies to Frankena and Broad are illuminating for the topics of concern in this chapter. He offers two chief reasons for thinking that intrinsic natural properties, though ought-implying, neither individually nor as part of an infinite disjunction could be identical with intrinsic value. Namely,

(1) that there are an immense number of natural intrinsic properties, all of which are 'ought-implying,' and (2) that there does not

seem to be any natural intrinsic property, other than (possibly) the disjunction of them all, which is both entailed by them all and also 'ought-implying.'

(pp. 604–605)

Orsi, Francesco, *Value Theory*, London: Bloomsbury, 2015. Good survey of contemporary debates in value theory, many of which revisit Moore's view of intrinsic value. Particularly relevant to the topics of this chapter are its discussions of normativity, intrinsic and conditional value, Geach's objection to the use of the term 'good' in *Principia Ethica*, and Moore's distinction of 'good' and 'good for.'

Paton, H. J., "The Alleged Independence of Goodness," in Paul Arthur Schilpp ed., *The Philosophy of G. E. Moore*, Lasalle, IL: Open Court, 1942, pp. 113–134. Takes issue with Moore's thesis that things that are good as ends in themselves are good intrinsically and independent of anything else. Goodness might be non-natural but need not be construed as an intrinsic non-relational property. It must be related to a mind if, as Moore says, it ought to exist, and to context, which is always relevant to determining whether a thing is good non-instrumentally.

Pigden, Charles R., "Geach on 'Good'," *The Philosophical Quarterly* 40(159) (1990): 129–154. Replies to Geach's claim that 'good' (or its counterpart 'bad') cannot convey a non-natural concept and property simply because there is no meaningful predicative use of this term. Not only does 'good' allow for legitimate predicative uses, but the neo-Aristotelian naturalistic project of Geach and others cannot get off the ground. Good discussion of the problem of the unavoidability of moral intuitions facing the neo-Aristotelian program of Geach and others. For an updated version, see Pigden's "Identifying Goodness' (2012).

10

MORAL OBLIGATION

As we saw earlier, given Moore's moral semantics, to say that an ethical term is simple is to say that neither its meaning nor its denotation admits of reductive definition or analysis. Although in his early writings Moore identified only *one* such irreducible ethical term, 'good' when used for intrinsic value, by 1910, Moore had added to his minimal list the term 'right' when used for moral obligation.[1] On this more expansive view, any other ethical term can be reduced at least in part to either 'good,' 'right,' or their converses. But, of course, not always may these terms and the complexes derived from them convey a normativity that is moral. Although the Moore of *Principia Ethica* did not draw a clear distinction between kinds of normativity, as I discuss in this chapter, in later writings he adopted the view that moral obligation is comparatively more astringent and authoritative than legal, conventional, and other kinds of obligation. In what follows, I first consider how in "The Nature of Moral Philosophy" he drew the line between different kinds of normativity and outlined some rules that he

DOI: 10.4324/9780429275975-10

took to govern two distinct types of moral obligation: obligations involving an act or omission, and obligations involving a propositional attitude or a feeling. Moore's treatment of moral obligation suggests that there is a problem facing Henry Sidgwick's attempt at producing a reductive definition of 'good' in terms of, roughly, 'what ought to be desired.' I argue that this definition fails to be reductive since given a certain conception of moral obligation endorsed by Moore, 'what ought to be desired' expresses an ideal duty. As such, it is closer to an evaluation than to a duty.

Next, I turn to a debate concerning whether an ought-first type of non-naturalism like Sidgwick's is better suited for avoiding some metaphysical puzzles facing the moral metaphysics of *Principia Ethica*. Moore would agree that intrinsic value metaphysically depends or supervenes on some of the natural properties of a thing, so that, for example, the badness of an agent's experience is determined by its being an experience of a toothache. But could he embrace the so-called buck-passing account (Scanlon 1998; 2014), according to which it is the natural property that provides a reason for action and fully explains why an agent acts in a certain way? Some critics think he cannot because, on his account, only the supervenient value provides a reason for action. But if on Moore's non-naturalism the reason for action stems from its intrinsic value instead of the natural property that metaphysically determines that value, this view appears to deepen the puzzle for Moorean non-naturalism about what anchors non-natural properties on the natural world.

10.1 MORAL AND NON-MORAL OBLIGATION

The Moore of *Principia* neither distinguished different kinds of normativity nor drew a sharp line between evaluative and deontological terms and judgments. Accordingly, some of the examples throughout his book involve the system of morality, others the systems of rationality, convention, or the law. Some are evaluative; others amount to prescriptions – as illustrated by these examples from the opening chapter of *Principia*:

1 So and so is a good man.
2 That fellow is a villain.

3   Temperance is a virtue.
4   Drunkenness is a vice.

Judgments 1–4 have evaluative meaning *in addition to* having an increasing degree of descriptive meaning. In terms of the normative concepts involved, 1 and 2 feature concepts 'good' and 'bad' that are thinner compared with 'virtue,' 'vice,' 'temperance,' and 'drunkenness' in 3 and 4. Suppose we recast 3 and 4 as the following prescriptions:

5   Be temperate.
6   Avoid drunkenness.

Judgments 5 and 6 have the force of obligations, duties, or oughts (all treated alike by Moore). Now it is unclear whether they qualify as deontic *moral* judgments since arguably they involve prudential obligation. But in *Principia* Moore did not distinguish normativity of this and some other common kinds from moral normativity, and that conflation is evident in other examples from Chapter 1 of *Principia* (§§3–4: 55) such as:

7   I am doing good now.
8   I had a good dinner.
9   Books are good.

Nevertheless, Moore found judgments 7 and 8 of no interest to ethics on the grounds that the term 'good' in each of them refers to facts that "are unique, individual, absolutely particular ..." while a "scientific" ethical theory should concern itself only with *general* judgments. After all, ethics aims at finding reasons and principles that are true of types of actions, things, and character traits (*PE*: §4, 56). Consistent with his view about normativity in *Principia Ethica*, Moore neglected to point out that none of these judgments appear to have moral normativity.

However, his later essay "The Nature of Moral Philosophy" (NMP) distinguishes several kinds of normativity and outlines some criteria for distinguishing two kinds of moral obligation. As in *Principia*, in NMP too, Moore started out by relying on the everyday practice of moral appraisal, which he took to provide a pre-theoretical grasp of what morality is. Since in his view this practice rests on generally correct intuitions about which concepts and judgments are moral and which aren't, the practice provides a "rough" understanding of morality and of what separates moral normativity from rational, epistemic, prudential, and legal normativity. Accordingly, Moore noted that:

> [w]e all make a distinction between a man's moral character, on the one hand, and his agreeableness or intellectual endowments on the other. We feel that to accuse a man of moral misconduct is quite a different thing from accusing him merely of bad taste, crude manners, stupidity or ignorance.
>
> (NMP: 311)

In this passage he is pressing a familiar, "overridingness" criterion for drawing the distinction between moral and non-moral normativity, according to which moral normativity is more authoritative and stringent than normativity of most other kinds, such as epistemic, conventional, and legal normativity. Moore appears to endorse a strong version of this criterion, one that vindicates the *universal* overridingness of morality (Gert and Gert 2016/2002). However, the overridingness criterion of moral normativity need not commit him to the controversial claim that moral rules are more authoritative than the rules of *any* other normative system, including the system of rationality. A weaker criterion of morality's overridingness may allow Moore to say that, in certain circumstances, the requirements of rationality might compete with moral requirements. Any such scenario creates a dualism of practical reason that, if Sidgwick was right, would amount to a problem for an impartialist utilitarian theory, including Moore's ideal utilitarianism. After all, it seems plausible that, in a circumstance there might not be a sufficient reason to choose between these two opposing principles,

1. Rational egoism – The principle that one ought to do only what's best for oneself.
2. Impartialist utilitarianism – The principle that one ought to do only what's impartially best for most concerned.

Consider a scenario where an agent faces the choice of saving herself or risking her life to save five other people, while the loss of her life would produce little pain (say, no one cares about this agent). What ought she to do? On Sidgwick's view, in a scenario of this sort there is an irresolvable standoff between two competing obligations, with no stronger reason for the agent to choose one obligation over the other. By contrast, the Moore of *Principia* is a consequentialist unwilling to grant that rational normativity might compete with moral normativity on occasion, thus failing to see the problem identified by Sidgwick's dilemma of practical reason.

Finally, note that, although Moore (like most non-naturalists of his time) did not address specifically the relation between morality and reasons for action, it is safe to say that he had an objectivist conception of that relation. Given that conception, any justified judgment of moral obligation counts as a categorical, decisive reason for acting in a certain way *provided the agent has no excuses*. Moore would have rejected conceptions restricting the source of reason for action to one's present or ideal desires, as Bernard Williams's desire-fulfillment theory of moral obligation maintains. In the current debate involving this subjectivist theory and its objectivist rivals, there is no doubt that Moore would have been in the objectivist camp.[2]

OBLIGATION AND ACCOUNTABILITY

Let's now turn to Moore's analysis of the relation between moral obligation and ascriptions of moral responsibility to agents. Some elements of this analysis support a conclusion considered in the next section, namely, that Sidgwick's famous attempt at analyzing 'good' in terms of 'ought' fails to produce the reductive analysis he had in mind.

Moore's analysis of obligation in NMP draws attention to the rules that govern deontic judgments about acts and omissions, on the one hand, and feelings and propositional attitudes (i.e., psychological attitudes, of which beliefs and desires are paradigms), on the other. Moore noted the differential strength of moral accountability associated with deontic judgments of either sort and attempted to account for this difference by holding that, under normal circumstances, agents often can (in some sense) act or refrain from acting if they choose to do so. But they cannot adopt or reject feelings and propositional attitudes voluntarily even if they choose to do so. As a consequence of this difference, the rules of moral duty governing deontic judgments vary accordingly, depending on whether they apply to either acts and omissions or feelings and propositional attitudes since

> [Our] feelings are not, as a rule, directly within the control of our will in the sense in which many actions are. I cannot, for instance, by any single act of will directly prevent from arising in my mind the desire for something that belongs to someone else ... But though I thus cannot prevent myself altogether from coveting my neighbour's possessions, I can altogether prevent myself from stealing them. The action of stealing, and the feeling of covetousness, are clearly on a very different level in this respect. The action is directly within the control of my will, whereas the feeling is not. If I will not to take the thing ... *it does in general follow directly* that I do not take it; whereas, if I will not to desire it, *it emphatically does not, even in general, follow directly* that no desire for it will be there.
>
> (NMP: 316–317, my emphasis)

Consistent with Kant's well-known principle that 'ought' implies 'can,' Moore writes "it cannot be true that you 'ought' to do a thing, unless it is true that you *could* do it, *if* you chose" (ibid.: 317). Given that principle, ascriptions of moral accountability are governed by different constraints depending on whether any given obligation involves an act/omission or a psychological state (a feeling or a propositional attitude). The constraint for psychological states concerns what an agent *can* do or feel/believe if she chooses to. The sense of 'can' relevant to this constraint is the one at work in the Kantian *dictum*, which, like other classical non-naturalists, Moore accepted (hereafter 'the Kantian sense').

Accordingly, a deontic moral judgment often expresses a decisive reason for an agent to act or refrain whenever the agent can (in the Kantian sense) if she chooses to. By contrast, in the case of a certain feeling or attitude any seemingly deontic moral judgment may *only* appear to express a decisive reason for an agent to either adopt or reject it. The judgment provides a weaker, subjunctive-conditional reason because the agent cannot (in the Kantian sense) adopt or reject that feeling or attitude even if she chooses to. Among Moore's favorite examples of judgments that express reasons of one type or the other figure,

10   Stealing is wrong.
11   Love your enemies.
12   Covetousness is wrong.

On this analysis of moral obligation, under normal circumstances judgment 10 would have the force of a decisive reason to avoid stealing (ibid.: 316–320). The same can be said *mutatis mutandis* of the force of proscriptions such as 'Thou shalt not lie' and 'Thou shalt not murder.'[3] However, under normal circumstances, 11 and 12 would not have the force of decisive reasons to love one's enemies and to avoid the feeling of covetousness respectively since, given the account above, the 'ought' featured in these judgments can amount only to a conditional reason for adopting or rejecting a certain feeling. A reason of this sort plays the role of an *ideal* that *would* entail an ascription of praise or blame only if the agent *could* (in the Kantian sense) love her enemies or avoid covetousness if she chooses to. By contrast, the acts and omissions subject to strictly deontic judgments "very often" are something "we could do, if we chose" (ibid.: 317). When an agent feels covetousness, there is no guarantee that she could cease to covet even if she chooses to. However, generally she *will* refrain from covetous *actions* if she chooses to.[4] In consequence, not all ascriptions of moral responsibility based on ought-judgments qualify for having decisive normative force. Only judgments involving acts or omissions generally do have such a force, while judgments involving feelings and attitudes may have only the force of an ideal obligation for the agent and may therefore be considered closer to evaluative judgments than to deontic ones.

Supporting an analysis of moral oughts along these lines are intuitions stemming from everyday moral appraisal, which suggest to Moore that, depending on whether a moral obligation concerns acts/omissions or feelings/propositional attitudes, one of the following rules would govern it:

A. *Rule of Duty* – A moral rule with the normative force of what an agent has a decisive reason to do or omit doing in the circumstances. Any qualifying acts or omissions must be such that, (1) the agent will act or refrain if she chooses to do so, and (2) she can (in the Kantian sense) act or refrain in the circumstances.
B. *Rule of Ideal Duty* – A moral rule with the force of a conditional reason to adopt or reject a certain feeling or propositional attitude. Any qualifying feeling or attitude must be such that, (1) there is no guarantee that the agent will adopt or reject it even if she chooses to do so, and (2) she cannot (in the Kantian sense) adopt or reject it in the circumstances.

Moore called these rules 'rule of duty' and 'ideal rule' respectively. All present, past, and future acts or omissions and feelings or propositional attitudes are governed by a rule of one or the other type. In an ordinary ascription of moral praise or blame, a type-A rule is at work. For example, when someone judges retrospectively, 'In that circumstance, she ought not to have Φ,' on the basis of a deontic judgment presupposing that there was a decisive reason for her not to Φ and she could have refrained from Φ-ing had she chosen to do so. A type-B rule is at work when someone judges, 'In that circumstance, she ought not to have had feeling Ψ,' on the basis of a quasi-deontic judgment presupposing an *ideal* reason for her not to adopt feeling Ψ. To paraphrase Moore's words above: had she *will* not to adopt Ψ, "it emphatically does not, even in general, follow directly" that a rejection of Ψ will follow.

However, finding moral normativity in certain mental states was not a new idea in Moore's time since we can trace ascriptions of moral normativity to mental states at least to Aristotle's *Nicomachean Ethics* and all subsequent developments in virtue theory. Neither were the two types of rule of moral obligation noted in NMP, a distinction with which the classical non-naturalists were familiar, at least from the work of Sidgwick. After all, in *Methods* (1967/1874: 33),

Sidgwick distinguished two kinds of ought-judgments, depending on whether an agent generally can or cannot (in the Kantian sense) act or feel in a certain way. For feelings and propositional attitudes, the 'ought' in the judgment represents an "ideal or pattern" that an agent must "imitate" when she could. Nevertheless, not only does Moore's analysis put Sidgwick's insight in a perspicuous way. As I show next, it can contribute a fine-grained distinction of evaluative and deontic judgments to discussions of the nature of moral language and thought, as well as dispel a misleading interpretation of Sidgwick's attempt at a reductive definition of 'good.'

THE EVALUATIVE/DEONTIC DISTINCTION

Let's first consider what Moore's analysis can contribute to Michael Smith's criterion for the evaluative/deontic distinction, which, painting with broad strokes, states "those normative claims that entail the possibility of holding some agent responsible are deontic, whereas normative claims that do not entail such a possibility are evaluative" (2005: 10). Smith goes on to consider deontic, as opposed to evaluative, any normative judgment that raises the issue of the agent's responsibility *immediately* or, as Moore would put it, *directly* in the sense of requiring no further premises. Given this criterion, from a judgment such as 10 above, if I nonetheless steal and lack an excuse, it follows *immediately* that I did something wrong and am the subject of moral blame. By contrast, in the case of an evaluative judgment, any attribution of responsibility requires further premises. Smith would agree, since he writes:

> Flowers and sunsets and some person's feeling a pain are all subject to evaluative judgments, while someone's having done something he ought not to have done is subject to a deontic judgment. Only in the latter case does the issue of the agent's responsibility arise immediately.
>
> (ibid.: 11)

Plausibly, such differential intuitions concerning moral accountability in the case of deontic and evaluative judgments rest on conceptual connections constitutive of the ordinary practice of normative appraisal.

Now Moore's analysis suggests that in the cases of deontic judgments concerning acts and omissions, ascriptions of responsibility to an agent *do* require at least the further premise that the agent can (in the Kantian sense) act or refrain if she chooses to. Therefore, appraisals of the agent's responsibility in these cases do not in fact follow *directly*. However, assuming that agents often can, say, refrain from stealing or breaking a promise if they choose to, we may ignore this complication in order to focus on how his analysis can be put at the service of rendering Smith's evaluative-deontic distinction more fine-grained. The key to this is Moore's ideal rule of duty, which govern normative judgments about feelings and propositional attitudes. Recall that according to Smith, ordinary intuitions about the concepts at stake in certain normative judgements are the key to distinguishing *evaluative* and deontic appraisals, with ascriptions of moral accountability justified directly only in the case of deontic appraisals. But there is a third category of judgment, arguably governed by an ideal rule: normative judgments about feelings and psychological attitudes. By contrast with evaluative judgments about sunsets and flowers, it makes sense to judge in retrospect that, for example, 'I ought not to have felt covetous in that circumstance if I could have avoided it.' In other words, 'I ought not to feel covetous' warrants a conditional ascription of blame even when it is closer to an evaluative judgment than to a deontic judgment. We should consider it a quasi-deontic judgment, given Moore's analysis of moral obligation.

That analysis thus contributes to an improved taxonomy of the evaluative/deontic distinction of judgments that features, at one extreme, deontic judgments involving acts and omissions, from which categorical ascriptions of accountability arise immediately in the sense of not requiring further premises except for the general assumption that, under normal circumstances, agents often can in a Kantian sense act or refrain if they choose to. At the other extreme are evaluative judgments, from which ascriptions of moral responsibility do not follow immediately. In between, there is a penumbra of *quasi*-deontic moral judgments involving feelings and propositional attitudes. About these, ascriptions of moral responsibility have the form of subjunctive conditionals about what an agent should feel or believe if she could (but she generally cannot even if she chooses to do so).

DID SIDGWICK REDUCE 'GOOD' TO 'OUGHT'?

An account of the evaluative/deontic distinction sensitive to Moore's analysis may also reveal the misleading character of a common contrast drawn between the goodness-first doctrine of *Principia Ethica* and Sidgwick's ought-first doctrine. It is often said that, unlike Moore, Sidgwick defined the evaluative in terms of the deontic. After all, he considered 'ought' definitionally prior to 'good,' and offered a seemingly reductive definition of 'good' in terms of 'ought' – roughly in terms of what ought to be desired by an agent with an ideal psychology. However, since desires are propositional attitudes, plausibly the 'ought' relevant to Sidgwick's definition is governed by Moore's ideal rule of moral duty. As argued above, such oughts have a quasi-deontic normative status since in their case the issue of an agent's accountability arises only ideally, thus warranting ascriptions of praise or blame of a subjective conditional form. 'What ought to be desired' is clearly closer to an evaluative predicate akin to 'what's desirable' and even 'what's good in itself' than to predicates that express a decisive obligation, one that is governed by a rule of duty of the sort stated by Moore. As a result, Sidgwick's definition of 'good' appears circular and by no means amounts to reducing 'good' to 'ought' as Darwall (2007) and other critics have thought. That is, Sidgwick can claim only to have offered a non-reductive definition of 'good' in quasi-deontic terms that are not radically different from the evaluative predicates 'desirable' and 'intrinsically good.' Arguably, other putative reductive definitions of 'good' into some other moral term or terms deemed more basic, such as Broad's (1942) in terms of 'what's fitting to desire as an end' are amenable to a Moorean reply along similar lines.

10.2 OBLIGATION, VALUE, AND PRACTICAL REASON

We now turn to a debate concerning what the Moore of *Principia* was committed to saying about the relation between moral obligation, intrinsic value, and reasons for action or attitude. Given the doctrines of moral semantics and metaphysics in this book, the term 'good' in its primary ethical use captures the sole basic ethical concept and property. By contrast, other key ethical terms such as 'right' and 'virtue' capture structured concepts and properties, which admit of reductive analyses by decomposition into the basic concept and property of ethics together with some naturalistic or metaphysical ethical concepts and properties. In the case of 'right,' *Principia* has it that, when used to express moral obligation, it is analyzable in terms of *the action that would produce the most intrinsic goodness among options available to an agent in the circumstances*.[5] But, as noted earlier, by 1912, in *Ethics*, Moore proposed a pluralism according to which there are two basic ethical terms, 'good' and 'right.' By his own recollection, Russell's (1904) review of *Principia* had persuaded him that his attempt in *Principia* to reduce 'right' in part in terms of 'good' was vulnerable to objection by the OQA. Russell argued:

> I hold that this is not a definition, but a significant proposition, and in fact a false one. It might be proved, in the course of moral exhortation, that such and such an action would have the best results; and yet the person exhorted might enquire why he should perform the action. The exhorter would have to reply: "Because you ought to do what will have the best results." And this reply distinctly adds something. The same arguments by which good was shown to be indefinable can be repeated here, *mutatis mutandis*, to show the indefinability of ought.[6]

To Moore's credit, he had abandoned the view that 'ought' can be defined at least in part in terms of 'good' in less than ten years after publication of *Principia Ethica*.

'GOOD' OR 'OUGHT'

In any case, contemporary critics, such as Darwall (2006; 2007), Parfit (2011), and Scanlon (1998), for a number of reasons disagree with Moore's early view about which term of ethics is definitionally prior, 'good' or 'ought.' Rejecting his view that the concept expressed by the term 'right,' when used to convey moral obligation, is reducible in part to intrinsic goodness, they find more perspicuous Henry Sidgwick's account of the matter.

According to this account, the sole simple concept of ethics is that expressed by the deontic term 'ought,' and 'good' is analyzable in terms of *what ought to be desired in a circumstance by an ideally rational agent* (Sidgwick 1967/1874: 92n, 112, 381, 388). In arguing for the definitional priority of 'ought' over 'good' Sidgwick had insightful comments on the distinctions between deontic and evaluative concepts as well as inside these categories of normative concepts. Prominent among them is that 'ought,' understood in a wide sense, expresses what an agent has *most* reason to do or refrain from doing in a circumstance, and therefore amounts to the most authoritative prescriptive concept. By contrast, 'good' expresses merely an "attractive" concept (ibid.: 105–106).[7] If a witness ought to tell the truth, that amounts to a decisive normative reason for the witness to tell the truth. However, if truth-telling is simply a good thing, that amounts to nothing more than having some reason for regarding their truth-telling *favorably*.

Another source of support for the definitional priority of 'ought' is the fact that this term does not admit degrees in ordinary speech and thought. By contrast, evaluative terms generally admit of positive, comparative, and superlative degrees – as exemplified by 'good'/'better'/'best' and their counterparts 'bad'/'worse'/'worst.' Moreover, as argued in Section 10.1, of normative judgments featuring one or the other type of normative terms, only those featuring deontic terms seem to warrant direct ascriptions of responsibility to agents. These sorts of features encourage critics like Darwall (2006; 2007) to consider 'ought' more suitable for grounding the reactive attitudes commonly associated with ordinary ethical reasoning, such as esteem, respect, benevolent concern, remorse, and contempt.

But Moore can resist these familiar reasons for the definitional priority of 'ought' and any other deontic term. After all, although *thin* evaluative terms, such as 'good' and 'bad,' may be less authoritative than 'ought,' *thick* evaluative terms such as 'cruel,' 'unjust,' 'abusive,' 'grateful,' 'compassionate,' and the like, may occur in judgments whose prescriptive force is as strong as that of an 'ought' judgment. For instance, if Hitler's actions were evil, that counts as a decisive reason to refrain from performing actions analogous to Hitler's. At the same time, not all 'oughts' have the prescriptive force of a duty, all things considered, since some may involve only the weaker notion of a Rossian *prima facie* duty or duty other things being equal. Moreover, as suggested by Thomas Hurka (2014: 51), for Moorean non-naturalists, intrinsic value can have the force of a decisive reason whenever it occurs in the superlative form *best*. After all, in their view, an action that maximizes goodness compared with any alternatives open to the agent in the circumstances is best in an objective, agent-neutral way that is consistent with Moore's own understanding of intrinsic value. Moore explicitly rejected an agent-relative notion of intrinsic goodness, especially in the course of attempting to show the incoherence of ethical egoism. However, since his argument to demonstrate the incoherence of ethical egoism is invalid, for no obvious reason some critics appear to have taken the failure of this argument to tip the scale in favor of Sidgwick's ought-first view.[8] Yet the invalidity of Moore's argument against ethical egoism is consistent with the truth of his agent-neutral notion of intrinsic goodness as well as with his claim about the definitional priority of 'good.'

In any case, those who favor Sidgwick's view over Moore's tend to think that a reductive definition of 'good' in terms of 'ought' is available, namely, Sidgwick's attempted definition. But if my discussion of that definition in Section 10.1 is on the right track, the term 'ought' in its *definiens* ('what ought to be desired') is governed by an ideal rule of duty and therefore falls short of expressing the kind of decisive reason of a truly deontic 'ought' governed by a rule of duty. As I argued above, the predicate 'what ought to be desired' does not differ greatly from 'desirable' -- and even from 'good in itself,' the very predicate Sidgwick was attempting to define in partly deontic terms.

CAN THE BUCK-PASSING ACCOUNT TIP THE SCALES?

Like Sidgwick, the early Moore also favored a monist view, according to which there is only one irreducible ethical property to which other ethical properties reduce in part. But while the term 'ought,' in its primary ethical sense, denotes that property in Sidgwick's ought-first monism, it is the term 'good' that plays that role in Moore's goodness-first monism. Our discussion in the previous section found no conclusive argument for preferring one monism over the other. However, given another line of argument, non-naturalists should prefer Sidgwick's ought-centered monism to solve a puzzle raised in Moore's *Principia* about how to anchor non-natural concepts and properties in the natural world. As an alternative to Moorean non-naturalism, Thomas Scanlon (1998; 2014) has proposed the so-called buck-passing account (BPA) of the relation between ought and reason. This account, combined with an ought-first monism, might better accommodate ordinary explanations of that relation and have less puzzling ontological implications. But why think that the BPA makes such a critical difference in favor of an ought-first non-naturalism? And is Moorean non-naturalism inconsistent with Scanlon's BPA?

Let's consider these questions in turn, beginning with a rough outline of what make some critics think that an ought-first non-naturalism enhanced with the BPA is comparatively better positioned (1) to meet objections from the alleged extravagant metaphysics of non-naturalism; and (2) to accommodate some common intuitions about the relation between value and practical reason (Stratton-Lake and Hooker 2006). In what follows I'll focus on these questions and omit any independent assessment of the BPA.[9] However, a rough approximation to it is needed first.

The BPA, though anticipated by a number of moral philosophers (Brentano 1969/1902; Broad 1933–1934; Ewing 1939; 1947; 1959; Frankena 1942) owes its present-day construal to Scanlon. Apparently, Scanlon arrived at it by reflecting on the OQA of *Principia Ethica*, which he reads as arguing for the non-naturalist thesis that there are irreducible ethical properties (1998: 19). Any attempted reductive analysis of ethical properties into purely naturalistic properties would fail because it would have an open "feel." In the course of presenting his take on the OQA, Scanlon also drew attention to what is in fact an old debate among classical non-naturalists about which ethical properties should count as basic or underivative. Of the two camps in this disagreement, theorists sympathetic to the BPA are in the deontic-property-first camp because they hold that only the property expressed by a deontic term (generally, 'ought' or 'fitting') can play that role.[10]

Concerning evaluative properties, the BPA theorists make two claims:

BPA's positive claim: Evaluative properties are higher-order properties of some lower-order natural properties.

BPA's negative claim: Evaluative properties are not reason-providing.

Given Moore's moral metaphysics, of necessity intrinsic goodness or value depends metaphysically on some of the natural properties of the object that has that value. Thus, it is unclear why a Moorean should reject the BPA's positive claim. About its negative claim, critics argue that the Moore of *Principia* was committed to rejecting this claim, which arguably is plausible. In order to assess this claim about the BPA's negative claim, let's take a quick look at Scanlon's two arguments for it. Following Roger Crisp (2005: 81), I call these arguments "Redundancy" and "Pluralism." Redundancy purports to show that it is always a certain natural property or other that amounts to what needs invoking in ordinary ascriptions of reasons for action or attitude. If so, then evaluative properties would be redundant. This argument proceeds by cases: if a resort is pleasant, it is its pleasantness that fully explains why one should visit or recommend it; if one's tooth is aching, it is its painfulness that fully explains why one should go to the dentist; and so on. For Scanlon, "it is not clear what further work could be done by special reason-providing properties of goodness and value, and even less clear how these properties could provide reasons" (1998: 97).

On the other hand, "Pluralism" has it that since the things that can be said to be good vary greatly (e.g., knowledge, pleasure, enjoyment of a friendship, benevolent concern, etc.), "[t]here does not seem to be a single, reason-providing property that is common to all these cases" (ibid.: 98). But now it is unclear what the objection is. Perhaps it charges that the pluralist normative theory of *Principia* conflicts with an attempt at having a parsimonious moral ontology behind Moore's monism about key ethical properties. However, there are reasons to think that Moorean non-naturalism is committed to neither monism nor pluralism in normative ethics. And in moral metaphysics, although *Principia* features a monist view of the simple properties of ethics, *Ethics* features a pluralist view of good and right. This change, which involved no substantive revision to Moore's non-naturalism, is consistent with a minimalist moral ontology. It appears, then, that Pluralism fails to get off the ground, leaving Redundancy as the only argument for the only building block of the BPA that appears incompatible with his doctrine.

Redundancy raises questions about Moore's actual commitments when it comes to explaining the relation of value and practical reason. Can Moore accommodate the intuitions fueling Scanlon's cases? Must he postulate a "special reason-providing" property of goodness or badness to account for the reason for recommending the resort or going to the dentist? I believe he can accommodate those intuitions by invoking the view noted above, according to which he treated intrinsic goodness (or its counterpart, badness) as a higher-order property of having some lower-order natural properties that are "ought-implying" and thus reason-providing – so that the pleasantness of the resort or the painfulness of the tooth is itself ought-implying. He held this view consistently in all his ethical writings, from *PE* (pp. 161–162) and *EE* (p. 44) to RC (p. 604). Even when he rejected the BPA theorists' attempt at reducing intrinsic value to ought or practical reason, he can accommodate the view that some natural properties are sources of normativity.

Supporting this line of reply are passages of *Principia* featuring goodness as equivalent to what ought to exist, ought to be, or ought to be promoted.[11] In Moore's view, the natural properties on which goodness thus conceived supervenes are associated with ought-to-be reasons that are normative.[12] Once the textual evidence from *Principia* is taken into consideration, it looks like Moore's view of the relation between value and practical reason is compatible with the BPA. After all, thus reconstructed, it holds that to say that a natural property of a thing is good is to say that there is a reason to pursue it, or to promote it, or to bring it into existence. If there is a reason to promote, say, states of admiration of beautiful objects, this reason is agent-neutral: the agent must promote these states whether she likes it or not. Any rational beings could become aware of this reason purely in virtue of their rationality. Thus, since the reason in question is of an objective, absolute kind, the view still comes out as incompatible with a number of naturalist outlooks in ethics, from non-cognitivism, metaethical relativism and fictionalism to relativism and naturalistic realism.

True, in §90 of *Principia*, Moore wrote that judgments about what's good in itself rest on no further reason, a statement that Stratton-Lake and Hooker (2006) interpret as supporting that he assigned no role to natural properties in explaining an agent's reason for action or attitude. But this interpretation misrepresents what Moore is up to in the relevant passages of *Principia Ethica*. According to Stratton-Lake and Hooker, he was committed to the view that if a certain experience contains some pleasure, the goodness of the pleasure is what fully explains why there is a reason for bringing that experience about whenever possible. Similarly, the badness of a toothache would fully explain why there is a reason for going to the dentist, etc. But in the section of *Principia* at stake here, Moore was unconcerned with the relation between value and practical reason. He was instead referring to the epistemic non-naturalist thesis that judgments about what's good in itself are self-evident or *a priori* in the sense that no reason or evidence is needed for their justification. Thus, Stratton-Lake and Hooker's attempt to argue for the incompatibility of Moore's non-naturalism with the BPA fails.

In conclusion, given the textual evidence, Moore was never committed to holding that the explanatory buck stops at intrinsic value: he could pass it to the natural properties on which the value of a thing supervenes. The key to this line of reply is his conception that some natural properties are ought-implying. Furthermore, the accounts of the relation of value to practical reason presented by Moore, Broad (1933–1934) and some other early non-naturalists or their non-cognitivist rivals (e.g., Hare 1952), who also vindicated the supervenience of the moral on the natural, need not raise more puzzles than Scanlon's. After all, we ordinarily explain that a certain action must be performed *because* it will produce greater happiness or that an action must be avoided because it will produce uncompensated pain, leaving implicit that happiness is good and pain bad. With regard to the issue of which of the two accounts scores highest in ontological parsimony, for the reasons discussed above, I agree with those who see no significant difference between the goodness-first non-naturalism of *Principia* and an ought-first non-naturalism enhanced with the BPA (Olson 2006). As noted above, in *Ethics*, Moore offered a less parsimonious ontology owing to his becoming a pluralist about unanalyzable normative properties. But perhaps the small price he thereby paid in parsimony was compensated by a reduction of the number of "confusions and invalid arguments" he later found in *Principia* (A: 27).

NOTES

1 Like some other classical non-naturalists, Moore did not draw a sharp line between Ought, Duty, and Obligation. On his view, several acts or omissions might be right if they equally maximize intrinsic value, but only one of them is the agent's duty in a circumstance (*E*: 14).

2 Moore's moral rationalism commits him to being in the objectivist camp of Derek Parfit (2011) and Thomas Scanlon (1998) rather than in the desire-based-theory camp of Bernard Williams (1985). He would have rejected Williams's claim that if a person is being given all the information about why she needs to take a certain medicine, and the person still doesn't want to take it, then she doesn't have any reason to take it.

3 Moore (*PE*: §94, 204). Arguably, one may have sufficient rational reasons to lie or to steal – say, to save one's children – and therefore one may have sufficient reason to do wrong morally. But as noted earlier, Moore focused narrowly on moral obligation and neglected to consider scenarios that featured a competing rational obligation, in fact, ruling out the dilemma of practical reason raised by Sidgwick.

4 Moore's analysis of moral obligation relies in part on his conception of free will, which has been very influential but falls beyond what I can consider in this chapter.

5 Moore (1903a: 122) offered a parallel, consequentialist definition of 'right' in an early review of Brentano's *The Origin of the Knowledge of Right and Wrong*, where he equates 'right' with action "which will cause the whole state of the Universe to have as much intrinsic value as possible."

6 See Russell's (1904) "The Meaning of 'Good.'" Moore's preface to the second edition of *Principia Ethica* (P2: 5) and his contribution to the Schilpp collection (RC: 558, 611) credited this objection by Russell with having prompted his change of mind about the definability of 'right.'

7 Sidgwick also recognized the especial or "narrow" sense that 'ought' has when ranging over feelings and propositional attitudes. He argued that an 'ought' of this sort amounts to an ideal or pattern that agents should "imitate" if they could. This sense of ought probably motivated Moore's distinction of rule of duty and rule of ideal obligation discussed here in Section 10.1.

8 Moore (*PE*: §59, 150). For more on Moore's rejection of ethical egoism in *Principia*, see Chapter 11.

9 For other objections facing the BPA, see Olson (2006; 2013).

10 In addition to Scanlon (1998; 2014), I include in this camp Crisp (2005; 2008), Stratton-Lake (2002b), and Stratton-Lake and Hooker (2006). The nomenclature used here to refer to Scanlon's arguments is from Crisp (2005: 81).

11 In *Principia Ethica*, Moore used a number of paraphrases of 'good' such as 'intrinsic value,' 'what ought to be and what ought to exist for its own sake' (as opposed to 'what ought to exist for the sake of some effect'). See, for example, Chapter 1 §13, Chapter 3 §§40 and 59, Chapter 4 §§68, 69, 70, and 76, and Chapter 5 §§90, 104, 109, and 134.

12 For more on this, see Chapter 9.

SUGGESTED READING

Chang, Ruth, "Practical Reasons: The Problem of Gridlock," in *The Bloomsbury Companion to Analytic Philosophy*, Barry Daiton and Howard Robinson eds., London: Bloomsbury Academic, 2014, pp. 474–499. An outline of normative practical reason, a comparatively recent area of metaethics, that pays some attention to the non-naturalists' commitment to *sui generis* moral facts in order to explain reasons for action or attitude.

Crisp, Roger, "Goodness and Reasons: Accentuating the Negative," *Mind* 117 (2008): 257–265. In reconstructing Scanlon's buck-passing account of the relation between value and practical reason, Crisp argues that to avoid eliminativism about goodness, a revised account should hold only that being good is not itself reason-providing.

Henne, Paul, Vladimir Chituc, Felipe de Brigard, and Water Sinnott-Armstrong, "An Empirical Refutation of 'Ought' Implies 'Can'," *Analysis* 76(3) (2016). An experimentalist critique of the Kantian rule that 'ought' implies 'can,' which the authors rightly associate with Moore's conception of moral obligation. Plausibly claims that Moore would regard that rule as having the status of a synthetic *a priori* truth, something that the authors challenge by appeal to empirical counterexamples.

Hurka, T., "'Ought' and 'Good'", in *British Ethical Theorists from Sidgwick to Ewing*, Thomas Hurka ed., Oxford: Oxford University Press, 2014, pp. 44–64. Excellent discussion of opposite claims made by classical non-naturalists about their underivative/derivative distinction of ethical concepts and properties. Hurka sees a circularity problem facing some reductive definitions of 'good' in terms of 'ought' or 'fitting.'

Olson, Jonas, "G. E. Moore on Goodness and Reasons," *Australasian Journal of Philosophy* 84 (2006): 525–534. Proponents of the buck-passing account regard its two core theses about the relation between value and practical reason as incompatible with Moore's account. According to one thesis, it is not value properties but rather the properties upon which value supervenes that provide reasons to respond in certain ways. According to the other, value reduces to practical reason. Olson argues that Moore's account is incompatible only with the latter thesis. See also Olson (2013).

Scanlon, T. M. *What We Owe to Each Other*, Cambridge, MA: Harvard University Press, 1998. *Locus classicus* for the buck-passing account of the relation between value and practical reason. Moore may accept most of Scanlon claims about moral obligation in Chapter 1 on reasons – except Scanlon's claim that some psychological attitudes such as contempt and admiration also support direct ascriptions of responsibility.

Smith, Michael, "Meta-ethics," in *The Oxford Handbook of Contemporary Philosophy*, Frank Jackson and Michael Smith eds., Oxford: Oxford University Press, 2005, pp. 3–30. Includes moral normativity within the broader class of normative reasons, which may be either deontological or evaluative. In moral appraisal, deontic judgments differ from evaluative judgments in that only the former judgments support direct ascriptions of responsibility to an agent. I argue above that Moore's analysis of moral obligation calls for a refinement of Smith's criterion for the evaluative/deontic distinction. Of interest in this chapter is also Smith's thesis that Moore and Sidgwick did not disagree about 'good' but had in mind different concepts of goodness.

Stratton-Lake, Philip and Brad Hooker, "Scanlon versus Moore on Goodness," in Terence Horgan, and Mark Timmons eds., *Metaethics after Moore*, Oxford: Clarendon Press, 2006, pp. 149–168. Contrasts Scanlon's buck-passing account of the relation between value and practical reason with what it takes to be Moore's buck-stopping account of that relation, charging that, of the two, it is only Moore's account that requires an appeal to spooky non-natural properties in order to explain common responses to some natural properties.

11

NORMATIVE ETHICS AND THEORY OF VALUE

11.1 IDEAL CONSEQUENTIALISM, CLASSICAL UTILITARIANISM, AND ETHICAL EGOISM

With Hastings Rashdall and John McTaggart, Moore was among the early classical non-naturalists who vindicated an ideal or agathistic variety of consequentialism, also known as 'ideal utilitarianism.' Like classical utilitarianism, this variety is a maximizing, impartialist, indirect, act consequentialist theory. But, as discussed in this chapter, ideal consequentialism has some substantive points of disagreement with other consequentialist theories, including classical utilitarianism and ethical egoism. Moore devoted Chapter 3 of *Principia Ethica* to object to the hedonism of Mill and Sidgwick and sharpened his objections to classical utilitarianism in two chapters of *Ethics*.[1] About ethical egoism, he went from regarding it as self-contradictory in *Principia* to claiming in *Ethics*, more modestly, that it is self-evidently mistaken.

DOI: 10.4324/9780429275975-11

This chapter first considers Moore's theory of right conduct in the context of other consequentialist theories. After establishing its merits and demerits, the chapter takes a closer look at Moore's theory of value.

THEORY OF RIGHT CONDUCT

Moore's ideal consequentialism takes the deontic status of an action to depend entirely on the value of its effects and is therefore a form of *act* consequentialism. Like classical utilitarianism, ideal consequentialism would agree with the following principles of conduct:

1. An act or omission is obligatory just in case (and because) it would produce the highest overall balance of intrinsic value for those most affected by it than would any alternative available to the agent in the circumstances.
2. An act or omission is permissible just in case (and because) it would produce at least as high an overall balance of value for those most affected by it as would any alternative available to the agent in the circumstances.
3. An act or omission is forbidden just in case (and because) it would fail to produce at least as high an overall balance of value for those most affected by it as would any alternative available to the agent in the circumstances.

Principles 1–3 are consistent with classical utilitarianism as well as with Moore's remarks in Chapter 5 of *Principia Ethica*, "Ethics in Relation to Conduct" (§§86–109). Given these principles, first, establishing the deontic status of an action involves piecemeal consideration of the value of its effects. Second, morality requires the maximization of value. That is, agents act wrongly *whenever they fail* to choose the action that produces most value or at least as much value as any alternative available to them in the circumstances. (In Moore's time, there was no satisficing competitor to maximizing forms of consequentialism, and he contemplated no such option.) Third, the weighing of the value of the effects that determine the deontic status of an action is agent-neutral, universalist, and impartialist.[2] The agent-neutrality of the principles entails that, *contra* relativism and subjectivism, ascriptions of value do not necessarily involve the perspective of the agent. Their universalism and impartialism entail that an action count as right only if it is the action that would produce at least as great a sum of value as any alternative actions available to an agent in a circumstance for the aggregate of all affected by it *without prioritizing the interests of any member of the aggregate.* Moore explicitly endorsed these features of consequentialism in the course of objecting to ethical egoism and when he said that the interests of no individual or group have more weight than anyone else's (*E*: 121) – as did Jeremy Bentham in his famous formula, "Everyone to count for one, no one to count for more than one."

Rule consequentialist or indirect-act consequentialist?

The above principles outline how ideal consequentialism goes about accounting for the deontic status of acts and omissions. But as a theory of general normative ethics, ideal consequentialism needs to provide, in addition to a criterion of right conduct, a decision procedure capable of offering determinate moral guidance to agents in situations where they must decide what to do or believe morally. A chief practical problem facing ideal consequentialism and other varieties of act consequentialism is their seeming failure to provide such guidance, especially in light of constraints in time and ability for calculating the effects of actions. Act consequentialism appears to require that agents be able to establish quickly all alternatives open to them and calculate their short- and long-term effects. This creates a practical problem that, as we'll see, Moore attempted to solve by appeal to the generally used rules of common morality. But there are other options. Motivated at least in part by the same problem is rule consequentialism, a family of consequentialist theories that determine the deontic status of any action according to whether the action conforms with a moral rule whose application over time, if nearly everyone conforms to it, would maximize value. A rule consequentialist may adopt these principles of right conduct,

1. An action is obligatory just in case (and because) it conforms with a moral rule which, if nearly everyone conforms to it, would produce the best outcome among all alternatives available to an agent.
2. An action is permissible just in case (and because) it conforms with a moral rule which, if nearly everyone conforms to it, would produce at least as high an overall balance of good outcome as would any alternative available to an agent.
3. An action is forbidden just in case (and because) it conforms with a moral rule which, if nearly everyone conforms to it, would produce an outcome less good than some alternative available to the agent.

Given principles along these lines, the deontic status of an action is not determined directly by the value of its effects but rather by whether in performing it the agent conforms or fails to conform with some moral rules that are themselves assessed in terms of their conduciveness to the maximization of value (Slote 1992: 58–59; Timmons 2013: 112–113). An agent may act rightly even where her action falls short of producing as much value as any alternative available to her in the circumstances.

Moore cannot accept such a verdict. Given his ideal consequentialism, if an agent failed to perform the action that would produce as much value as any alternative available to her in the circumstances, she acted wrongly. In determining the deontic status of an action, besides the value of its 'total' effects, other considerations do not matter: neither that an action may fall within a class of actions that typically have the best outcome, nor that it may be an application of a moral rule whose systematic observance would maximize value over time. Yet as previously noted, aware of the practical problem facing any attempt to determine the total effects of an action, given act consequentialism, Moore recommended that in deciding what to do or believe morally in a situation agents follow the generally used rules of common morality (*PE*: §91, 198/201; §§95/98, 205/211). On his view, act consequentialism provides what is now known as a criterion of rightness (i.e., an explanation of why an act is right or a duty) while the generally used rules of common morality provide a decision procedure (i.e., moral guidance and justification for ascriptions of praise or blame to an agent). Traceable to Mill and Sidgwick but first clearly articulated by Moore, this indirect or 'two-level' theory became a key feature of some later attempts to solve the practical problem facing act consequentialism.[3]

Moore recommended the generally accepted rules of common morality as a decision procedure on the grounds that doing so is conducive to best results over time. He probably joined the camp of indirect consequentialism motivated by his expansive view of the effects that matter in determining the deontic status of an action, according to which they extend infinitely into the future. Moreover, he was skeptical about agents' ability to identify accurately all alternatives available to them in a circumstance and to predict the immediate and future value of the effects of each of them. Here is how he described these difficulties:

> In order to shew that any action is a duty, it is necessary to know both what are the other conditions, which will, conjointly with it, determine its effects; to know exactly what will be the effects of these conditions; and to know all the events which will be in any way affected by our action throughout an infinite future. We must have all this causal knowledge, and further we must know accurately the degree of value both of the action itself and of all these effects; and must be able to determine how, in conjunction with the other things in the Universe, they will affect its value as an organic whole. And not only this: we must also possess all this knowledge with regard to the effects of every possible alternative; and must then be able to see by comparison that the total value due to the existence of the action in question will be greater. But it is obvious that our causal knowledge alone is far too incomplete for us ever to assure ourselves of this result, that an action is our duty: we can never be sure that any action will produce the greatest value possible.[4]

True, Moore also thought that the effects of an action get somewhat diluted over time, as other contributory causes intervene. But they do not disappear. Furthermore, there is the additional problem of agents' biases, which might lead them, for example, to underestimate the pain their actions would inflict on others, or exaggerate their good effects when the agents themselves or their nearest and dearest stand to benefit from an action.

All these practical difficulties suggested to Moore that the observance of some general rules of common morality is the best consequentialist policy. On his account, although such rules cannot compare with the laws of science, which express empirically necessary truths, they can compare with scientific predictions, which express generalizations from experience about certain effects and have greater probability of being true than any known alternative. These rules of thumb (Smart 1956) have the force of guidelines prescribing refraining from killing, keeping promises, telling the truth, and so on. Although they by no means prescribe courses of action in all situations, they do issue prescriptions for a limited set of types of action that are *"likely to occur to any one and to* produce the greatest sum of good" (ibid.). Moore considered these rules not only helpful in compensating for our epistemic limitations and biases but also necessary for social stability – or as he put it, for the preservation of civilized society. In fact, contributing to this end is necessary for any rules of common morality to be eligible as an action-guiding rule. Qualifying rules must also have universality in the sense of being generally accepted at all times and places. Rules of common morality that lack universality merely express the "ideals" of isolated groups and often remain unobserved even by members of the groups who have them. In *Principia*, the prescription to preserve chastity illustrates rules of this idiosyncratic kind. According to Moore, while agents may flout such rules, they must always observe the universal rules of common morality without exception. They must do so even in a situation where they have a high degree of confidence that some action other than the one prescribed by a certain generally used rule of common morality is more likely to produce a greater sum of value.

At the same time, on this account the rules of common morality fall short of warranting that the action they prescribe in a particular situation is in fact a duty, since

> [I]f we are subsequently persuaded that any possible action would have produced more good than the one we adopted, *we admit that*

we failed to do our duty. It will, however, be a useful task if Ethics can determine which among alternatives likely to occur will produce the greatest total value. For, though this alternative cannot be proved to be the best possible, yet *it may be better than* any course of action which we should otherwise adopt.

(PE: §91, 199; my emphasis)

To sum up, given Moore's ideal consequentialism, in deciding how to act, an agent must follow any generally accepted rules of common morality relevant to the situation at hand simply because actions in conformity with these rules *are more likely* to produce the most value. She should observe these rules even in situations where she confidently predicts that such rules prescribe an action that will fail to produce as much value as some alternative available to her in the circumstances. In a case of this sort, Moore can accommodate the commonsense intuition that her decision was justified and she is not blameworthy if she acted in conformity with a qualifying rule. But he would say that her action was wrong, since some available alternative with a better outcome *was in fact her duty.* To account for the agent's justification, Moore would *not* invoke the expected outcome of her action since, like the classical utilitarians, he was in the actualist camp of the actualist/expectabilist debate within consequentialism. His account falls within an actualist consequentialism because it holds that what makes an action right or wrong is the objective, total value of its consequences, not what an agent believes that its value might be. And since it separates the question of what determines an action's deontic status from the question of how to decide what to do in a circumstance, it is a form of act consequentialism akin in this respect to classical utilitarianism.

Urmson on Moore's consequentialism

J. O. Urmson takes Moore's ideal consequentialism to open up a new possibility for utilitarians: they can consistently combine act consequentialism and rule consequentialism depending on whether they are concerned with a criterion of rightness or a decision procedure.[5] According to Urmson, Moore has shown not only that these aspects of a moral theory are distinct but also that there is no inconsistency in invoking act consequentialism as a criterion of rightness and rule consequentialism as a decision procedure.

Yet arguably Moore has nothing to gain by following Urmson's casting of ideal consequentialism since he then would need to meet some common objections facing rule consequentialism, which range from problems of coherence and indeterminacy to the charge that it is extensionably equivalent to act consequetialism.[6] Although a full discussion of these objections would carry us far afield from our present concern, we can nonetheless note that Urmson's suggestion conflicts with the textual evidence from *Principia Ethica*. For its Chapter 5 makes clear that, on Moore's ideal consequentialism, deontic status is contingent on the value of outcomes and the observance of commonly accepted rules of common morality never determines whether any action counts as right or a duty. Thus, an action may be wrong even if the agent was justified in taking it because she observed a commonly used, universal rule of common morality. To illustrate this interpretation of ideal consequentialism, consider a scenario inspired in one of Urmson's cases. Suppose you find young Adolf Hitler drowning in a ditch, recognize him, and save him. In doing saw, you followed a generally used rule of common morality prescribing something like, 'Whenever you can save someone at no great risk of your own, you ought to do so.' Given ideal consequentialism as outlined in *Principia*, your action was justified and you are blame-free. But since it failed to maximize value over time for most concerned, your action was morally wrong. After all, the world was not made better off by your failing to let Hitler die at a young age. Moore is committed to these judgments since his ideal consequentialism combines each of these theses:

A. The deontic status of an action rests entirely on the value of its effects.
B. For some classes of action, ascriptions of moral responsibility (praise or blame) rest entirely on an agent's observance of any generally used rules of common morality that applies in the circumstance.

C. In the absence of any generally used rules of common moral-
    ity relevant to the circumstance, agents must calculate for
    themselves the action that, among alternatives available to
    them, maximizes intrinsic value.

Rule consequentialists need not accept B and would definitely
reject A and C. Their key disagreement with Moore is on what
determines the deontic status of an action. He holds that it is
something along A's lines and therefore qualifies as an act consequentialist. Accordingly, rule consequentialists and Moore need
not agree about the deontic status of your action in the Hitler scenario. For Moore, since you complied with an appropriate rule of
common morality, you are not blameworthy but your action was
morally wrong because it failed to maximize value. For the rule
consequentialists, its deontic status depends on whether it instan-
tiates a rule that, if generally observed, maximizes value over time.
  Of course, avoiding the problems facing rule consequentialism
does not rid ideal consequentialism of some problems of its own.
Among these, let's briefly consider indeterminacy and conservatism. The problem of indeterminacy concerns a theory's ability to
guide action. It arises for ideal consequentialism because, besides a
few examples of the rules of common morality that agents should
strictly follow such as 'Do not murder,' Moore provided neither
determinate criteria for inclusion of a rule within the set of relevant
rules, nor determinate criteria for ranking these rules. The lack of
such criteria entails that on occasion, when two or more rules of
common morality pull in opposite directions, agents would be left
without guidance about what to do or believe morally. And since
on Moore's view the rules of common morality can provide guidance only for some classes of action, arguably in many cases an
action would fall outside those classes, and agents would be left to
calculate by themselves which of the alternatives available to them
in the situation would maximize value. In consequence, given ideal
consequentialism, agents would often lack guidance about which,
if any, such rules best applies to a situation. Thus, Moore's appeal
to the generally used rules of common morality hardly solves the
practical problem facing his normative theory and other types of
act consequentialism, such as classical utilitarianism.

A conservatism problem also arises in connection with Moore's appeal to the generally used rules of common morality as a decision procedure. Some critics take his appeal to have reformist, even liberating, implications; others find its implications exceedingly conservative.[7] Although the textual evidence from Moore's writings does not support a strong conclusion either way, I believe it provides more ammunition for the conservatism camp. True, it follows from Moore's view on what correct the procedure for moral decision-making is that agents very often must calculate the value of outcomes by themselves, and this "liberates" them from the strictures of moral principles (except of course for the act consequentialist principles outlined at the beginning of this chapter). But it is hard to square this liberationist interpretation with Moore's defense of the observance of the relevant rules of common morality, namely, that these rules prescribe what is best for the preservation of the social order. As argued earlier in Chapter 2, this defense tips the scale in favor of the conservatism objection to his normative theory.

AGAINST ETHICAL EGOISM

For the Moore of *Principia Ethica*, consequentialism is true by definition of the key deontological concepts 'right' and 'duty.' That is, consequentialism is analytically true. Accordingly, assertions such as 'I am morally bound to perform this action' and 'This action will produce the greatest amount of good in the Universe' are semantically identical.[8] But after agreeing with Bertrand Russell that this early attempt at defining 'right' is vulnerable to an Open Question Argument, in *Ethics*, he compared the truth of consequentialism with some self-evident, though synthetic, truths of math and logic (*E*: 26–27). Either way he begged the question against critics of consequentialism in general, and of his preferred brand in particular. For if ideal consequentialism is self-evident, just by understanding it, any rational thinker would grasp its truth. Its truth would then count as *a priori* in the sense of being accessible just by thinking.[9] Yet as some critics point out (Gert 2007; Shaw 2000), by holding the self-evidence of his brand of consequentialism, Moore simply rejected without argument a long and varied history of rival consequentialist and non-consequentialist normative theories, from ethical egoism to deontology and virtue ethics. Each of these would be self-evidently false, given Moore's claim. In fact, he embraced such immodest implications here:

> It seems to me *self-evident* that knowingly to do an action which would make the world, on the whole, really and truly worse than if we had acted differently, must always be wrong. And if this be admitted, then *it absolutely disposes of the view that there are any kinds of action whatever, which it would always be our duty to do or to avoid, whatever the consequences might be.*
>
> (*E*: 94, my emphasis)

Accordingly, Moore also regarded as self-evidently true the maximizing, universalist, consequentialist principle "that it must always be our duty to do what will produce the best effects upon the whole" (ibid.: 100). However, Moore needs an independent argument if he is to rule out representative competitors of this principle, such as ethical egoism, whose central principle he construed in this way:

> The principle of Ethical Egoism – What's good for me (or my own good) is the sole ultimate good.

From this principle, the ethical egoist can infer rules of right conduct according to which, in any particular circumstance,

A. A moral agent has a *direct* duty to promote her own interests and no one else's.
B. A moral agent has at most only an *indirect* duty to promote anyone else's interests: she must promote such interests if and only if (and because) by doing so she promotes her own interests.

Given A and B, each agent has a duty only to herself and not to others *as such*. A and B make up an ethical egoist theory incompatible in at least two points with some of Moore's central views in metaethics and normative ethics. First, it conflicts with his conception of goodness as a simple, indefinable and unanalyzable intrinsic property since, thus construed, ethical egoism defines intrinsic value in terms of *what's good from the first person's perspective*. Second, it conflicts with his view that intrinsic value ought to be promoted universally (i.e., for all affected by the consequences of our acts and omissions) and impartially (i.e., in non-prioritarian and agent-neutral ways). On ideal consequentialist assumptions, an agent's duty is always to act in the way that would produce the greatest possible balance of intrinsic goodness over intrinsic evil, regardless of the individual interests of those affected by the action. Accordingly, there is only one justification for producing the greatest sum of goodness for a restricted group, such as the agent herself and/or her family, friends, country, and the like. It consists in the indirect justification that by producing the greatest sum of goodness for a restricted group, agents would produce the greatest net balance of goodness over evil on the whole. Like the classical utilitarians, Moore was committed to invoking such indirect justification in order to accommodate intuitions from commonsense morality and considered judgment that support the existence of special obligations to restricted groups, the so-called nearest and dearest. But unlike his rival ethical egoists, Moore would have difficulties in accommodating those intuitions and also runs into the so-called demandingness problem facing also other proponents of universalist, impartialist forms of consequentialism.

Without acknowledging this advantage of ethical egoism, the Moore of *Principia Ethica* focused on charging that this ethical theory is self-contradictory since it allegedly entails that a thing that is good absolutely must belong to the agent exclusively. On his charge, assuming that happiness is the sole intrinsic good, ethical egoism is committed to simultaneously affirming and denying the proposition 'My own happiness or interest is [the sole] good.' But if happiness were the sole good, it would be good absolutely, and therefore "it would be strange that other people's happiness should not be good too" (*PE*: §59, 149/150). The problem for this line of objection is that it relies on a construal of the egoist's principle according to which the term 'good' stands for a complex predicate that is analyzable in terms of 'x is good absolutely and is mine.' Moore thus conflates the ethical egoist's agent-relative concept of goodness with his own agent-neutral concept. As a result, he mistakenly charged that ethical egoism is self-contradictory since surely, nothing that is good absolutely can be 'private' in the sense that others should not have it too. Here is how Moore stated this objection:

> The only reason I can have for aiming at my own good, is that it is good absolutely ... But if it is good absolutely that I should have it, then everyone else has as much reason for aiming at my having it, as I have myself. If, therefore, it is true of any single man's interest or happiness that it ought to be his sole ultimate end, this can only mean that that man's interest or happiness is the sole good, the Universal Good, and the only thing that anybody ought to aim at. What Egoism holds, therefore, is that each man's happiness is the sole good—that a number of different things are each of them the only good thing there is—an absolute contradiction!
>
> (*PE*: §59, 150/151)

But the objection seems a strawman argument because except for a vague reference to some "English Hedonists" of the seventeenth and eighteenth centuries, Moore provides no evidence for thinking that in fact there are proponents of the ethical egoist doctrine he is attempting to refute in this passage. Furthermore, as noted in C. D. Broad's "Certain Features in Moore's Ethical Doctrines" (1942), Moore fails to articulate a reason against ethical egoism since his argument in *Principia Ethica* has not shown it to be *self-contradictory* but merely *contrary* to his brand of consequentialism. As a result, both Moore's "ethical neutralism" and ethical egoism can be false. In addition, if Broad is right, there is a modest ethical altruism that is a better alternative to Moore's ideal consequentialism because it can accommodate common intuitions about special obligations to the nearest and dearest.

Moore later avoided charging ethical egoism with self-contradiction. In *Ethics*, he claimed instead that it is *self-evidently* mistaken though it can be neither decisively proved nor decisively refuted (*E*: 120–121). Yet if self-evidently mistaken, ethical egoism would be *a priori* false. Its falsity would be graspable directly to any rational thinker who has thought hard enough about this moral theory – something that seems implausible in light of the long and varied history of ethical egoism. Once again, Moore begged the question against a rival normative theory.

11.2 VALUE PLURALISM AND HOLISM

Besides the theory of right conduct outlined in Section 11.1, Moore's practical ethics rests on an objectivist, pluralist theory of simple things that have intrinsic value and an invariabilist, holistic, or non-additive approach to the value of wholes. Thus supplemented, ideal consequentialism avoids one of the problems facing classical utilitarianism: how to accommodate the intuitions of common morality in the case of deserved retributive punishment. However, as discussed later here, Moore's alternative account of the justification of retributive punishment, together with the value pluralism and holism that fuel it, is far from being objection-free.

WHAT'S WRONG WITH SIDGWICK'S ARGUMENT FOR HEDONISM

Classical utilitarianism and ideal consequentialism share among other defining features their being value-based, maximizing, impartialist forms of act consequentialism. Nevertheless, these moral theories disagree about the number and nature of the non-moral properties that have intrinsic value. Moore rejected the value monism as well as the hedonism of classical utilitarianism, which we may construe as the following theses:

> Value Monism – The thesis that there is just one intrinsic value, and one intrinsic evil.
> Hedonism – The thesis that intrinsic value consists exclusively or primarily in pleasure, and intrinsic disvalue consists exclusively or primarily in pain.

Classical utilitarianism's combination of value monism and hedonism conflicts with common morality, which rules out the idea that nothing but pleasure may increase the intrinsic value of a complex state of affairs or "whole": not an addition of knowledge, or virtue, or the enjoyment of human affection, or the appreciation of beauty (*PE*: §50, 113; *E*: 123). It conflicts also with the value judgments of some major moral theories, from natural law theory and Aristotelian virtue ethics to Kantian and Rossian ethics. Nevertheless, the reasons for the above theses may be strong enough to outweigh any objection from such conflicts. Among them, Moore examined and rejected two reasons. One was Mill's attempted "proof" of hedonistic utilitarianism, considered here in Chapter 6, which he showed to be invalid. The other was Sidgwick's argument for hedonism, to which we now turn. Given this argument, although besides pleasure there are other states of consciousness that seem good, their value must be instrumental since pleasure is the sole part that *no* whole may lack if it is to have any intrinsic value. Moore must object to this argument owing to the following three theses of his own theory of value:

> Value Pluralism – The thesis that there is more than one intrinsic good and one intrinsic evil.
> Impersonal Perfectionism – The thesis that some moral ideals or perfections are objective ultimate ends, completely independent of how they might affect the welfare of persons.
> Value Holism – The "principle of organic unities" sanctioning that the value of a whole need not be equal to the sum of the value of each part.

Given value pluralism and impersonal perfectionism, intrinsic value consists neither exclusively nor primarily in pleasure or any other welfarist value postulated by a standard utilitarian theory. Given value holism, the value of some wholes may arise in the combination of parts that have little or no value on their own. Unless Sidgwick could rule out value holism, the following objection gets off the ground:

> The argument [Sidgwick's] is calculated to mislead, because it supposes that, if we see a whole state to be valuable, and also see that one element of that state has no value by itself, then the other element, by itself, must have all the value which belongs to the whole state. The fact is, on the contrary, that, since the whole may be organic, the other

element need have no value whatever, and that even if it has some, the value of the whole may be very much greater.

(*PE*: §55, 144)

If a certain valuable whole containing some pleasure is governed by the principle of organic unities, then it is possible that pleasure has little or no value on its own even if removing it from the whole would result in a complete loss of value. Moore can accept that the addition of pleasure to, say, the contemplation of a beautiful object makes a substantial difference in the value of the whole, while insisting that this does nothing to support hedonism. After all, the value of the aggregate need not hinge on pleasure but rather on the combination of its parts itself: what determines value may be the unity of *pleasure-in-the-contemplation-of-beauty* even if each of the parts of this whole on its own has little or no value at all.

For the Moore of *Principia* that is precisely the case of pleasure, to which he ascribed little or no value on its own. "It is quite possible," writes Moore, "that this constituent [pleasure] also has no value in itself; that value belongs to the whole state, and to that only ..." (ibid.: §55, 144). He was skeptical also about the value of any whole consisting in a cognitive state without the right emotion such as a state of contemplation of beauty without an appreciation of it. By contrast, pleasure *in* the contemplation of beauty, a whole made up of a cognition and the right emotion, has great value. About any valuable whole, Moore countenanced two ways in which its value may be calculated: *as a whole* and *on the whole* – where the relevant distinction runs this way:

> Value as a whole – The value of a whole regarded as a new complex state of affairs. It need not be equal to the sum of the value of each part.
> Value on the whole – The value that results from the sum of the value of a whole as a whole plus any value of its parts.[10]

For example, suppose pleasure-in-the-contemplation-of-beauty has great value as a whole. It would have even greater value on the whole if it turns out that pleasure and beauty have some intrinsic value on their own. The value of this unity on the whole would be calculated by adding to its value as a whole whatever values these parts may have. (But recall that in Moore's view, contemplation is a cognition and cognitions have no independent value.) The value of pleasure or of beauty on its own seems comparable to the value of a pinch of salt. Having little culinary value on its own, when mixed with other ingredients, a pinch of salt may create a meal that's tasty as a whole. Now suppose no other ingredients of some meal have value on their own. Furthermore, if the salt is removed, the meal would cease to be tasty. To claim from these premises that salt is the only valuable culinary element in the meal would seem as fallacious as Sidgwick's argument to the conclusion that pleasure is the sole intrinsic value. Undermining his argument seems to be the so-called fallacy of division, or the mistake of thinking that, since a whole has a certain property, therefore one or more of its parts must have that property.

Finally, is the consciousness of pleasure, or more generally consciousness itself, always required for intrinsic value? To these questions, Moore gave inconsistent answers. On the one hand, in *Principia Ethica*, he ran a thought experiment that entails that the intrinsic value of beauty and disvalue of ugliness are independent of any consciousness of them.[11] On the other, in *Ethics*, he wrote:

> [i]t does seem as if nothing can be an intrinsic good unless it contains both some feeling and also some other form of consciousness; and, as we have said before, it seems possible that amongst the feelings contained must always be some amount of pleasure.
>
> (*E*: 129)

ORGANIC UNITIES AND VINDICTIVE PUNISHMENT

Given Moore's principle of organic unities, the value of a whole need not be proportional to the value of any of its parts, whether these be pleasure, beauty, knowledge, or any other simple intrinsic good (*E*: 126–128). Chapter 6 of *Principia* offers a sophisticated taxonomy of complex goods in the course of which Moore made insightful points about "unmixed" and "mixed" goods and evils. To the category of "unmixed" goods (§§113/122) belong two wholes he considered ideal or good *to the highest degree*: aesthetic enjoyments and the pleasures of human intercourse or personal affection. The category of mixed goods comprises wholes that "though intrinsically good *as wholes*, nevertheless contain, as essential elements, something positively evil or ugly ...." Similarly, mixed evils are wholes that are bad but also "contain, as essential elements, something positively good or beautiful" (*PE*: §124: 256–257). This holistic, pluralist conception of value allows Moore to account for a number of cases of practical ethics that raise problems for standard utilitarian theories. He can explain, for example, the evil of sadistic pleasure or any other whole made up entirely of an experience of pleasure, something that has some intrinsic good, toward what intentionally causes pain and is wicked or cruel.

Most notably, unlike standard utilitarians, Moore can accommodate the retributivist intuitions of commonsense morality about "vindictive" or deserved punishment.[12] According to those intuitions, any scenario featuring someone who has inflicted pain on an innocent party but is later caught and punished adequately is far better than another scenario featuring a miscreant who goes unpunished. Classical utilitarians generally face a problem in accommodating such judgments because, arguably, punishment maximizes pain for all concerned. On Moore's account, retributive punishment qualifies as a mixed good in which the pain of the punishment and the wickedness of the crime are each bad on its own, but their combination results in something better as a whole than an alternative scenario of crime without punishment. This account has three building blocks: Moore's intrinsicalist conception of the supervenience of the moral on the purely descriptive (considered here in Chapter 8), his principle of organic unities, and his invariablitist approach to the value of the parts of a whole. According to this approach, the following is true:

> Invariabilism – A part of a whole retains its value as the part travels from whole to whole.

Invariabilism follows from Moore's narrow intrinsicalist conception of moral supervenience whereby what determines value necessarily is one or more of the natural properties of a thing. Any two things that are identical in their intrinsic natural properties must have exactly the same value and to the same degree.[13] Suppose that pain equals C-fibers firing and pain is bad. It follows from Moore's intrinsicalist supervenience thesis that any identical states of C-fiber firings must be equally bad. But given his holistic (non-additive) view of organic unities, a whole containing parts that are bad on their own may nonetheless be good as a whole and sometimes also good on the whole – provided it has some valuable parts whose values, when added to the value as a whole, are great enough to outweigh the badness of some or all of its parts. The standard competitor of invariabilism is variabilism, construed as the following claim:

> Variabilism – A part may change its value as it travels from whole to whole.

Variabilists reject the three theses underwriting Moore's account of retributive punishment: invariabilism about the value of parts of wholes, a non-additive conception of organic unities, and intrinsicalism about the supervenience of value on the purely descriptive. They combine variabilism together with an additive conception of the value of wholes, and an extrinsicalist or externalist supervenience thesis, according to which the value of a thing may necessarily supervene more broadly on some of its external properties. To support an externalist conception along these lines, Jonathan Dancy (2007) appeals to cases suggesting that context has a bearing on value since, for example, a joke about someone may be funny if told behind that person's back, but not funny if told to the person's face. If so, the property of being funny for a joke necessarily depends at least in part on factors outside, or external to, the joke.

   These rival accounts of the value of wholes make up a current organicity debate about which more needs to be said in order to decide which of the competitors is more plausible. But of concern to us here is the more modest question of whether Moorean invariabilism or its variabilist rival can better accommodate common morality's retributivist intuitions about deserved punishment.

Variabilism has implications that conflict not only with common morality but also with many philosophical traditions. For it is committed to the provocative claim that pain changes its value from bad to good as it enters, for example, a scenario of vindictive punishment. Yet it offers no explanation of how pain, widely considered bad (in common morality as well as moral theory) could become something good as it enters this whole. Furthermore, if pain does become something good, then as pointed out by Thomas Hurka (2003), inflicting it on the guilty cannot count as punishment. It seems less puzzling to say, following Moorean invariabilism, that, although pain is always bad, a whole containing it as retributive punishment for a crime is good as a whole and better on the whole than the scenario of a crime without punishment (*PE*: §128, 262; *E*: 130). This view can accommodate intuitions about retributive justice while at the same time being in a position to explain why punishing the innocent seems always wrong, something that creates trouble for standard utilitarian theories.

THE IDEAL

In Chapter 6 of *Principia Ethica*, "The Ideal" (§§110–135), Moore looked closely not only at a number of simple goods that appear to have no other single feature in common except for each being worth pursuing as an ultimate end. In this category fall pleasure, beauty, and knowledge, among other simple intrinsic goods.[14] He also paid attention to some complex intrinsic goods, a category that comprises any state that combines a cognition with some positive feeling or attitude toward what is intrinsically good or beautiful, such as the admiration of a beautiful object and the enjoyment of a friendship. Moore claimed that qualifying complex states of affairs such as these have more value when the feelings or attitudes apply to objects that are real rather than imaginary. Furthermore, although some of these goods require for their instantiation a conscious experience (aesthetic pleasures and the pleasures of "human intercourse"), a thought-experiment to be considered in the last section of this chapter suggests that for Moore beauty may amount to a simple good that is independent of any state of consciousness. Yet on his account, beauty does not have great intrinsic value on its own, even when its value may be greater than that of pleasure or knowledge (*PE*: §50, 135). However, the *appreciation* of beauty has great value (ibid.: §113, 237/238). In fact, this complex good, together with the pleasures of personal relationships, "among all the wholes composed of elements known to us ... seems to be 'better than all the rest'" (ibid.: §111, 234). In the case of each of these complex goods, Moore held that although its parts have little or no value on their own (except for the persons who are the object of pleasure in human intercourse), their combination creates a whole that is ideal or good to the highest degree. Here is his claim:

> By far the most valuable things, which we know or can imagine, are certain states of consciousness, which may be roughly described as the pleasures of human intercourse and the enjoyment of beautiful objects. *No one, probably, who has asked himself the question, has ever doubted* that personal affection and the appreciation of what is beautiful in Art or Nature, are good in themselves; nor, if we consider strictly what things are worth having purely for their own sakes, does it appear probable that any one will think that anything else has nearly so great a value as the things which are included under these two heads.
>
> (ibid.: §113, 237; my emphasis)

Needless to say, a perfectionism of this sort is vulnerable to a number of objections. To begin with, it is unclear why a whole consisting in the appreciation of a beautiful object is more valuable when involving a real rather than a fictional object: Moore offered no supporting reason for such a Platonist claim that might have bridled with his art-obsessed friends in Bloomsbury. Second, there is a tension between one of Moore's two ideal goods and his maximizing, impartialist, act consequentialism. After all, this normative theory requires maximizing what is good impartially considered, and this on occasion might conflict with the maximization of a personal good such as the enjoyment of an interpersonal relationship (Hooker 2000: 139). Third, a puzzle arises for Moore's claim that pleasure and even beauty, each of which has at most little value on its own, can render a whole good to the highest degree when combined with a cognition that has no value on its own. Moore needs a strong reason to the effect that this excess in value results from the emergence of a new, complex relational property such as experiencing-pleasure-in-the-contemplation-of-beauty.

Fourth, Moore's choice of the things that are intrinsically good to the highest degree conflicts with intuitions from common morality as well as from several major moral theories. Accordingly, some critics, such as Bertrand Russell in a 1903 review of *Principia Ethica*, have questioned that choice, even when Russell agreed with Moore that "it is the whole as such, namely, the emotion towards an appropriate object, which has value." But Russell found Moore's choice of values for the role of the ideal too narrow in that it leaves out many other things that better qualify for being good to the highest degree. In my view, it leaves out most notably complex states involving the right attitude toward non-maleficence, broadly construed as the avoidance and prevention of uncompensated harms.

Fifth, on Stuart Hampshire's (1987) related critique, Moore's conception of the ideal in *Principia* results from his personal failure to address the most pressing issues of practical ethics of his time. True, Moore's ethical writings fail to engage ethical issues concerning massacres, genocide, torture, corruption, and other social ills of the early twentieth century. And unlike Russell, Moore failed to denounce promptly the moral wrongness of World War I. But Hampshire seems to have no strong *ad hominem* here since, as noted in Chapter 2, some of his disciples were able to put the normative theory in Chapters 5 and 6 of *Principia* at the service of justifying their own progressive social and political agendas. They were able to do so because, by contrast with standard utilitarian theories, Moore's normative theory has the resources to prioritize the avoidance and prevention of harm over the promotion not only of simple intrinsic values (pleasure, knowledge, and the like) but also of complex intrinsic values such as the ideal. After all, we'll see next that on that theory, given equal amounts of pleasure and pain, the intrinsic evil of pain far outweighs the intrinsic value of pleasure.

AN ASYMMETRICAL ACCOUNT OF THE VALUE OF PLEASURE AND THE EVIL OF PAIN

Chapter 6 of *Principia Ethica* features a particularly insightful discussion of the value of pleasure and the disvalue of (intense) pain in which Moore plausibly maintains that, given equal units of pleasure and pain, the disvalue of pain far outweighs the value of pleasure. More precisely, the consciousness of pain is by far a greater evil than the consciousness of pleasure a good (*PE*: §127: 260/261). On this account, pain and pleasure differ at least in two respects: (1) the proportion of disvalue and value that each respectively determines; and (2) the contribution each makes to the organic whole in which they occur. Pleasure is not a great good on its own "even if it has some slight intrinsic value ... [but] pain (if we understand by this expression, the consciousness of pain) appears to be a far worse evil than pleasure is a good" (ibid.: §127: 260). Furthermore, pleasure adds great value to a good whole while pain need not make an evil whole more evil. On the contrary, as we saw in the case of the pain inflicted as deserved punishment for a crime: in Moore's account, the pain contained in this organic whole contributes to its goodness as a whole.

There is abundant evidence that Moore's asymmetric assessment of the value of pleasure and the disvalue of pain better accommodates commonsense and considered judgment. As illustrated in many ethical codes of the professions from medicine and biomedical research to the law and journalism, the disvalue of causing uncompensated harms counts more morally than the value of promoting beneficial outcomes. Professional ethical codes accordingly assign greater stringency to duties of nonmaleficence over duties of beneficence. In medicine, for instance, the rule 'First, do no harm' is widely regarded as expressing a weightier duty than 'Promote well-being.'[15] While classical utilitarianism cannot accommodate such asymmetrical assessments of the value and disvalue of pleasure and pain, ideal utilitarianism can. Although Moore may acknowledge that a symmetrical account of the value of pleasure and the disvalue of pain seems neater, he can insist that this amounts to no objection to his account. After all, as he famously put it in *Principia*, "[t]o search for unity and system, at the expense of truth, is not, I take it, the proper business of philosophy, however universally it may have been the practice of philosophers" (ibid.: §134: 270).

On this issue, then, Moore's intuitions about value have the virtue of accommodating commonsense and considered judgment. Even so, his theory of value faces an indeterminacy problem similar to the problem facing other pluralist theories of value that do not rank the basic values they countenance. Since such values on occasion may come into conflicts, absent a principled way to resolve those conflicts, the theory cannot provide normative guidance. True, Moore's discussion of the ideal can be considered a (failed) attempt to offer guidance on how to rank complex states of affairs that are intrinsically good. And his discussion of the comparative value and disvalue of pleasure and pain contains subtle points for any welfarist conception of value. But more is needed to conclude that Moore's theory can help agents decide what to do or believe morally.

11.3   THE METHOD OF ISOLATION

However, Moore thought he had an intuition-based method for determining whether a thing has intrinsic value and to what degree, the so-called *method of isolation* (*PE*: §§55, 57, 112; *E*: 28). To see how it works, let's consider some examples. Suppose we want to determine by means of his isolation test which of two effects, A or B is intrinsically better. Our first step would be to use reflective judgment to decide whether A considered in isolation (i.e., on its own) has intrinsic value. That is, we want to know whether A is good in itself "quite apart from any accompaniments or further effects which it might have." Next, we would make an analogous inquiry about B. If it turns out that both A and B have intrinsic value, we would need to make a comparative judgment of their respective degrees of value. This judgment would hinge on the correct answer to the question, 'If A existed "quite alone" as the only thing in a universe, would that universe be better than a different universe containing only B?' According to the method of isolation, an affirmative answer entails that A is intrinsically better than B, while a negative answer leaves underdetermined whether A and B have the same degree of intrinsic value, or B is intrinsically better than A. Other inquiries to determine the intrinsic value of a simple property or a whole would proceed along relevantly similar lines.

In *Principia Ethica*, Moore deployed this method to argue against another pillar of Sidgwick's hedonist utilitarianism: the thesis that value is contingent on conscious experiences of pleasure and pain (ibid.: §50, 133/136). To show that a thing's intrinsic value need not depend on any state of consciousness, Moore invited his readers to consider two worlds, one very beautiful, the other very ugly. *Ex hypothesi*, in neither of these worlds are there any beings capable of having conscious experiences. He then asked which of these two worlds ought to exist and submitted that the obvious answer points exclusively to the beautiful world.[16] Once we assumed, as Moore did, that beauty is a type of moral goodness, then this thought experiment, if compelling, would provide a strong objection not only to Sidgwick but also to the entire classical utilitarian tradition that links right conduct to some form of conscious experience. For, given Moore's conclusion from his thought experiment, beauty is metaphysically independent of any such experience.

Yet Moore's reasoning is not compelling. A first line of reply simply rejects his thought experiment altogether, since there is logical space to insist that "we are in a position to make a judgment of intrinsic value only if we have experienced (or can imaginatively reconstruct) what it is like to be or to have what is being judged" (Kupperman 1982: 327). A second line of reply explains away Moore's intuitions about the two worlds by invoking, for example, our evolutionary history. On this reply, some Darwinian adaptations fully account for our aversion to ugliness and attraction to beauty: while ugliness lacks instrumental value, beauty is conducive to pleasure, preference satisfaction, or whichever natural property utilitarians associate with intrinsic value (Mulgan 2007: 22). And given a third line of reply, Moore was right that, of the two worlds in his thought experiment, the beautiful one ought to be real. But this reaction is consistent with a relativistic construal of beauty according to which beauty is an intrinsic value *for us*. Moore accepted without argument that beauty has absolute value, not just value for us. Once this assumption is abandoned, his thought experiment does nothing to support his view that intrinsic value need not depend on conscious experience (Kraut 2011). Either way, Moore's two-empty-worlds thought experiment seems viciously circular: its conclusion requires the assumption that some things are good or bad independent of anyone's states of consciousness, which amounts to the conclusion the thought experiment was intended to support.

NOTES

1 The term 'consequentialism' best captures Moore's normative theory because, as standardly construed, 'utilitarianism' denotes a monist consequentialist theory within which some welfarist value is the sole intrinsic value that can determine the deontic status of an action. By contrast, ideal consequentialism is a pluralist theory within which welfare, understood as pleasure and the absence of pain, is one among other intrinsic values. Moore's objections to standard welfarist forms of utilitarianism, focused on Mill and Sidgwick, appear mostly in Chapters 1 and 2 of *Ethics* and Chapter 3 of *Principia*.

2 For more on utilitarianism and the agent-neutral/agent-relative distinction, see Timmons (2013: 114–115) and Ridge (2005/2017).

3 R. M. Hare (1981) is commonly credited with first using the expression 'two-level theory' to characterize his own version of indirect consequentialism. Although Moore used neither of these terms of art, he showed more reflective awareness of this type of consequentialism than his predecessors Mill and Sidgwick.

4 Moore (*PE*: §91, 198/199). See also *PE*: §17, 74–75.

5 Urmson (1970: 345). See also Shaw (2000: 6).

6 For some of the problems facing rule consequentialism, see Smart (1956), Slote (1992), and Timmons (2013).

7 For Regan (1986), Shaw (2000), and Woolf (1960), Moore's practical ethics has reformist implications because in fact few rules of common morality satisfy his conditions to qualify as a decision procedure. Agents must then make their own decisions guided only by consequentialist calculations of the effects of their actions. By contrast, Hutchinson (2001), Hurka (2011b), and Russell (1903a) consider its implications too conservative because it recommends agents observe rules that may be in need of either revision or rejection even if they satisfy Moore's conditions.

8 Moore (*PE*: §89, 198). Similarly, Moore writes that "in asserting that a certain action is the best thing to do we assert that it together with its consequences presents a greater sum of intrinsic value than any possible alternative" (ibid.: §17, 76).

9 Cf. Shaw (2000), who argues that since in *Principia Ethica* consequentialism figures as true by definition, Moore is committed to its being provable. But he isn't, because Moore can say (and, in fact, he did assume) that consequentialism is self-evident, with neither *inference* nor evidence necessary for grasping its truth.

10 Thomas Hurka (2005/2015) outlines the relevant distinction in this clear way: "if x and y have values a and b on their own, and x-plus-y has value c as a whole," the value of x-plus-y "on the whole" is a + b + c. The value of the whole is therefore not equal to the sum of the values of its parts, but equal to a sum of which those values are constituents.

11 See Moore's two-empty-worlds thought experiment in the final section of this chapter.

12 Moore (*PE*: §§128/130). Critics of Moore's account of vindictive punishment and the invariabilist, holistic view of value that fuels it, include Hurka (2003) and Lemos (2015) in the sympathetic camp, Dancy (2007) and Zimmerman (2015) in the critical camp.

13 For more on Moore's commitment to invariabilism, see Heathwood (2013) and Dancy (2007). As formulated by Moore, the supervenience thesis that generates this commitment reads:

> it is impossible for what is strictly one and the same thing to possess ... [intrinsic] value at one time, or in one set of circumstances, and not to possess it at another; and equally impossible for it to possess it in one degree at one time, or in one set of circumstances, and to possess it in a different degree at another, or in a different set.
>
> (CIV: 260–261)

14 Although Moore's account of these intrinsic goods occurs chiefly in Chapter 6 of *Principia Ethica*, see also *Ethics*, pp. 128–129.

15 Some bioethicists further claim that nonmaleficience is the sole fundamental duty in medicine, and all other duties are derivative. See, for instance, "Principlism", in Gert, Culver, and Clouser (2006: 99–128).

16 In *Principia Ethica*, this rhetorical question is cast in terms of *rationality* for it reads "is it irrational to hold that it is better that the beautiful world should exist than the one which is ugly? Would it not be well, in any case, to do what we could to produce it rather than the other?" (*PE*: §50, 135). But as noted earlier, Moore drew no distinction between the normative concepts of rationality and morality.

SUGGESTED READING

Broad, C. D., "Certain Features in Moore's Ethical Doctrines," in Paul Arthur Schilpp ed., *The Philosophy of G. E. Moore*, Lasalle, IL: Open Court, 1942, pp. 41–67. Exposes the question-begging character of Moore's objection to ethical egoism in *Principia Ethica*. According to Broad, his own "self-referential altruism" can better accommodate common intuitions about agents' special moral obligations (toward their family, friends, community, etc.) than both Moore's "ethical neutralism" and ethical egoism.

Dancy, Jonathan, "Moore's Account of Vindictive Punishment: A Test Case for Theories of Organic Unities," in Susana Nuccetelli and Gary Seay eds., *Themes from G. E. Moore: New Essays in Epistemology and Ethics*, Oxford: Oxford University Press, 2007, pp. 325–342. Charges that Moore's invariabilism faces the problem of explaining how retributive punishment could turn out to be good when its parts are bad. By contrast, Dancy's variabilism avoids that problem because it allows for holding that in the context of retributive punishment the inflicted pain is good.

Driver, Julia, "The History of Utilitarianism," in *Stanford Encyclopedia of Philosophy*, Edward Zalta ed., 2014, https://plato.stanford.edu/entries/utilitarianism-history/ Detailed account of the development of standard utilitarian theories. Has a section outlining the core claims of Moore's ideal consequentialism as well as the challenges facing them.

Eggleston, Ben, "Act Utilitarianism," in *The Cambridge Companion to Utilitarianism*, Ben Eggleston and Dale E. Miller eds., Cambridge: Cambridge University Press, 2014, pp. 125–145. Good summary of act utilitarianism and the problems facing it. Offers an account of *indirect* consequentialism that is consistent with the account offered in this chapter.

Gert, Joshua, "Beyond Moore's Utilitarianism," in Susana Nuccetelli and Gary Seay eds., *Themes from G. E. Moore: New Essays in Epistemology and Ethics*, Oxford: Oxford University Press, 2007, pp. 307–324. Rehearses some of the standard objections to ideal consequentialism, such as that it neglects to consider moral obligation as a species of rational obligation and assumes the truth of utilitarianism. Agrees with Urmson on the view that Moore equivocated between act and rule utilitarianism (cf. Section 11.1).

Hurka, Thomas, "Moore in the Middle," *Ethics* 113(3) (2003): 599–628. Argues that Moore's invariabilism accounts for certain wholes such as retributive punishment better than his variabilist critics because these must say that in this context pain is good. But if so, inflicting it would not amount to punishment. Furthermore, Moore can better explain why the appropriate reactive attitude to deserved punishment is a mix of satisfaction with regret for causing pain.

Hurka, Thomas, "Common Themes from Sidgwick to Ewing," in Thomas Hurka ed., *Underivative Duty: British Moral Philosophers from Sidgwick to Ewing*, New York: Oxford University Press, 2011, pp. 6–25. Interprets the value pluralism of Moore as a moderate position that avoids the monism of standard utilitarian theories as well as the ultra-pluralism of particularist theories.

Kraut, Richard, "The Enjoyment of Beauty," in *Against Absolute Goodness*, New York: Oxford University Press, 2011, pp. 107–111. Partly agrees with Moore that, in his two-empty-worlds thought experiment, it is the beautiful, rather than the ugly, unexperienced world that ought to be real. But disagrees with him about the nature of beauty: instead of an absolute intrinsic value, it may have value *just for us*.

Kupperman, Joel J., "Utilitarianism Today," *Revue Internationale de Philosophie* 36(141) (1982): 318–330. A challenge to Moore's two-empty-worlds scenario from a utilitarian perspective. Contends that, first, our preference for beauty over ugliness is an automatic habitual attitude that has no tendency to support Moore's conclusion; and second, a real or imaginary experience of the thing being judged always fuels a judgment of intrinsic value.

Moore, G. E., Chapters 3, 5, and 6 of *Principia Ethica*, Cambridge: Cambridge University Press, rev. ed., Thomas Baldwin ed., 1993/1903. Key primary sources for Moore's ideal consequentialism. Chapter 3, "Hedonism" (§§36–65), takes issue with hedonistic utilitarianism, especially as formulated by Mill and Sidgwick. Chapter 5, "Ethics in Relation to Conduct" (§§86–109), outlines the ideal consequentialist alternative. Chapter 6, "The Ideal" (§§110–135) is the best source for a closer look at Moore's value pluralism and holism.

Moore, G. E., *Ethics*. London: Williams & Norgate, 1912, New York: Henry Holt, 1912 (page numbers to reprint Oxford: Clarendon Press, 2005). Perhaps the best source for Moore's critique of classical utilitarianism. Chapters 1 and 2 examine the challenges facing this normative theory and offer insightful accounts of the differential strength of moral right and Mill's view that some pleasures are intrinsically better than others. Chapter 7, the last in the book, offers a defense of Moore's ideal consequentialist alternative to hedonistic utilitarianism.

Mulgan, Tim, *Understanding Utilitarianism*, Stocksfield: Acumen, 2007. Excellent introduction to utilitarianism, especially classical utilitarianism. *Contra* Moore's two-empty-worlds thought experiment, Mulgan argues that humans may have an evolutionary built-in preference for beautiful over ugly things because beauty is a means to happiness.

Shaw, William H., "Between Act and Rule: The Consequentialism of G. E. Moore," in *Morality, Rules, and Consequences: A Critical Reader*, Brad Hooker, Elinor Mason, and Dale E. Miller eds., Edinburgh: Edinburgh University Press, 2000, pp. 6–26. Good outline of Moore's ideal consequentialism. About the controversy over whether this theory has conservative or reformist implications, Shaw supports the reformist-implications camp. True, for Moore only moral rules that are generally used must be observed without exceptions, and this seems to have conservative implications. But he also said that such rules are in fact very few in number and scope and this promotes individual decision-making.

Skelton, Anthony, "Ideal Utilitarianism: Rashdall and Moore," in Thomas Hurka ed., *Underivative Duty: British Moral Philosophers from Sidgwick to Ewing*, New York: Oxford University Press, 2011, pp. 45–65. Mostly devoted to the analysis of Rashdall's ideal utilitarianism. Argues that Moore's objection to Sidgwick's attempt to prove hedonism can be used against his own attempt to prove the truth of consequentialism in *Principia Ethica*. After all, from the fact that all right actions must produce some good outcomes, it does not follow that only good outcomes determine the deontic status of actions. However, as I discuss in Chapter 7, Moore considered consequentialism self-evident and therefore in no need of any proof.

Sylvester, Robert Peter, *The Moral Philosophy of G. E. Moore*, Ray Perkins and R. W. Sleeper eds., Philadelphia, PA: Temple University Press, 1990. An introduction to Moore's ethical writings up to the 1920s. Contains insightful comments and a critical bibliography compiled by the editors. *Contra* some critics, Sylvester sees a continuity between the moral metaphysics and epistemology of *Principia Ethica* and Moore's discussion of utilitarianism, egoism, and relativism in *Ethics*. Good source for a closer look at Moore's critique of Sidgwick.

Urmson, J. O., "Moore's Utilitarianism," in Alice Ambrose and Morris Lazerowitz eds., *G. E. Moore: Essays in Retrospect*, London: George Allen & Unwin, 1970, pp. 343–349. A classic of the literature on Moore's ideal consequentialism. Argues that Moore was able to meet a practical objection concerning the poor performance of consequentialism as a decision procedure by combining an act-consequentialist criterion of right conduct with a rule-consequentialist decision procedure. By contrast, on the interpretation proposed here, Moore proposes a consistent act consequentialism of the form sometimes called 'indirect' or 'two-level theory.'

EPILOGUE

The legacy of G. E. Moore and *Principia Ethica*

In his autobiography, G. E. Moore remarked that he was by disposition lazy. That assessment is, according to G. J. Warnock, consistent with the fact that Moore's philosophical writings were not "copious" compared with those of some of his contemporaries.[1] Together with Stuart Hampshire (1987), Warnock is perhaps one of the rare harsh critics of Moore's works within the ordinary language tradition of analytic philosophy, whose followers generally viewed favorably Moore's ability to accommodate intuitions from common sense and language use as well as to discover philosophical puzzles involving relations between propositions other than logical entailment and implication. Chapters 1 and 2 of the present book, largely focused on Moore's philosophical development and influence, offer evidence that counts for that positive reception of his works and against Warnock's comment, at least in the case of Moore's epistemological and ethical writings. For one

DOI: 10.4324/9780429275975-12

thing, the closer look at the philosophical development of Moore in Chapter 1 suggests that he was in fact a prolific writer in ethics whose works spanned two periods, the first commencing in 1898, the second marked roughly by the expiration of his six-year fellowship at Cambridge in 1904. Among his early writings, *Principia Ethica* of 1903 stands out as a significant source of radical changes in the ways philosophers approached ethical inquiry during most of the twentieth century. In this first published monograph, Moore devoted four of its six chapters to advancing his positions on foundational issues of metaethics. There is consensus now among critics that, for better or worse, by vigorously and persuasively arguing for those positions, he was influential in the switch of the general focus to metaethics and the consequent neglect of practical ethics that characterized the discipline until at least the 1970s. An earlier monograph he produced in this period, *The Elements of Ethics*, was published only in 1991 probably due to its partial overlap with some chapters of *Principia*. In 1912, Moore published a short monograph, *Ethics*, which includes new arguments against subjectivism, relativism, and classical utilitarianism – together with some significant reflections on issues left altogether out of *Principia*, such as the problem of free will and determinism. During the second period he also wrote substantive replies to his critics in the Schilpp volume of 1942 and some influential essays that appeared in two edited volumes of his works, *Philosophical Studies* of 1922 and *Philosophical Papers* of 1959. In addition, during both periods Moore produced miscellaneous ethical writings consisting of reviews, lecture notes, entries in reference volumes, and journal articles. Such a corpus of ethical writings I would not hesitate to call 'copious' compared with the ethical writings of many of his contemporaries.

Moreover, needless to say, in scholarly works, quality matters more than quantity. In the case of Moore, considerations of the quality of his ethical writings, especially that of *Principia Ethica*, far outweigh any considerations of their quantity. Attesting to *Principia*'s quality is its almost immediate impact on philosophy and beyond, which was unusual for a monograph mostly devoted to questions of metaethics. Gary Seay and I discuss *Principia*'s structure and the reactions of early readers in Chapter 2 of the present book. Following some standard historical accounts, we take its influence to consist primarily in supporting not only the early Moore's core ethical doctrines and themes but also his style of conducting philosophical inquiry, which I take up in Chapter 3. Each of these achievements of Moore's first published monograph needs be in clear view for a correct assessment of his contributions to the development of analytic ethics. The present book considers at length his core ethical doctrines and themes in Chapters 3 through 11. Its study reveals a long and varied history of critical responses largely focused on his non-naturalist moral semantics and metaphysics. But, as Chapter 11 shows, neither his ideal consequentialism nor his holistic theory of value has gone without criticisms and re-evaluations. And his moral intuition-ism, examined here in Chapter 7, has attracted some attention too even when in the Preface of *Principia* Moore had a cagey attitude toward moral intuition and attempted to deflate any extravagant implications of his moral epistemology.

Nevertheless, by far the most critical attention has been devoted to Moore's moral semantics and metaphysics. In each of these areas, Moore launched a critique of naturalistic and metaphysical ethics that for a long time was regarded as having inflicted fatal blows to a range of reductionist ethical theories, from Spencer's evolutionary ethics and various forms of naturalistic ethical real-ism to Kantian rationalism and the divine command theory. That Moore's naturalistic fallacy charge killed Spencer's evolutionary ethics is now a familiar refrain inside and outside philosophy. Stephen Pinker (2003: 162–163), for example, makes this claim and even friends of evolutionary ethics like Michael Ruse (1995; 2019) concur (with some qualifications). On the other hand, Moore's positive doctrine of non-naturalism elicited numerous attempts at revisions by other non-naturalists and refutations by its rivals, especially the subjectivists and emotivists of the first half of the twentieth century. In the second half, the group of crit-ics of non-naturalism grew larger with the addition of new rivals from the camps of prescriptivism and expressivism within moral non-cognitivism as well as moral fictionalism, constructivism, and realism of either reductive or non-reductive naturalistic persua-sions. Early this century, when ethical naturalists and evolution-ary "debunkers" joined the fray, it became obvious that neither naturalistic ethical realism nor evolutionary ethics was dead but simply dormant after the blow inflicted in *Principia Ethica.*

I have agreed with many of these critics that the truth of ethical non-naturalism does not follow from any of the arguments Moore offered in that book. Furthermore, his charge that any naturalistic or metaphysical theory in ethics commits a "naturalistic" fallacy was too ambitious, given that arguably only semantical reductive theories of either sort might fall within the scope of that charge. Yet, on my assessment, the Open Question Argument (OQA) does succeed in supporting a restricted version of the naturalistic fallacy, which nonetheless is strong enough to raise a puzzle for certain reductive naturalistic and metaphysical theories in ethics. After all, these theories respectively maintain that moral terms are reducible without any ethical remainder to purely descriptive and metaphysical terms. The OQA undermines that claim. It does so by invoking some standard, non-disjunctive, reductive analyses of key moral vocabulary and showing that in each case a conflict arises between the attempted reductive analysis and the robust semantical intuitions of competent speakers of the relevant moral and non-moral vocabularies. Unless proponents of such reductive analyses could explain away those intuitions, it seems plausible that the key moral vocabulary is irreducibly moral. This negative conclusion is (and has been) the most appealing doctrine of *Principia*.

However, Moore also took his chief argument for this conclusion to support the more controversial, positive claim that non-naturalism offers the correct metaphysical account of the nature of moral properties and truths. But, as argued in Chapters 5 and 6, the OQA fails to do this: once Moore's conflation of reductive and non-reductive varieties of naturalism is eliminated, reasoning along the lines of the OQA falls short of being compelling either against non-reductive naturalistic ethics or for Moore's own non-naturalistic alternative. Thus, together with many critics, I reject Moore's expansive view of the naturalistic theories vulnerable to his argument, since moral properties might be reducible to natural properties even if moral terms are irreducible to purely descriptive terms. Moore's ambitious conclusion from the OQA founders on the widely accepted view that conceptual non-identity fails to entail non-identity of reference. Moreover, as noted by his rivals among the non-cognitivists, fictionalists, and non-reductive naturalists, they can accommodate Moore's negative conclusion from that argument and consistently subscribe to a moral ontology opposite to his non-naturalism.

Note finally that, given the approach in the present book, Moore's early reasons against naturalistic and metaphysical ethics must play a prominent role in any assessment of his legacy in ethics. But this approach seems incompatible with a recent call for "de-emphasizing" the significance of those reasons in order to clear the way for re-assessing the many other valuable aspects of *Principia Ethica* (Hutchinson 2001: 4). Perhaps it was Moore himself who initiated that de-emphasizing tendency when in later writings he largely ignored his chief reasons against naturalistic and metaphysical ethics in that early work. Accordingly, in a now published, incomplete preface for *Principia*'s second edition of 1922, he mentions the naturalistic fallacy only for the purpose of clarifying what he should have said about the problem identified in that book as a "fallacy." In addition, when wondering about the best objection to naturalistic ethics in a reply to William Frankena (Schilpp 1942), none of his formulations of the OQA in his early book came to his mind. Evidently *Principia* has many philosophically interesting aspects beyond those arguments and I have done my best to provide a thorough discussion of them in the preceding chapters. But it seems possible to attend to all its valuable aspects without de-emphasizing Moore's chief reasons against naturalistic or metaphysical reductionism in ethics. If the present study of *Principia Ethica* is on the right track, he succeeds in getting some of those arguments off the ground and fails in propelling others. Either way, there is much to be learned from a close examination of his efforts.

NOTE

1   Warnock made his unsympathetic comment in a review of *Lectures on Philosophy*, a volume containing some of Moore's lecture notes (1968: 435). For sympathetic comments about Moore's work from followers and friends of ordinary language philosophy, see, for instance, J. L. Austin (1963), R. M. Hare (1952: 82), Gilbert Ryle (1957; 1971), and J. O. Urmson (1958; 1970). However, unlike the Wittgenstein of the *Philosophical Investigations*, neither the early nor the mature Moore fits nicely within that school of analytic philosophy.

BIBLIOGRAPHY

WRITINGS OF G. E. MOORE

Note: This list does not contain *all* works by G. E. Moore but only those works to which we refer in this book. See Schilpp (1942) for a complete list of Moore's writings published up to 1966.

Moore, G. E., "In What Sense, If Any, Do Past and Future Time Exist?" *Mind* 6 (1897): 235–240.

Moore, G. E., "Freedom," *Mind* 7 (1898): 179–204.

Moore, G. E., "The Nature of Judgement," *Mind* 8(30) (1899): 176–193.

Moore, G. E., "The Value of Religion," *International Journal of Ethics* 12 (1901): 81–98.

Moore, G. E., "Truth," in *Dictionary of Philosophy and Psychology*, vol. 2, James Mark Baldwin ed., London: Macmillan & Co., 1902. [Reprinted in Moore 1993b, pp. 20–22.]

Moore, G. E., "Experience and Empiricism," *Proceedings of the Aristotelian Society* 3 (1902–1903): 80–95.

Moore, G. E., "The Refutation of Idealism," *Mind* 12(48) (1903a): 433–453.

Moore, G. E., "*The Origin of the Knowledge of Right and Wrong* by Franz Brentano," *International Journal of Ethics* 14(1) (1903b): 115–123.

Moore, G. E., "Mr. McTaggart's Ethics," *International Journal of Ethics* 13(3) (1903c): 341–370.

Moore, G. E., "Kant's Idealism," *Proceedings of the Aristotelian Society* 4 (1903–1904): 127–140.

Moore, G. E., *Ethics*, London: Williams & Norgate, 1912; New York: Henry Holt, 1912 [page numbers to reprint New York: Clarendon Press, 2005].

Moore, G. E., "External and Internal Relations," *Proceedings of the Aristotelian Society* 20 (1919–1920): 40–62.

Moore, G. E., *Philosophical Studies*, London: Routledge & Kegan Paul, 1922.

Moore, G. E., "The Conception of Intrinsic Value," in Moore 1922, pp. 253–275. [Reprinted in Moore 1993, pp. 280–298.]

Moore, G. E., "The Nature of Moral Philosophy," in Moore 1922, pp. 310–339.

Moore, G. E., "A Defence of Common Sense," in *Contemporary British Philosophy*, 2nd series, J. H. Muirhead ed., London: Allen and Unwin, 1925, pp. 193–223. [Reprinted in *Philosophical Papers* 1959, pp. 32–59.]

Moore, G. E., "Is Goodness a Quality?" *Proceedings of the Aristotelian Society*, Suppl. vol. 11 (1932): 116–131 [References to reprint in Moore 1959, pp. 89–105.]

Moore, G. E. (with Margaret Masterman), "The Justification of Analysis," *Analysis* 1 (1933–1934): 28–30.

Moore, G. E., "Proof of an External World," *Proceedings of the British Academy* 25 (1939): 273–300. [Reprinted in *Philosophical Papers* 1959.]

Moore, G. E., "An Autobiography," 1942a, in Schilpp 1942, pp. 3–39.

Moore, G. E., "A Reply to My Critics," 1942b, in Schilpp 1942, pp. 533–677.

Moore, G. E., "Russell's 'Theory of Descriptions,'" in *The Philosophy of Bertrand Russell*, edited by Paul Arthur Schilpp, Evanston, IL: Northwestern University, 1944, pp. 175–225.

Moore, G. E., *Some Main Problems of Philosophy*, London: Allen & Unwin, 1953. [Page numbers to the Collier Book Edition, New York, 1962.]

Moore, G. E., "What Is Philosophy?" [1910], in Moore 1953, pp. 1–27.

Moore, G. E., *Philosophical Papers*, Casimir Lewy ed., London: George Allen & Unwin, 1959.

Moore, G. E., "Four Forms of Scepticism," in Moore 1959, pp. 196–226.

Moore, G. E., "Certainty," in Moore 1959, pp. 226–252.

Moore, G. E., *The Commonplace Book, 1919–1953*, Casimir Lewy ed., London: Allen & Unwin, 1962.

Moore, G. E., *Lectures on Philosophy*, Casimir Lewy ed., London: Allen & Unwin; New York: Humanity Press, 1966.

Moore, G. E., *The Elements of Ethics*, Tom Regan ed., Philadelphia, PA: Temple University Press, 1991/1898.

Moore, G. E., *Principia Ethica*, Cambridge: Cambridge University Press, rev. edn., Thomas Baldwin ed., 1993a/1903.

Moore, G. E., "Preface," written for *Principia Ethica*'s 2nd edn. of 1922, in Moore 1993a./1903, pp. 1–32.

Moore, G. E., *G. E. Moore: Selected Writings*, Thomas Baldwin ed., London: Routledge, 1993b.

Moore, G. E., *G. E. Moore: Early Philosophical Writings*, Thomas Baldwin and Consuelo Preti eds., Cambridge: Cambridge University Press, 2011.

Moore, G. E., "The 1897 Dissertation: The Metaphysical Basis of Ethics," in Moore 2011, pp. 2–94.

Moore, G. E., "The 1898 Dissertation: The Metaphysical Basis of Ethics," in Moore 2011, pp. 117–244.

GENERAL REFERENCES

Ambrose, Alice and Morris Lazerowitz, eds., *G. E. Moore: Essays in Retrospect*, London: George Allen & Unwin, 1970.

Aristotle, *Nicomachean Ethics* (H. Rackham trans.), Cambridge, MA: Harvard University Press, 1926.

Armstrong, D. M., *Universals and Scientific Realism*, 2 vols., Cambridge: Cambridge University Press, 1978.

Audi, Robert, "Intuitionism, Pluralism, and the Foundations of Ethics," in *Moral Knowledge*, Walter Sinnott-Armstrong and Mark Timmons eds., Oxford: Oxford University Press, 1996, pp. 101–136.

Audi, Robert, "Can Normativity Be Naturalized?" in Nuccetelli and Seay 2012, pp. 169–193.

Austin, J. L., "Performative-Constative," in *Philosophy and Ordinary Language*, Charles E. Caton ed., Chicago: University of Illinois Press, 1963, pp. 22–54. [Reference to reprint in *Philosophy of Language*, Susana Nuccetelli and Gary Seay eds., Lanham, MD: Rowman & Littlefield, 2008, pp. 329–337.]

Ayer, A. J., *Language, Truth and Logic*, New York: Dover, 1952/1936.

Ayer, A. J., *Philosophical Essays*, London: Macmillan, 1954.

Ayer, A. J., *Russell and Moore*, Cambridge, MA: Harvard University Press, 1971.

Baldwin, Thomas, "Review of *Bloomsbury's Prophet*. Tom Regan," *Mind* 385 (1988): 129–133.

Baldwin, Thomas, *G. E. Moore*, London: Routledge, 1990.

Baldwin, Thomas, "Appendix: '*Principia Ethica*' and '*The Elements of Ethics*'," in Moore 1993/1903, pp. 312–313.

Baldwin, Thomas, "G. E. Moore," *Philosophy* 71(276) (1996): 275–285.

Baldwin, Thomas, "The Open Question Argument," in John Skorupski ed., *The Routledge Companion to Ethics*, London: Routledge, 2010, pp. 286–296.

Baldwin, Thomas and Consuelo Preti, eds., *G. E. Moore: Early Philosophical Writings*, Cambridge: Cambridge University Press, 2011.

Baldwin, Thomas and Consuelo Preti, "Editor's Introduction," in Baldwin and Preti 2011, pp. xii–lxxxv.

Ball, S. W., "Reductionism in Ethics and Science: A Contemporary Look at G E. Moore's Open Question Argument," *American Philosophical Quarterly* 25 (1988): 197–213.

Beaney, Michael, "Analysis," in *Stanford Encyclopedia of Philosophy*, Edward Zalta ed., 2014/2003, https://plato.stanford.edu/entries/analysis/

Beaney, Michael, "Moore," in "Annotated Bibliography on Analysis §6: Conceptions of Analysis in Analytic Philosophy," Supplement 2014, in *Stanford Encyclopedia of Philosophy*, Edward Zalta ed., 2014/2003, https://plato.stanford.edu/entries/analysis/bib6.html#

Bentham, Jeremy, *Introduction to the Principles of Morals and Legislation*, Buffalo, NY: Prometheus Books, 1988/1789.

Bergmann, Michael and Patrick Kain, eds., *Challenges to Moral and Religious Belief: Disagreement and Evolution*, Oxford: Oxford University Press, 2014.

Blackburn, Simon, *Spreading the Word*, Oxford: Clarendon Press, 1984.

Blackburn, Simon, "How to Be an Ethical Antirealist," in *Midwest Studies in Philosophy*, vol. II: *Realism and Antirealism*, Peter A. French, Theodore E. Uehling, Jr., and Horward Wettstein eds., Bloomington, IN: University of Notre Dame Press, 1987, pp. 361–375.

Blackburn, Simon, "Review of Tom Regan, *Bloomsbury's Prophet: G.E. Moore and the Development of His Moral Philosophy*," *Times Literary Supplement* 4 (1988): 99–100.

Blackburn, Simon, "Supervenience Revisited," in *Essays in Quasi-Realism*, Oxford: Oxford University Press, 1993, pp. 130–148.

Blackburn, Simon, *Ruling Passions*, Oxford: Clarendon Press, 1998.

Bosanquet, Bernard, "*Principia Ethica* by G. E. Moore," *Mind* 13(50) (1904): 254–261.

Boyd, Richard, 'How to Be a Moral Realist,' in *Essays on Moral Realism*, Geoff Sayre-McCord ed., Ithaca, NY: Cornell University Press, 1988, pp. 181–228.

Bradley, Francis Herbert, *The Principles of Logic*, 2nd edn., London: Oxford University Press, 1922/1883.

Brady, Michael, ed., *New Waves in Metaethics*, Basingstoke: Palgrave Macmillan, 2011.

Braithwaite, R. B., "George Edward Moore 1873–1958," *Proceedings of the British Academy* 47 (1961): 293–309. [References to reprint pp. 17–33 in Ambrose and Lazerowitz, 1970.]

Brentano, Franz, *The Origin of the Knowledge of Right and Wrong*, London: Routledge, 1969/1902.

Bridge, Ursula, *The Correspondence of W. B. Yeats and T. Sturge Moore*, London: Routledge: 1953.

Brink, David O., *Moral Realism and the Foundations of Ethics*, Cambridge: Cambridge University Press, 1989.

Brink, David O., "Realism, Naturalism and Moral Semantics," *Social Philosophy & Policy* 18 (2001): 154–76. http://davidobrink.com/sites/default/files/publications/RealismNaturalismMoralSemantics_0.pdf

Brink, David O., *Mill's Progressive Principles*, Oxford: Clarendon Press, 2013.

Broad, C. D., "Critical and Speculative Philosophy," in *Contemporary British Philosophy: Personal Statements*, J. H. Muirhead ed., London: Allen and Unwin, 1924, pp. 77–100.

Broad, C. D., *Five Types of Ethical Theory*, London: Routledge & Kegan Paul, 1930.

Broad, C. D., "Is 'Goodness' a Name of a Simple Non-Natural Quality?" *Proceedings of the Aristotelian Society* 34 (1933–1934): 249–268.

Broad, C. D., "Certain Features in Moore's Ethical Doctrines," in Schilpp 1942, pp. 41–67.

Broad, C. D., "G. E. Moore's Latest Published Views on Ethics," *Mind* 70(280) (1961): 435–457. [References to pp. 350–373 in Ambrose and Lazerowitz, 1970.]

Broad, C. D., "Obligations, Ultimate and Derived," in *Broad's Critical Essays in Moral Philosophy*, David R. Cheney ed., New York: Routledge, 2013/1971, pp. 351–368.

Bruening William H., "Moore and "Is-Ought," *Ethics* 81(2) (1971): 143–149.

Buchanan, Emerson and G. E. Moore, "Bibliography of the Writings of G. E. Moore," in Schilpp 1942, pp. 689–701.

Chalmers, David, *The Conscious Mind*, New York: Oxford University Press, 1996.

Chang, Ruth, "Practical Reasons: The Problem of Gridlock," in *The Bloomsbury Companion to Analytic Philosophy*, Barry Daiton and Howard Robinson eds., London: Bloomsbury Academic, 2014, pp. 474–499.

Copp, David, *Morality, Normativity, and Society*, New York: Oxford University Press, 2001.

Copp, David, "Why Naturalism?" *Ethical Theory and Moral Practice* 6 (2003): 179–200.

Copp, David, ed., *The Oxford Handbook of Ethical Theory*, Oxford: Oxford University Press, 2006.

Copp, David, *Morality in a Natural World: Selected Essays in Metaethics*, Cambridge: Cambridge University Press, 2007.

Cox, H. H., "Warnock on Moore," *Mind* 79 (1970): 265–267.

Crimmins, James E., ed., *The Bloomsbury Encyclopedia of Utilitarianism*, London: Bloomsbury Academic, 2017.

Crisp, Roger, "Value, Reasons and the Structure of Justification: How to Avoid Passing the Buck," *Analysis* 65 (2005): 80–85.

Crisp, Roger, "Goodness and Reasons: Accentuating the Negative," *Mind* 117 (2008): 257–265.

Crisp, Roger, "Naturalism: Feel the Width," in Nuccetelli and Seay 2012, pp. 58–69.

Cuneo, Terence, "Ethical Nonnaturalism," in LaFollette ed., 2013, pp. 3641–3652, DOI: 10.1002/ 9781444367072.wbiee134.

Cuneo, Terence and Russ Shafer-Landau, "The Moral Fixed Points: New Directions for Nonnaturalism," *Philosophical Studies* 171 (2014): 399–443.

Dancy, Jonathan, *Moral Reasons*, Oxford: Blackwell, 1993.

Dancy, Jonathan, *Ethics without Principles*, Oxford: Oxford University Press, 2004.

Dancy, Jonathan, "Should We Pass the Buck?" in *Recent Work on Intrinsic Value*, Toni Ronnow-Rasmussen and Michael J. Zimmerman eds., Dordrecht, the Netherlands: Springer Verlag, 2005, pp. 33–44.

Dancy, Jonathan, "Nonnaturalism," in Copp 2006, pp. 122–145.

Dancy, Jonathan, "Moore's Account of Vindictive Punishment: A Test Case for Theories of Organic Unities," in Nuccetelli and Seay 2007, pp. 325–342.

Darwall, Stephen, "How Should Ethics Relate to (the Rest of) Philosophy?" in Horgan and Timmons 2006, pp. 17–38.

Darwall, Stephen, "How is Moorean Value Related to Reasons for Attitudes?" in Nuccetelli and Seay 2007, pp. 183–202.

Darwall, Stephen, Allan Gibbard, and Peter Railton, "Toward *Fin de Siècle* Ethics: Some Trends," *Philosophical Review* 101 (1992): 115–189.

Darwall, Stephen, Allan Gibbard, and Peter Railton, eds., *Moral Discourse and Practice: Some Philosophical Approaches*, New York: Oxford University Press, 1997.

Darwin, Charles, *The Descent of Man, and Selection in Relation to Sex*, Princeton, NJ: Princeton University Press 1981/1891.

Donnini Macciò, Daniela, "G.E. Moore's Philosophy and Cambridge Economics: Ralph Hawtrey on Ethics and Methodology," *The European Journal of the History of Economic Thought* 22(2) (2015): 163–197.

Donnini Macciò, Daniela, "Ethics, Economics and Power in the Cambridge Apostles' Internationalism between the Two World Wars," *European Journal of International Relations* 22(3) (2016a): 696–721.

Donnini Macciò, Daniela, "The Apostles' Justice: Cambridge Reflections on Economic Inequality from Moore's *Principia Ethica* to Keynes's General Theory (1903–1936)," *Cambridge Journal of Economics* 40 (2016b): 701–726.

Dreier, Jamie, "Was Moore a Moorean?" in Horgan and Timmons 2006, pp. 191–207.

Dreier, Jamie, "Quasi-Realism and the Problem of Unexplained Coincidence," *Analytic Philosophy* 53(3) (2012): 269–287.

Driver, Julia, "The History of Utilitarianism," in *Stanford Encyclopedia of Philosophy*, Edward Zalta ed., 2014, https://plato.stanford.edu/entries/utilitarianism-history/

Dummett, Michael, *Origins of Analytical Philosophy*, London: Duckworth & Co., 1993.

Durrant, R. G., "Identity of Properties and the Definition of 'Good'," *Australasian Journal of Philosophy* 48(3) (1970): 360–361.

Eggleston, Ben, "Act Utilitarianism," in *The Cambridge Companion to Utilitarianism*, Ben Eggleston and Dale E. Miller eds., Cambridge: Cambridge University Press, 2014, pp. 125–145.

Elstein, Daniel Y. and Thomas Hurka, "From Thick to Thin: Two Moral Reduction Plans," *Canadian Journal of Philosophy* 39(4) (2009): 515–536.

Enoch, David, *Taking Morality Seriously*, Oxford: Oxford University Press, 2011.

Ewing, A. C., "A Suggested Non-Naturalistic Analysis of Good," *Mind* 48 (1939): 1–22.

Ewing, A. C., *The Definition of Good*, London: Routledge & Kegan Paul, 1947.

Ewing, A. C., *Ethics*, London: English University Press, 1953.

Ewing, A. C., *Second Thoughts in Moral Philosophy*, London: Routledge & Kegan Paul, 1959.

Ewing, A. C., "G. E. Moore," *Mind* 71(282) (1962): 251.

Feldman, Fred, "The Naturalistic Fallacy: What It Is, and What It Isn't," in Sinclair 2019, pp. 30–72.

Field, Hartry, *Science Without Numbers*, 2nd edn., Oxford: Oxford University Press, 2016.

FitzPatrick, William J., "Robust Ethical Realism, Non-Naturalism, and Normativity," in *Oxford Studies in Metaethics* 3, Russ Shafer-Landau ed., Oxford: Oxford University Press, 2008, pp. 159–206.

FitzPatrick, William J., "Ethical Non-Naturalism and Normative Properties," in Michael Brady ed., *New Waves in Metaethics*, Basingstoke: Palgrave Macmillan, 2011, pp. 7–35.

FitzPatrick, William J., "Skepticism about Naturalizing Normativity: In Defense of Ethical Nonnaturalism," *Res Philosophica* 91(4) (2014): 559–588.

FitzPatrick, William J., "Debunking Evolutionary Debunking of Ethical Realism," *Philosophical Studies* 172(4) (2015): 883–904.

FitzPatrick, William J., "Open Question Arguments and the Irreducibility of Ethical Normativity," in Sinclair 2019, pp. 138–161.

Fletcher, Guy, "Brown and Moore's Value Invariabilism vs Dancy's Variabilism," *The Philosophical Quarterly* 60(238) (2010): 162–168.

Foot, Philippa, "Moral Arguments," *Mind* 67 (1958): 502–513.

Foot, Philippa, *Virtues and Vices and Other Essays in Moral Philosophy*, Oxford: Blackwell, 1978.

Foot, Philippa, *Natural Goodness*, Oxford: Clarendon Press, 2001.

Foot, Philippa, *Moral Dilemmas and Other Topics in Moral Philosophy*, Oxford: Clarendon Press, 2002.

Frankena, William K., "The Naturalistic Fallacy," *Mind* 48 (1939): 464–477.

Frankena, William K., "Obligation and Value in the Ethics of G. E. Moore," in Schilpp 1942, pp. 93–110.

Frankena, William K., *Ethics*, 2nd edn., Englewood Cliffs, NJ: Prentice-Hall, 1963.

Frankena, William K. and John T. Granrose, eds., *Introductory Readings in Ethics*, Englewood Cliffs, NJ: Prentice-Hall, 1974.

Geach, Peter T., "Good and Evil," *Analysis* 17 (1956): 33–42.

Geach, Peter T., *Truth, Love, and Immortality*, London: Hutchinson, 1979.

Gert, Bernard, Charles M. Culver, and K. Danner Clouser, *Bioethics: A Systematic Approach*, New York: Oxford University Press, 2006.

Gert, Bernard and Joshua Gert, "The Definition of Morality," in *Stanford Encyclopedia of Philosophy*, Edward N. Zalta ed., 2016/2002, https://plato.stanford.edu/entries/morality-definition/#NormDefiMora

Gert, Joshua, "Beyond Moore's Utilitarianism," in Nuccetelli and Seay 2007, pp. 307–324.

Gibbard, Allan, *Wise Choices, Apt Feelings*, Oxford: Clarendon Press, 1990.

Gibbard, Allan, *Thinking How to Live*, Cambridge, MA: Harvard University Press, 2003.

Goodman, Nelson, *Fact, Fiction, and Forecast*, Cambridge, MA: Harvard University Press, 1954.

Greig, Gordon, "Moore and Analysis," in Ambrose and Lazerowitz, 1970, pp. 242–268.

Griffin, Nicholas, "Moore and Bloomsbury," *Russell* 9(1) (1989): 80–93.

Griffin, Nicholas, *Russell's Idealist Apprenticeship*, Oxford: Clarendon Press, 1991.

Hall, E., 'The 'Proof' of Utility in Bentham and Mill," *Ethics* 61 (1950–51): 66–68.

Hampshire, Stuart, "Liberator, Up to a Point," *The New York Review of Books* 34(March 26) (1987): 37–39.

Hare, R. M., *The Language of Morals*, Oxford: Clarendon Press, 1952.

Hare, R. M., *Freedom and Reason*, Oxford: Oxford University Press, 1963.

Hare, R. M., *Moral Thinking*, Oxford: Oxford University Press, 1981.

Harman, Gilbert, *The Nature of Morality*, New York: Oxford University Press, 1977.

Harman, Gilbert, "Moral Relativism," in *Moral Relativism and Moral Objectivity*, G. Harman and J. J. Thompson eds., Malden, MA: Blackwell, 1996, pp. 3–64.

Harman, Gilbert, "Naturalism in Moral Philosophy," in Nuccetelli and Seay 2012, pp. 8–23.

Heathwood, Chris, "Organic Unities," in LaFollette ed., 2013, pp. 1–3, DOI: 10.1002/ 9781444367072.wbiee362

Henne, Paul, Vladimir Chituc, Felipe de Brigard, and Water Sinnott-Armstrong, "An Empirical Refutation of 'Ought' Implies 'Can'," *Analysis* 76(3) (2016).

Hooker, Brad, *Ideal Code, Real World*, Oxford: Clarendon Press, 2000.

Hooker, Brad, "Rule Consequentialism," in *Stanford Encyclopedia of Philosophy*, Edward N. Zalta ed., 2015, https://plato.stanford.edu/entries/consequentialism-rule/

Horgan, Terence, "From Supervenience to Superdupervenience: Meeting the Demands of a Material World," *Mind* 102(408) (1993): 555–586.

Horgan, Terence and Mark Timmons, "New Wave Moral Realism Meets Moral Twin Earth," *Journal of Philosophical Research* 16 (1991): 447–465.

Horgan, Terence and Mark Timmons, "Troubles for New Wave Moral Semantics: The Open Question Argument Revived," *Philosophical Papers* 21(3) (1992): 153–175.

Horgan, Terence and Mark Timmons, eds., *Metaethics after Moore*, Oxford: Clarendon Press, 2006.

Horgan, Terence and Mark Timmons, "Introduction," in Horgan and Timmons 2006, pp. 1–6.

Hudson, W. D., "Did Mill Commit the Naturalistic Fallacy?" in *Modern Moral Philosophy* Garden City, NY: Doubleday, 1970, pp. 74–79.

Huemer, Michael, *Ethical Intuitionism*, New York: Palgrave Macmillan, 2005.

Huemer, Michael, "A Liberal Realist Answer to Debunking Skeptics: The Empirical Case for Realism," *Philosophical Studies* 173 (2016): 1983–2010.

Hume, David, *A Treatise of Human Nature*, Project Gutenberg EBook, 2010/1739, www.gutenberg.org/files/4705/4705-h/4705-h.htm#link2H_4_0008

Hurka, Thomas, "Moore in the Middle," *Ethics* 113(3) (2003): 599–628.

Hurka, Thomas, "Moore's Moral Philosophy," in *Stanford Encyclopedia of Philosophy*, Edward Zalta ed., 2005/2015, https://plato.stanford.edu/entries/moore-moral/

Hurka, Thomas, "Soames on Ethics," *American Philosophical Association*, Pacific Division Author-Meets-Critics Session, Portland, OR, Mar. 24, 2006, https://thomashurka.com/writings/papers-in-progress/2020/1739

Hurka, Thomas, ed., *Underivative Duty: British Moral Philosophers from Sidgwick to Ewing*, New York: Oxford University Press, 2011.

Hurka, Thomas, "Common Themes from Sidgwick to Ewing," in Hurka 2011, pp. 6–25.

Hurka, Thomas, ed., *British Ethical Theorists from Sidgwick to Ewing*, New York: Oxford University Press, 2014.

Hutchinson, Brian, *G. E. Moore's Ethical Theory: Resistance and Reconciliation*, Cambridge: Cambridge University Press, 2001.

Huxley, Thomas H., *Evolution and Ethics*, London: Macmillan and Co., 1894. [References to selection, pp. 111–150 in Thompson 1995.]

Hylton, Peter, "The Nature of the Proposition and the Revolt against Idealism," in Richard Rorty, J. B. Schneewind, and Quentin Skinner eds., *Philosophy in History: Essays on the Historiography of Philosophy*, Cambridge: Cambridge University Press, 1984, pp. 376–397.

Hylton, Peter, *Russell, Idealism, and the Emergence of Analytic Philosophy*, Oxford: Clarendon Press, 1990.

Hylton, Peter, "Idealism and the Origins of Analytic Philosophy," in *Analytic Philosophy: An Interpretive History*, Aaron Preston ed., New York: Routledge, 2017, pp. 20–33.

Jackson, Frank, *From Metaphysics to Ethics: A Defence of Conceptual Analysis*, Oxford: Clarendon Press, 1998.

Jackson, Frank, "On Ethical Naturalism and the Philosophy of Language," in Nuccetelli and Seay 2012, pp. 70–88.

Jackson, Frank, "The Autonomy of Ethics," in LaFollette 2013, pp. 459–465.

Jonsen, Albert R., "Strong on Specification," *Journal of Medicine & Philosophy* 25(3) (2000): 348–360.

Jonsen, Albert and Stephen Toulmin, *The Abuse of Casuistry*, Berkeley, CA: University of California Press, 1988.

Joyce, Richard, *The Evolution of Morality*, Cambridge, MA: MIT Press, 2006.

Katz, Jerrold D., *Sense, Reference, and Philosophy*, New York: Oxford University Press, 2004.

Kerner, George C. *The Revolution in Ethical Theory*, New York: Oxford University Press, 1966.

Keynes, John Maynard, "My Early Beliefs," in *Two Memoirs*, New York: A. M. Kelley; London, Rupert Hart-Davis, 1949, pp. 78–103.

Kim, Jaegwon, *Supervenience and Mind*, Cambridge: Cambridge University Press, 1993.

Kim, Jaegwon, "Moral Kinds and Natural Kinds – What's the Difference for a Naturalist?" *Philosophical Issues* 8 (1997): 293–301.

Kim, Jaegwon, *Mind in the Physical World*, Cambridge, MA: MIT Press, 1998.

Kitcher, Philip, *The Ethical Project*, Cambridge, MA: Harvard University Press, 2011.

Klagge, James C., "Review of Tom Regan, *Bloomsbury's Prophet: G.E. Moore and the Development of His Moral Philosophy* and *G.E. Moore, Early Essays*, edited by T. Regan," *Ethics* 3 (1988): 582–584.

Kramer, M., *Moral Realism as a Moral Doctrine*, Oxford: Blackwell, 2009.

Kraut, Richard, *Against Absolute Goodness*, New York: Oxford University Press, 2011.

Kripke, Saul, *Naming and Necessity*, Cambridge, MA: Harvard University Press, 1972.

Kupperman, Joel J., "Utilitarianism Today," *Revue Internationale de Philosophie* 36(141) (1982): 318–330.

LaFollette, Hugh, ed., *The International Encyclopedia of Ethics*, Oxford: Blackwell, 2013.

Langford, C. H., "Moore's Notion of Analysis," in Schilpp 1942, pp. 319–342.

Lemos, Noah, "A Defense of Organic Unities," *Journal of Ethics* 19 (2015): 125–141.

Lewy, Casimir, "G. E. Moore on the Naturalistic Fallacy," in *Studies in the Philosophy of Thought and Action*, P. F. Strawson ed., London: Oxford University Press, 1968, pp. 134–146. [Reprint pp. 292–303 in Ambrose and Lazerowitz 1970.]

Levy, Paul, *G. E. Moore and the Cambridge Apostles*, London: Weidenfeld and Nicolson, 1979.

Lubenow, W. C., *The Cambridge Apostles 1820–1914*, Cambridge: Cambridge University Press, 1998.

Malcolm, Norman, "George Edward Moore," in *Knowledge and Certainty*, Englewood Cliffs, NJ: Prentice-Hall, 1963, pp. 163–183.

Malcolm, Norman, *Ludwig Wittgenstein: A Memoir*, Oxford: Oxford University Press, 2nd edn., 1984.

McDowell, John, "Virtue and Reason," *The Monist* 62 (1979): 331–350.

McDowell, John, "Non-Cognitivism and Rule-Following," in Steven H. Holtzman and Christopher M. Leich eds., *Wittgenstein: To Follow a Rule*, London: Routledge, 1981, pp. 141–162. [References to reprint pp. 198–219 in McDowell's *Mind, Value, and Reality*, Cambridge, MA: Harvard University Press, 1998].

McGrath, Sarah and Thomas Kelly, "Soames and Moore on Method in Ethics and Epistemology," *Philosophical Studies* 172(6) (2015): 1661–1670.

McGuinness, Brian. *Wittgenstein, a Life: Young Ludwig, 1889–1921*, London: Duckworth, 1988.

Mackenzie, J. S., "*Principia Ethica* by George Edward Moore," *International Journal of Ethics* 14(3) (1904): 377–382.

Mackie, J. L., "Edward Alexander Westermarck," in *Encyclopedia of Philosophy*, vol. 8, Paul Edwards ed., New York: Macmillan, 1967, pp. 284–286.

Mackie, J. L., *Ethics: Inventing Right and Wrong*, Harmondsworth: Penguin, 1977.

McLaughlin, Brian, "Supervenience," in *Stanford Encyclopedia of Philosophy*, Edward Zalta ed., 2005/2018. https://plato.stanford.edu/entries/supervenience/#SupeEnta

McPherson, Tristram, "Ethical Non-Naturalism and the Metaphysics of Supervenience," in *Oxford Studies in Metaethics* 7, R. Shafer-Landau ed., Oxford: Oxford University Press, 2012, pp. 205–234.

McPherson, Tristram, "Supervenience in Ethics," in *Stanford Encyclopedia of Philosophy*, Edward Zalta ed., 2015. https://plato.stanford.edu/entries/supervenience-ethics/

McTaggart, John McTaggart Ellis, *Studies in Hegelian Cosmology*, Cambridge: Cambridge University Press, 1901.

Mill, John Stuart, *Utilitarianism*, Indianapolis: Hackett, 1979/1863.

Mulgan, Tim, *Understanding Utilitarianism*, Stocksfield: Acumen, 2007.

Nelson, John O., "George Edward Moore 1873–1958," in *Encyclopedia of Philosophy*, vol. 5, Paul Edwards ed., New York: Macmillan, 1967, pp. 372–381.

Nowell-Smith, P. H., *Ethics*, Harmondsworth: Penguin, 1954.

Nuccetelli, Susana, "Should Analytical Descriptivists Worry about the Naturalistic Fallacy?," in Sinclair 2019, pp. 162–178.

Nuccetelli, Susana and Gary Seay, eds., *Themes from G. E. Moore: New Essays in Epistemology and Ethics*, Oxford: Oxford University Press, 2007.

Nuccetelli, Susana and Gary Seay, "What's Right with the Open Question Argument?" in Nuccetelli and Seay 2007, pp. 261–282.

Nuccetelli, Susana and Gary Seay, "Is There a Naturalistic Fallacy?" Unpublished manuscript, read at the American Philosophical Association's Eastern Division Meeting, Philadelphia, Dec. 2008.

Nuccetelli, Susana and Gary Seay, eds., *Ethical Naturalism: Current Debates*, Cambridge: Cambridge University Press, 2012.

Nuccetelli, Susana and Gary Seay, "Does Analytical Ethical Naturalism Rest on a Mistake?" in *Ethical Naturalism: Current Debates*, Susana Nuccetelli and Gary Seay eds., Cambridge University Press, 2012, pp. 131–143.

Olson, Jonas, "G. E. Moore on Goodness and Reasons," *Australasian Journal of Philosophy* 84 (2006): 525–534.

Olson, Jonas, "Buck-Passing Accounts," in *The International Encyclopedia of Ethics*, Hugh LaFollette ed., Oxford: Blackwell, 2013, pp. 625–636. DOI: 10.1002/ 9781444367072.wbiee083.

Orsi, Francesco, *Value Theory*, London: Bloomsbury, 2015.

Parfit, Derek, *On What Matters*, vols. 1 and 2, Oxford: Oxford University Press, 2011.

Passmore, John Arthur, *A Hundred Years of Philosophy*, London: Gerald Duckworth, 1957.

Paton, H. J., "The Alleged Independence of Goodness," in Schilpp 1942, pp. 113–134.

Pears, David F., "Logical Atomism: Russell and Wittgenstein," in Ryle 1957, pp. 41–55.

Perry, Ralph Barton, *General Theory of Value: Its Meaning and Basic Principles Construed in Terms of Interest*, Cambridge, MA: Harvard University Press, 1926, pp. 138–151. [References to "Value as Any Object of Any Interest," in *Readings in Ethical Theory*, 2nd edn., W. Sellars and J. Hospers eds., New York: Appleton-Century-Crofts, 1970.]

Perry, Ralph Barton, *Realms of Value: A Critique of Human Civilization*, Cambridge, MA: Harvard University Press, 1954.

Pigden, Charles R., "Logic and the Autonomy of Ethics," *Australasian Journal of Philosophy* 67(2) (1989): 127–151.

Pigden, Charles R., "Geach on 'Good'," *The Philosophical Quarterly* 40(159) (1990): 129–154.

Pigden, Charles R., ed., *Russell on Ethics: Selections from the Writings of Bertrand Russell*, New York: Routledge, 1999.

Pigden, Charles R., "Desiring to Desire: Russell, Lewis and G.E Moore," in Nuccetelli and Seay 2007, pp. 244–260.

Pigden, Charles R., "Identifying Goodness," *Australasian Journal of Philosophy* 90(1) (2012): 93–109.

Pigden, Charles R., "No-Ought-From-Is, the Naturalistic Fallacy and the Fact/ Value Distinction: The History of a Mistake," in Sinclair 2019, pp. 73–95.

Pinker, Steven, *The Blank Slate: The Modern Denial of Human Nature*, New York: Penguin, 2003.

Prior, Arthur N., *Logic and the Basis of Ethics*, Oxford: Clarendon Press, 1949.

Prior, Arthur N., "The Autonomy of Ethics" *Australasian Journal of Philosophy* 38(3) (1960): 199–206.

Putnam, Hilary, "The Meaning of 'Meaning'," in Hilary Putnam, *Mind, Language and Reality: Philosophical Papers*, Cambridge: Cambridge University Press, 1975, vol. 2, pp. 215–271.

Putnam, Hilary, *Reason, Truth and History*, Cambridge: Cambridge University Press, 1981.

Quine, Willard V. O., "Two Dogmas of Empiricism," *Philosophical Review* 60(1) (1951): 20–43.

Railton, Peter, "Moral Realism," *Philosophical Review* 95 (1986): 163–207.

Railton, Peter, "Moral Factualism," in *Contemporary Debates in Moral Theory*, James Dreier ed., Oxford: Blackwell, 2006, pp. 201–219.

Railton, Peter, "Realism and Its Alternatives," in *The Routledge Companion to Ethics*, John Skorupski ed., New York: Routledge, 2010, pp. 297–320.

Rashdall, Hastings, "Professor Sidgwick on the Ethics of Religious Conformity: A Reply," *International Journal of Ethics* 7 (1897): 137–168.

Rashdall, Hastings, "The Commensurability of All Values," *Mind* 11 (1903): 145–161.

Rashdall, Hastings, *The Theory of Good and Evil*, 2 vols., London: Oxford University Press, 1907.

Rawls, John, *A Theory of Justice*, 2nd edn., Cambridge, MA: Harvard University Press, 1971.

Rees, Goronwy, "A Case for Treatment: The World of Lytton Strachey," *Encounter* 30(3) (1968): 71–83.

Regan, Tom, *Bloomsbury's Prophet*, Philadelphia, PA: Temple University Press, 1986.

Regan, Tom, "Editor's Introduction," in *The Elements of Ethics*, G. E. Moore, Philadelphia, PA: Temple University Press, 1991/1898b, pp. xiii–xxxiix.

Ridge, Michael, "Moral Non-Naturalism," in *Stanford Encyclopedia of Philosophy*, Edward N. Zalta ed., 2003/2014, https://plato.stanford.edu/entries/moral-non-naturalism/

Ridge, Michael, "Reasons for Action: Agent-Neutral vs. Agent-Relative," in *Stanford Encyclopedia of Philosophy*, Edward N. Zalta ed., 2005/2017, https://plato.stanford.edu/entries/reasons-agent/

Ridge, Michael, "Supervenience and the Nature of Normativity," in Nuccetelli and Seay 2012, pp. 144–168.

Rosenbaum, S. P., "Moore," in *The Early Literary History of the Bloomsbury Group*, vol. 1, New York: St. Martin's Press, 1987, pp. 214–238.

Ross, W. D., *Aristotle*, London: Methuen, 1923.

Ross, W. D., *The Right and the Good*, Oxford: Clarendon Press, 1930.

Ruse, Michael, "Evolutionary Ethics: A Phoenix Arisen," *Zygon* 21 (1986): 95–112. [Reprint in Thompson 1995, pp. 225–247.]

Ruse, Michael, "Evolution and the Naturalistic Fallacy," in Sinclair 2019, pp. 96–116.

Ruse, Michael and Edward O. Wilson, "Moral Philosophy as Applied Science," *Philosophy* 61 (1986): 173–192.

Russell, Bertrand, "Review of G. E. Moore, *Principia Ethica*," *The Cambridge Review* 25, lit. suppl., 12(3) (1903a): 37–38.

Russell, Bertrand, "Preface," *The Principles of Mathematics*, Cambridge: Cambridge University Press, 1903b. http://fair-use.org/bertrand-russell/the-principles-of-mathematics/preface

Russell, Bertrand, "The Meaning of Good: Review of G. E. Moore, *Principia Ethica*," *The Independent Review* 2(March 1904): 328–333. https://users.drew.edu/jlenz/br-moore-review2.html

Russell, Bertrand, "My Mental Development," in *The Philosophy of Bertrand Russell*, P. A. Schilpp ed., vol. 1, New York: Harper & Row, 1944, pp. 1–20.

Russell, Bertrand, *Portraits from Memory and Other Essays*, New York: Simon & Schuster, 1951a.

Russell, Bertrand, *The Autobiography of Bertrand Russell, 1872–1914*, London: Allen and Unwin, 1951b. [References to the 1967 edn, Boston: Little, Brown and Company.]

Russell, Bertrand, "The Elements of Ethics," in *Bertrand Russell on Ethics, Sex, and Marriage*, Al Seckel ed., Buffalo, NY: Prometheus, 1987/1910, pp. 15–108.

Russell, Bertrand, "Is Ethics a Branch of Empirical Psychology?" in *Russell on Ethics: Selection from the Writings of Bertrand Russell*, Charles R. Pigden ed., New York: Routledge 1999, pp. 71–78.

Ryle, Gilbert, ed., *The Revolution in Philosophy*, London: Macmillan, 1957.

Ryle, Gilbert, "G. E. Moore," in *Collected Papers: Critical Essays*, vol. 1, London: Hutchinson & Co., 1971, pp. 268–271.

Sainsbury, R. M., *Russell*, London: Routledge & Kegan Paul, 1979.

Santayana, George, "Russell's Philosophical Essays: III Hypostatic Ethics," *The Journal of Philosophy, Psychology and Scientific Methods* 8(16) (1911): 421–432.

Sayre-McCord, Geoffrey, ed., *Essays on Moral Realism*, Ithaca, NY: Cornell University Press, 1988.

Sayre-McCord, Geoffrey, "'Good' on Twin Earth," *Philosophical Issues* 8 (1997): 267–292.

Sayre-McCord, Geoffrey, "Mill's 'Proof' of the Principle of Utility: A More than Half-Hearted Defense," *Social Philosophy & Policy* 18(2) (2001): 330–360.

Scanlon, T. M., *What We Owe to Each Other*, Cambridge, MA: Harvard University Press, 1998.

Scanlon, T. M., "Rawls on Justification," in *The Cambridge Companion to Rawls*, S. Freeman ed., Cambridge: Cambridge University Press, 2002, pp. 139–167.

Scanlon, T. M., "Metaphysics and Morals," *Proceedings and Addresses of the American Philosophical Association* 77(2) (2003): 7–22.

Scanlon, T. M., *Being Realistic about Reasons*, Oxford: Oxford University Press, 2014.

Schilpp, Paul Arthur, ed., *The Philosophy of G. E. Moore*, Lasalle, IL: Open Court, 1942.

Schneewind, J. B., *Sidgwick's Ethics and Victorian Moral Philosophy*, Oxford: Clarendon Press, 1977.

Shaver, Robert, "Non-Naturalism," in Nuccetelli and Seay 2007, pp. 283–306.

Shaver, Robert, "Ethical Non-Naturalism and Experimental Philosophy," in Nuccetelli and Seay 2012, pp. 194–210.

Shaver, Robert, "George Edward Moore (1873–1958)," in Crimmins 2017, pp. 356–359.

Shafer-Landau, Russ, *Moral Realism: A Defence*, Oxford: Oxford University Press, 2003.

Shafer-Landau, Russ, *Whatever Happened to Good and Evil?* Oxford: Oxford University Press, 2004.

Shafer-Landau, Russ, "Ethics as Philosophy: A Defense of Ethical Nonnaturalism," in Horgan and Timmons 2006, pp. 209–232.

Shafer-Landau, Russ, "Moral and Theological Realism: The Explanatory Argument," *Journal of Moral Philosophy* 4(3) (2007): 311–329.

Shafer-Landau, Russ, "Evolutionary Debunking, Moral Realism and Moral Knowledge," *Journal of Ethics and Social Philosophy* 7(1) (2012): 1–37.

Shaver, Robert, "Non-naturalism," in Nuccetelli and Seay 2007, pp. 283–306.

Shaw, William H., "Between Act and Rule: The Consequentialism of G. E. Moore," in *Morality, Rules, and Consequences: A Critical Reader*, Brad Hooker, Elinor Mason, and Dale E. Miller eds., Edinburgh: Edinburgh University Press, 2000, pp. 6–26.

Shaw, William H., "Editor's Introduction," in *Ethics*, G. E. Moore, New York: Clarendon Press, 2005/1912, pp. vii–xxxix.

Shaw, William H., "The Consequentialist Perspective," in Jamie Dreier ed., *Contemporary Debates in Moral Theory*, Malden, MA: Blackwell, 2006, pp. 5–20.

Sidgwick, Henry, "The Theory of Evolution and Its Application to Practice," *Mind* 1 (1876): 52–67.

Sidgwick, Henry, *Henry Sidgwick, a Memoir*, Arthur Sidgwick and Eleanor Mildred Sidgwick eds., London: Macmillan, 1906.

Sidgwick, Henry, *The Methods of Ethics*, 7th edn, London: Macmillan, 1967/1874.

Sidgwick, Henry, "The Establishment of Ethical First Principles," *Mind* o.s. 4 (1879): 106–111. [Reprinted in Sidgwick 2000.]

Sidgwick, Henry, *Essays on Ethics and Method*, M. G. Singer ed., Oxford: Oxford University Press, 2000.

Sidorsky, David, "The Uses of the Philosophy of G. E. Moore in the Works of E. M. Forster," *New Literary History* 38(2) (2007): 245–271.

Sinclair, Neil, ed., *The Naturalistic Fallacy*, Cambridge: Cambridge University Press, 2019.

Sinnott-Armstrong, Walter, "Moral Intuitionism Meets Empirical Psychology," in Horgan and Timmons 2006, pp. 339–365.

Sinnott-Armstrong, "Consequentialism," in *Stanford Encyclopedia of Philosophy*, Edward N. Zalta ed., 2019, https://plato.stanford.edu/entries/consequentialism/

Skarsaune, Knut Olav, "Darwin and Moral Realism: Survival of the Iffiest," *Philosophical Studies* 152 (2010): 2229–2243.

Skelton, Anthony, "Ideal Utilitarianism: Rashdall and Moore," in Hurka 2011, pp. 45–65.

Skelton, Anthony, "Ideal Utilitarianism," in Crimmins 2017, pp. 261–264.

Skorupski, John, ed., *The Routledge Companion to Ethics*, London: Routledge, 2010.

Slote, Michael, *From Morality to Virtue*, Oxford: Oxford University Press, 1992.

Smart, J. J. C., "Extreme and Restricted Utilitarianism," *The Philosophical Quarterly* 6(25) (1956): 344–354.

Smart, J. J. C., *Philosophy and Scientific Realism*, New York: Routledge & Kegan Paul and The Humanities Press, 1963.

Smith, Michael, *The Moral Problem*, Oxford: Blackwell, 1994.

Smith, Michael, "Moral Realism," in *The Blackwell Guide to Ethical Theory*, H. LaFollette ed., Oxford: Blackwell, 2000, pp. 15–37.

Smith, Michael, "Meta-ethics," in *The Oxford Handbook of Contemporary Philosophy*, Frank Jackson and Michael Smith eds., Oxford: Oxford University Press, 2005, pp. 3–30.

Smith, Michael, "On the Nature and Significance of the Distinction between Thick and Thin Ethical Concepts," in *Thick Concepts*, Simon Kirchin ed., Oxford: Oxford University Press, 2013, pp. 97–120.

Soames, Scott, *Philosophical Analysis in the Twentieth Century*, vol. 1, *The Dawn of Analysis*, Princeton, NJ: Princeton University Press, 2003.

Spencer, Herbert, *Principles of Ethics*, London: Williams and Norgate, 1893.

Star, Daniel and Roger Crisp, *History of Ethics: Essential Readings with Commentaries*, Chichester: John Wiley and Sons, 2020.

Stebbing, Susan, "Moore's Influence," in Schilpp 1942, pp. 515–532.

Stevenson, Charles Leslie, "The Emotive Meaning of Ethical Terms," *Mind* 46(181) (1937): 14–31.

Stevenson, Charles Leslie, *Ethics and Language*, New Haven, CT: Yale University Press, 1944.

Stich, Stephen, *The Fragmentation of Reason: Preface to a Pragmatic Theory of Cognitive Evaluation*, Cambridge, MA: MIT Press, 1990.

Stratton-Lake, Philip, "Why Externalism Is Not a Problem for Ethical Intuitionists," *Proceedings of the Aristotelian Society* (New Series) 99 (1999): 77–90.

Stratton-Lake, Philip, ed., *Ethical Intuitionism: Re-evaluations* Oxford: Clarendon Press, 2002.

Stratton-Lake, Philip, "Introduction," in Stratton-Lake 2002, pp. 1–28.

Stratton-Lake, Philip, "Intuitionism in Ethics," in *Stanford Encyclopedia of Philosophy*, Edward N. Zalta ed., 2003/2014, https://plato.stanford.edu/entries/intuitionism-ethics/

Stratton-Lake, Philip, "G. E. Moore: *Principia Ethica*," in John Shand ed., *Central Works of Philosophy, The Twentieth Century: Moore to Popper*, Chesham: Acumen Publishing Ltd., 2005–2006, pp. 20–37.

Stratton-Lake, Philip, "Intuition, Self-Evidence, and Understanding," in *Oxford Studies in Metaethics* 11, R. Shafer-Landau ed., Oxford: Oxford University Press, 2016, pp. 28–44.

Stratton-Lake, Philip, and Brad Hooker, "Scanlon Versus Moore on Goodness," in Horgan and Timmons 2006, pp. 149–168.

Street, Sharon, "A Darwinian Dilemma for Realist Theories of Value," *Philosophical Studies* 127 (2006): 109–166.

Sturgeon, Nicholas, "Moral Explanations," in *Morality, Reason and Truth*, D. Copp and D. Zimmerman eds., Totowa, NJ: Rowman and Allanheld, 1985, pp. 49–78. [References to reprint pp. 229–255 in Sayre-McCord 1988.]

Sturgeon, Nicholas, "Ethical Intuitionism and Ethical Naturalism," in Stratton-Lake 2002, pp. 184–211.

Sturgeon, Nicholas, "Moore on Ethical Naturalism," *Ethics* 113(3) (2003): 528–556.

Sturgeon, Nicholas, "Ethical Naturalism," in *The Oxford Handbook of Ethical Theory*, David Copp ed., Oxford: Oxford University Press, 2006, pp. 91–121.

Sturgeon, Nicholas, "Doubts on the Supervenience of the Ethical," in *Oxford Studies in Metaethics 4*, Russ Shafer-Landau ed., Oxford: Oxford University Press, 2009, pp. 53–92.

Sylvester, Robert Peter, *The Moral Philosophy of G. E. Moore*, Ray Perkins and R. W. Sleeper eds., Philadelphia, PA: Temple University Press, 1990.

Thompson, Paul, *Issues in Evolutionary Ethics*, Albany, NY: SUNY Press, 1995.

Timmons, Mark, *Moral Theory*, 2nd edn., Lanham, MD: Rowman & Littlefield, 2013.

Urmson, J. O., *Philosophical Analysis*, London: Oxford University Press, 1958.

Urmson, J. O., "Moore's Utilitarianism," in Ambrose and Lazerowitz, 1970, pp. 343–349.

van Roojen, Mark, *Metaethics: A Contemporary Introduction*, New York: Routledge, 2015.

Väyrynen, Pekka, "Thick Ethical Concepts," in *Stanford Encyclopedia of Philosophy*, Edward Zalta ed., 2016, https://plato.stanford.edu/entries/thick-ethical-concepts/

Warnock, G. J., *Contemporary Moral Philosophy*, New York: St. Martin's Press, 1967.

Warnock, G. J., "*The Commonplace Book* of G. E. Moore 1919–1953. Casimir Lewy," *Mind* 77(307) (1968): 431–436.

Warnock, Mary, *Ethics since 1900*, London: Oxford University Press, 1960.

Wedgwood, Ralph, *The Nature of Normativity*, Oxford: Oxford University Press, 2007.

Wedgwood, Ralph, "Moral Disagreement among Philosophers," in Bergmann and Kain 2014, pp. 23–39.

Welchman, Jennifer, "G. E. Moore and the Revolution in Ethics: A Reappraisal," *History of Philosophy Quarterly* 6(3) (1989): 317–329.

West, Henry R., "Mill's 'Proof' of the Principle of Utility," in *Mill's Utilitarianism: Critical Essays*, David Lyons ed., Lanham, MD: Rowman & Littlefield, 1997, pp. 85–98.

West, Henry R., "The Proof," in *A Companion to Mill*, Christopher Macleod and Dale E. Miller eds., Chichester: Wiley Blackwell, 2017, pp. 328–341.

White, Alan R., *G. E. Moore: A Critical Exposition*, Oxford: Basil Blackwell, 1958.

Williams, Bernard, *Ethics and the Limits of Philosophy*, Cambridge, MA: Harvard University Press, 1985.

Williamson, Timothy, "Ethics, Supervenience, and Ramsey Sentences," *Philosophy and Phenomenological Research* 62 (2001): 625–630.

Wilson, Edward O., *Sociobiology: The New Synthesis*, Cambridge, MA: Harvard University Press, 1975.

Wisdom, John, "Moore's Technique," in Schilpp 1942, pp. 419–450.

Wisdom, John, "G. E. Moore," *Analysis* 19(3) (1959): 49–53.

Woolf, Leonard, *Sowing: An Autobiography of the Years 1880 to 1904*. London: The Hogarth Press, 1960.

Zimmerman, Aaron, *Moral Epistemology*, London: Routledge, 2010.

Zimmerman, Michael J., "On the Nature, Existence and Significance of Organic Unities," *Journal of Ethics & Social Philosophy* 8(3) (2015): 1–24.

INDEX

Made in the USA
Las Vegas, NV
07 November 2021

33871933R00164